PROFESSOR W. G. ELMSLIE, D. D.
MEMOIR AND SERMONS

WILLIAM GRAY ELMSLIE

Published by Left of Brain Books

Copyright © 2021 Left of Brain Books

ISBN 978-1-396-32015-6

First Edition

All rights reserved. No part of this publication may be reproduced, distributed, or transmitted in any form or by any means, including photocopying, recording, or other electronic or mechanical methods, without the prior written permission of the publisher, except in the case of brief quotations embodied in critical reviews and certain other noncommercial uses permitted by copyright law. Left of Brain Books is a division of Left of Brain Onboarding Pty Ltd.

Table of Contents

MEMOIR.	1
I. From the Rev. Professor Marcus Dods, D. D.	46
II. From Professor Henry Drummond.	47
III. From the Rev. John Smith, M. A.	49
IV. From the Rev. James Stalker, D.D.	51
SERMONS.	55
I. Christ at the Door.	55
II. The Dark Enigma of Death.	63
III. The Story of Dorcas.	74
IV. Unfulfilled Christian Work.	81
V. A Lesson in Christian Help.	91
VI. Joseph's Faith.	102
VII. The Brazen Serpent.	111
VIII. The Gradations of Doubt.	120
IX. The Story of Queen Esther.	131
X. The Example of the Prophets.	140
XI. The Making of a Prophet.	151
XII. For and Against Christ.	158
XIII. The Prophecy of Nature.	165
XIV. Christian Giving.	171
XV. Our Lord's Treatment of Erring Friends.	184
XVI. A Hymn of Heart's Ease.	196
XVII. The First Chapter of Genesis.	209

MEMOIR.

ALTHOUGH Dr. Elmslie was not destined to a long career, and died with the greater purposes of his life work almost entirely unfulfilled, very few men in the Nonconformist churches of Great Britain were better known and loved. The expectations of many in his native Scotland were fixed on him from the first; in England no preacher of his years had a larger or more enthusiastic following. Among students of the Old Testament he was beginning to be known as a master in his own subject, and as one likely to accomplish much in the reconciliation of criticism and faith. Add to this that he possessed the rarer charm of an almost unique personal magnetism—that many were attached to him by the chain which is not quickly broken, the bond of spiritual affinity, and it becomes necessary to apologise only for the imperfections, not for the existence, of this memorial.

WILLIAM GRAY ELMSLIE was born in the Free Church Manse of Insch, Aberdeenshire, October 5th, 1848, the second son of the Rev. William Elmslie, M.A., and May Cruickshank, his wife. Writing to his parents from Berlin more than twenty years after, he says, "How thankful I ought to be that I was born in dear old Scotland, and in the humble little Free Church manse of Insch!" His father was famous for his shrewd, homely, genial wisdom. He was a native of Aberdeen, and had the strong sense and quick perception for which Aberdonians are known. By no means without the nobler enthusiasms of Christianity, he had shared in the fervour of the Disruption movement, and was the popular and successful minister of a congregation large for the district, and including many members of earnest Christian principle. Mr. Elmslie was the father and counsellor of the whole parish; his advice was sought by members of all Churches, and cheerfully given. If there was any danger of his practical nature becoming somewhat too hard and worldly, the influence of his wife was a corrective. Dr. Elmslie's mother—a beautiful and accomplished woman—was a religious enthusiast. "I recognised," writes her son, from the New College, Edinburgh, "mamma's review in the *Free Press* by the words 'wrestling believing prayer.'" They were indeed characteristic, and it was the rare union of mystic elevation and warmth with perfect comprehension of ordinary life that gave Dr. Elmslie his separate and commanding place among the teachers of his time. The austerity, the somewhat chilly rigour which characterised manse life in the Free Church were not found at Insch. The children never suffered from the want of affection—what the French call *le besoin d'être aimé*. All the best was brought out in them, and in the case of our subject the brightness and sweetness of his disposition procured for him more than ordinary endearments. Two lovingly preserved letters in a large round child's hand give a better idea of the home than anything I can say. The first describes a visit to Huntly and the home of Duncan Matheson, the great evangelist, who did yeoman service in the Crimean War.

"INSCH, *July* 14*th*, 1856.

"MY DEAR MAMMA,—I am always glad when I hear that you are all keeping well. I have such a long string of news that I do not know where to begin, for I was at Huntly, and saw so many things there. I will now tell you the most of what I saw. I first saw the Bogie, and a few sheep being washed in it. When I arrived at Huntly, and had walked a short distance, Mr. Matheson and I met his dog Dash. When I got to the house I was first shown the Bugle, then the Drum, and three swords; one was broken after killing five Rusians, and the man who had used it killed. And then I saw the Rifle, and fired it off, though without shot. When I got out of the house I went to a shop where I bought a gun and Almonds, and on our way home Miss Matheson and I called on the Lawsons, and brought Johny and Jamie home, where we met William Brown, with his Aunt Mrs. Douglas, waiting us. When we went into the house there were two pistols which William and I took, and frightened some boys with them. I saw a piece of the rock of Gibralter. I saw a piece of wood made into stone, and two teeth—one a shark's, and the other an Alligator's—hardened into stone. There were medals and coins of the various countries of Europe, a piece of a church in Sevastopool, and a thing which the Russian soldiers wear on their coats. I also saw a brush which the Turks use for brushing themselves. I also saw an idol and a great many pictures of the Virgin Mary. I saw a small picture-book with all the different priests of Rome. Our Rabbits are all quite well and growing. I am yours aff^{te} Son,

"WILLIAM GRAY ELMSLIE."

"MY DEAR MAMA,—I am glad to hear that Papa is keeping better. How I would like to be with you, and see the beautiful scenery and the many rabbits. Tell our cousins to come here some time soon, and let them see our rabbits if they will come. I send some Heather and some broom which we got on the hill beside John davison, and took tea with him. I enclose what I got down of the forenoon sermon. I am your aff^{te} son,

"W. G. ELMSLIE."

P.S.—We sometimes receive to small dinners, but sometimes pretty good.

"W. G. ELMSLIE."

The religious forces of the time were those of that Evangelicalism which has been the base of so many powerful characters, even among those who have afterwards rejected it, like Cardinal Newman and George Eliot. These were reinforced by the influences of the Disruption, then at their strongest. It was something to be born at such a time, a time when, to use the words of Lacordaire, there was a noble union of heroic character and memorable achievement. The pecuniary poverty and spiritual opulence of Scotland, on which Carlyle has said so much, were then seen at their best. If a cautious, reticent race, impatient of extravagant action and unmeasured speech, is to be found anywhere, it is among the peasants of Aberdeenshire; but when possessed and stirred by religious feeling they are capable of unyielding firmness and unstinted devotion. These qualities were remarkably brought out at the Disruption. The religious life of New England, pictured by Harriet Beecher Stowe, must have been similar in many things, and Dr. George Macdonald, who was born in Huntly, a few miles from Insch, has rendered some aspects with incomparable beauty and tenderness in his first works. The preaching was intensely theological. The great highways of truth were trodden and retrodden. Texts were largely taken from the Epistles, and the doctrines of grace were accurately and thoroughly expounded. Freshness, style, and the other qualities now held essential to popular sermons were unknown. But the preaching did its work, nevertheless, as Dr. Macdonald says, because it *was* preaching—the rare speech of a man to his fellows, whereby they know that he is in his inmost heart a believer. As the result, every conscience hung out the pale or the red flag. Dr. Macdonald complains of the inharmonious singing, but others will testify with Mrs. Stowe that the slow, rude, and primitive rendering of the metrical Psalms excited them painfully. "It brought over one, like a presence, the sense of the infinite and the eternal, the yearning, and the fear, and the desire of the poor finite being, so ignorant and so helpless." Not less impressive was the piety to be found among the peasants. There were David Elginbrods in their ranks, men among whom you felt in the presence of the higher natures of the world—and women delivered from lonely, craving solitude by the Eternal Love that had broken through and ended the dark and melancholy years. These were to be found not only among the prominent Church members, but among others willing to be unknown, to be stones sunk in the foundation of the spiritual building. Under such influences the boy became a Christian almost unconsciously. There was no crisis in his life, that I can trace. When a mere boy he writes to his parents, during their absence from Insch, that he had conducted family worship according to their desire. "It required a great deal of previous thought and prayer, too, for I have found that is useful, and not study only, in preparing for the service of God. Yet I have good cause to be glad and thankful that I am able to do it; and I feel it a real relief and privilege to commit all to the care of God." At this time he visited an aged member of his father's Church, and prayed with her. He repeats with pride the compliment paid him in return, "Ye ken hoo to be kind and couthy wi' a puir auld body." His faith and vision grew clearer, but in cruder shape those thoughts were his from the beginning that haunted him to the very end.

The intellectual atmosphere of the place was much more quickening than might be thought. Insch is a cosy little village enough, and though not in itself beautiful, has picturesque bits near it. But even in summer sunshine it can hardly be called lively, and in winter, when the snow is piled for weeks on hill and field, and the leaden-coloured clouds refuse to part, it could not well look duller. But the Free Church manses of the district were full of eager inquiry. The ministers were educated men, graduates of the University, and in some cases had swept its prizes. Their ambition was satisfied in the service of Christ. There was a noble contentment with their lot which it is inspiring to think of; but they cherished a righteous ambition for their children, and spared no toil and no self-denial to open the way for them. From three Free Church manses in that neighbourhood, all at first included in the same Presbytery, have gone forth men whose names are familiar to the English people. From the manse of Keig, Professor Robertson Smith; from Rhynie, Mr. A. M. Mackay, of

Uganda, the true successor to Livingstone, whose early death is announced as these sheets are passing through the press; and from Insch, Professor Elmslie. The educational facilities of the district were of almost ideal excellence. The parish teachers, when salaries were increased by certain wise and liberal bequests, were almost without exception accomplished scholars. They took pride in a promising pupil, and would cheerfully work extra hours to ensure his success. Their fees were sufficiently moderate, one pound being enough to cover all expenses for a year. At these schools a boy might remain till he had reached the age, say, of fourteen or fifteen, when he might go to Aberdeen to compete for a scholarship, or "bursary" as it was called. Of these, perhaps forty were offered every year, varying from £35 a year for the University course, downwards. It was thought wiser to go for the last year or two to the Grammar School in Aberdeen, to receive the last polish; but often lads went in from their native glens, and defeated all competitors. Elmslie was trained at first in the Free Church school at Insch, then at the parish school, under the Rev. James McLachlan. He then proceeded to the Aberdeen Grammar School, where he was two years, under the Rev. William Barrack, a teacher of rare attainments and enthusiasm. He carried off one of the highest honours, and in 1864 entered the University of Aberdeen.

It is, or was, the ambition of every hopeful youth in the North to wear the student's gown. "Oh that God would spare me to wear the red cloakie!" said John Duncan, afterwards the well-known Professor of Hebrew in the New College, Edinburgh, when weakened by an early illness. The life of the Aberdeen student has never, perhaps, been rendered with sufficient fidelity, save in "Alec Forbes," and Dr. Walter Smith's "Borland Hall," and it may have changed in some respects since Elmslie's time. Then it was emphatically a period of plain living and hard work. Eight shillings a week sufficed to cover many a student's expenses for board and lodging, amounting to less than £10 for the twenty weeks of the session, and the summer was spent at home. The spirit of the place was democratic in the extreme. There were a few students who came out of wealthy families, but any claim to respect on this ground would have been fiercely resented. George Macdonald tells of an aristocrat among the students condemned and sentenced by a meeting presided over by "the pale-faced son of a burly ploughman." The high spirits of youth would at times break out in coarse and even ferocious excesses, but these were rare, and the characteristic of the place was a limitless persistency of application. Most of the men felt that this was their one chance. If they could distinguish themselves, there were scholarships to be had which would open the path to Oxford or Cambridge, or give them a fair chance in other fields of life. Some yielded to temptation, and became wrecks; others, after a period of obscuration, recovered themselves; a few soon abandoned the quest for University honours, and busied themselves with other lines of reading and study; but Elmslie set himself, without flinching or turning aside, to his task. Evil did not lure him. There was no stamp of moral *défaillance* on that clear brow. His watchful parents were still with him, for they set up another home in Aberdeen, and were constantly with their children. It ought, perhaps, to be mentioned that Elmslie's father was an enthusiastic total abstainer, in days when the practice was quite unfashionable, and in many parts of the country entirely unknown. In this his son warmly sympathised, maintaining the principle of abstinence to the end of his life, and carrying out the practice even during his studies in Germany. He wrote home, when assistant in Regent Square, "Glad you are getting on so famously in the temperance line, and do hope it will have a permanent and wide influence." But the secret of his University success was his indefatigable labour at the prescribed tasks. Although he might well be termed *l'esprit soudain*, he was capable of the long-continued and daily application which belongs to the rare union of ardour and patience. He had the characteristic of his countrymen—nothing could daunt him from fighting the battle out. His success accordingly was great and growing. In a class which numbered, perhaps, an unusual proportion of brilliant men, he steadily made his way to the front. He distinguished himself by taking prizes in almost every department of study, specially excelling in mathematics, and closed his career by carrying off the gold medal awarded by the Aberdeen Town Council to the first student of the year, in April, 1868. The victory was not gained without a price. From the first his studies brought on some occasional headaches, and the first triumph resulted in a serious illness, which his wise and skilful physician, Dr. Davidson, of Wartle, warned him would reappear twenty years later—an ominous prophecy, which was but too exactly fulfilled. The chief intellectual force in the Northern University at that time and long after was Dr. Alexander Bain, the Professor of Logic. In after life Dr. Elmslie frequently referred to his influence. But other chairs were also occupied by powerful men. Geddes infected many with his own enthusiasm for Greek literature; Fuller and Thomson were admirably efficient teachers of mathematics; and to name no more, "Jeems" Nicol, the Professor of Natural History, with his hoarse voice, his homely kindness, and his thorough knowledge of his subject, was a universal favourite. Thomson was, perhaps, the most original and cynical character of them all, and his dry wit had a great attraction for Elmslie.

The Rev. Thomas Nicol, of Tolbooth, Edinburgh, a distinguished minister of the Church of Scotland and one of the most outstanding of Professor Elmslie's classfellows, wrote thus to his father: "Since Dr. Elmslie's death I have often gone back to the days, just twenty-five years ago, when we first met at the bursary competition, and in the Bageant class at King's College, Aberdeen. Even from the first he was one of the most winsome and attractive members of the class, full of fun and mirth, with a perennial smile on his beautiful and finely formed face, and with a cheery word for everybody. I can see him to-day, with his neat Highland cape and the college gown over it, coming through the quadrangle, as distinctly as if it were yesterday, and it is easier for me preserving that picture because we have met so seldom of recent years. He is associated in my mind with another of our classfellows, who achieved distinction early, and early met an heroic and tragic death—I mean Mr. William Jenkyns, C.I.E, who died with Sir Louis Cavagnari, at Cabul. Your son and he were unlike in some things, but in delicacy of features, and expressiveness of countenance, and slimness of figure one associates them at once together. When I was helping to get up funds for the memorial of Mr. Jenkyns now in the University Library at Aberdeen I well remember the cheerfulness with which Mr. Elmslie contributed, and the kindly words of affection and esteem which accompanied his contribution. Of both it might most truly be said that 'being made perfect, in a short time they fulfilled a long time.' Like others of my classfellows, Mr. Bruce, our first Bursar, now minister of Banff, W. L. Davidson, LL.D., minister of Bourtie, and our mutual friend John Smith, of Broughton Place Church here, and many more, I watched your son's career with the deepest interest, and as I have said, took quite a pride in the career of usefulness and honour which by his ability and hard work he shaped for himself in London. We really felt as if he were our own somehow, and as if we had a share in all the honours he was gaining, both as a literary and as a public man." The Rev. W. A. Gray, of Elgin, who was brought up in a neighbouring Free Church manse, says, "What characterised him then was his intense sense of fun, his perception of the comic side of things, especially in regard to people, and his never-failing stock of anecdotes, almost always humorous, never malicious." Coming several years after Elmslie to the University of Aberdeen, I only knew him from a distance. To an outsider his prominent quality was winsomeness. There was no jealousy in Aberdeen of fairly won success; if there had been, Elmslie would have disarmed it. Then, as always, he took his victories with the utmost simplicity. He was always humble, with the humility which is very consistent with strenuous effort and even great ambition.

The sons of Free Church ministers in those days, however great their University successes might have been, generally desired no higher position than that of their fathers. It was, no doubt, the wish of his parents that Elmslie should be a minister, and his inclination fell in with that. At the same time there were counter-inducements; for one, many Aberdeen students had been winning high distinction at Cambridge, the senior wranglership having fallen to some of them, and his teacher and some of his relatives were anxious that he should try his fortunes there. He had himself a strong bent to the medical profession. Whatever line he had taken in life he would have been successful. A well-known revivalist preacher, also a professional man, is understood to have counselled him to go in for a business life. One who knew him well has remarked to me, since his death, that his true pre-eminence would have been shown in a scientific career. But his life, and especially its closing years, made it plain that his own choice was wise.

A new era opened for him when he went as a theological student to the New College, Edinburgh. The Free Church possesses a theological seminary in Aberdeen which assuredly did not lack for able Professors, but the number of students is small, and the more ambitious men usually go to Edinburgh. In Edinburgh the Free Church College (known as New College) had for its first Principal Dr. Chalmers, and in succession Dr. Cunningham and Dr. Candlish, the three greatest of the Disruption worthies. It had also some notable men among its Professors. When Elmslie went up Candlish was at the head. His appearances were only occasional, as he was also minister of Free St. George's, Edinburgh. But although his contribution to the vitality of the New

College was necessarily small, it was real. Mr. Gray writes: "He gave no lectures, his work being confined to the examining and criticising of the students' discourses. There was always a considerable interest in these criticisms, and a good turn out to hear them. They were usually strongly put, both in the direction of censure and of praise; but any one who knew the Doctor's methods, and made allowance for vigour of phrase, could depend on a true and perceptive estimate of the merits or demerits of a sermon. Sometimes he could be savage enough. Fancy a man tomahawked with the following, delivered with the well-known burr, flash of eye, and protrusion of underlip: 'All I have got to say about this discourse is' (raising his voice) 'that one half should be struck out, and' (lowering it again) 'it doesn't matter which half.' This may have compared with another historic criticism, attributed to Dr. Cunningham when addressing the author of a certain Latin thesis: 'Of this discourse I have only to say two things—the writer has murdered the Latin tongue, and perverted the glorious Gospel of Christ.' But Candlish was one of the kindest of men. How well I remember the little figure, with the gold spectacles flashing beneath the big hat; the loosely fitting coat; the wide trousers, lapping two or three inches above the shoes, which were usually set off by a foot of loose lace; the gruff greeting, which usually changed into a warm, hearty smile if he were accosted."

Among the Professors, Elmslie evidently appreciated Dr. Davidson and Dr. Rainy, while conscious of receiving benefit from others. The longest personal sketch he ever wrote was an article on Professor Davidson in the *Expositor* (January, 1888). In this he says, "His singular and significant influence does not consist in what he does, but in what he is. It is not the quantity or the contents, but the quality and kind of the thinking. It is not even the thought, so much as the mind that secretes it. It is not its clearness nor its profundity, not its reserve nor its passion, not its scepticism nor its superiority of spiritual faith; but it is the combination of all these, and the strange, subtle, and fascinating outcome of them. The central and sovereign spring of Dr. Davidson's unique influence in the literature, scholarship, and ministry of the Church is his personality. ... If the Church of Christ within our borders should pass through the present trial of faith without panic, without reactionary antagonism to truth, and without loss of spiritual power, a very large part of the credit will belong to the quiet but commanding influence of the Hebrew chair in that college which rises so picturesquely on the ancient site of Mary of Guise's palace in Edinburgh." Of Dr. Rainy he has nowhere written at length, but he was wont to speak of his "smouldering passion," and the great ideas with which he inspired the receptive among his students. Dr. Elmslie, though resolute and even daring on occasion, was a warm admirer of statesmanship, and Dr. Rainy's skilful piloting of the Free Church through many troubles he would often praise, emphasizing strongly, at the same time, his belief in the Principal's perfect honesty and singleness of purpose.

There are many kind allusions in his letters to Dr. Blaikie, to whom he was specially grateful for having introduced him to practical mission work. In this he was always intensely interested, maintaining that on this ground the true battle of Christ must be fought.

"Blaikie gave us a capital lecture, its only fault being that there was too much matter, so that we could not get down even a mere abstract of the substance."

"EDINBURGH, 1868.

"Things are still going on capitally. At the hall Davidson is most admirable, and Blaikie every day coming out even better and better. For instance, speaking of the fondness the early apologists displayed at pointing not to the lives, but to the deaths of Christians, he added, 'And indeed, gentlemen, I cannot help saying that in the course of my experience as a minister I have always noticed the hush and breathless attention such a subject ever commands, and I have found nothing make a deeper impression, or act more powerfully as a means of producing good, than a description of a triumphant death-bed.' This is practical, true, and useful."

Elmslie threw himself with intense energy into the work of his classes. At first he found it difficult to maintain the place he had achieved at Aberdeen, for he had able competitors, but his unweariable diligence and quick apprehension soon put him at the head.

In one of his earliest letters from Edinburgh he writes, "On Wednesday evening I did first copy of my essay with a headache coming on, which came on with such heartiness that I went to bed, and I could not go to college on Thursday. (N.B. It is remarkable that when I have no mamma to nurse me my headaches never come to such extremes as they do when I have a fall-back. This one was bad enough, but not one of the desperate kind.)"

There was only one cure for these headaches, and he could never bring himself to take it. It would be tedious to go over the story of his successes. By this time his younger brother, Leslie, had entered the University of Edinburgh, where his triumphs were scarcely less than those of his senior at the New College. So used did the household at Insch become to telegrams announcing new prizes and scholarships, that at certain periods of the year the faithful mother had telegrams of congratulation already filled up, waiting to be despatched.

Many students of theology are more impressed by the preaching they hear than by their Professors, and Edinburgh has always been known for pulpit eloquence. But it was the reverse with Elmslie. No preacher seems to have had any great power over him. He attended the Free High Church, then ministered to by Mr. William Arnot; but though he admitted the freshness and fertility of the preacher's mind, he was not a warm admirer of his sermons. He often listened to Dr. Charles J. Brown, in the Free New North, and liked him: "he seems such a fine-hearted man." One day he went to hear a fellow-student, and missed the way to the church. He turned aside into the Barclay Church, where Mr. (now Dr.) Wilson was preaching. "I like Mr. Wilson very much. He is thoroughly practical, both in his preaching and in his prayers. For instance, in the one after the chapter he prayed for boys and girls at school, that they might be helped with their lessons when they were difficult, and that they might learn obedience and courtesy and be made blessings to their teachers; also for those persons who had not had a good training in their youth, and felt it now in showing a good example to the children, and especially for those parents and children who were troubled with bad tempers." After remarking on the great predominance of young people in the congregation, he says that the sermon was delivered with a great deal of energy and action, and that the idea of the preacher seemed to be to bring religion down on the every-day life, that it might become the motive power in work. "On coming out I accosted an intelligent-looking man, and said, 'Was that Mr. Wilson?' 'Yes,' he said, and added, with a proud smile, 'And didn't you like him?' I answered, 'Very much indeed,' whereupon he looked exceedingly gratified and prouder than ever. I wish there were more such pride."

On another occasion he writes, "At present I had sooner hear Dr. Candlish than any one. He is so strong and honest, and wide in his sympathies. His address to the students was full of passion and feeling, and sympathy with the difficulty of believing some of our Calvinistic doctrines, such as eternal ruin, heathens' doom, etc. He went a very great length indeed, and ended by saying it was too hard for him, and his heart drew him the other way, and all he could do was to fall back on his loyalty to Christ. It was more a picture of his own heart's struggles than the Principal's address." But his usual note is, "Heard ——, in —— Church: middling."

In 1871 he gained the Hamilton Scholarship in a most brilliant manner, his marks being so extraordinary that as they came in the secretary of the Senatus thought there must be some mistake. His fellow-students, he writes, were overwhelmingly kind in their congratulations, and he himself seems to have rejoiced in this success more than in any other of his life. One thing was that in his after-work he would not have the same amount of anxiety and despair that weighed him down in his preparations. But the chief thing was the joy it would give at home. "I need not tell you," he writes to his mother, "how *sweet* your letter was to me, telling me of your joy on receipt of the telegram. When no letter came in the morning you cannot think how disappointed I was, for, to confess the truth, I had been thinking all Sabbath of the pleasure of reading the home letters, and in them getting the real joy of the scholarship. For, except the pleasure of knowing the gladness caused at home, there is not much satisfaction otherwise in it. It is strange how soon, after the first surprise of getting it, the delight of getting it passed away, and I think there was more enjoyment in the working for it than in the having it."

This incident may stand as typical of many others, and of his prominent place among men not a few of whom were of real mark. His comradeships among the students filled a large place in his life. Of all his friends the most intimate and best loved was Mr. Andrew Harper, now Lecturer on Hebrew in Ormond College, Melbourne. I regret much that exigencies of time make it impossible to include, for the present at least, any of his letters to this brother of his heart. They were always together, for ever disputing, and never quarrelling, very close to one another in heart and mind. Two years before Dr. Elmslie's death Mr. Harper visited this country. The friends resumed their ancient intercourse, visited Switzerland in company, and found that the changes of the years had only drawn them nearer. Some of the best life in the New College has always been found in the Theological Society—an association of the students who gather to discuss controverted questions, and do not fear to go into them thoroughly. These meetings were greatly relished by Elmslie. Among the leading members in his time was Professor Robertson Smith, whose amazing keenness in debate is often admiringly mentioned in his letters home. The first time Elmslie spoke in the Society was in connection with a discussion whether the Free Church should return to the Establishment on the abolition of patronage. He took the negative side, and was complimented on both sides for the ability and ingenuity of his speech. The speculative daring in the Society at a time when outside the old orthodoxy was hardly questioned partly amused and partly pleased him. He speaks of entertaining Dr. Davidson very much by telling him that the men at the Theological fathered all their heresies on Dr. Candlish's "Fatherhood of God," by, as they expressed it, carrying out its principles to their logical conclusions. The subjects themselves, however, were the main thing and took abiding possession of his heart. "I intend," he says, "to still go on studying these themes of Christ more deeply, for they have interested me intensely. By the way, I believe what will be of more value to me than the scholarship, and also far more satisfactory, is the feeling I have that in preparing for it I have made an immense addition to my knowledge in several departments, and done it so thoroughly that it will never pass away. Two subjects have so interested me that I mean to go on studying them—namely, the Person of Christ, and the Early Apostolic Church."

On his work and influence at New College the letters of Professor Drummond and Dr. Stalker will give a distinct impression, but I cannot leave the subject without giving room to what was almost before everything with him—his work among the poor, and especially among their children. They show the brilliant and courted student in another light, and it is worth mentioning that the larger proportion of his letters home is made up of such stories. His pupils in the ragged school greatly interested him, and his letters from Edinburgh are largely filled with picturesque incidents of his experience among them.

Edinburgh seemed to him more terrible in its undress than Aberdeen. "I never saw such miserable squalid faces, intermingled with roughs and coarse-looking women." There was a humorous side to it, also, which he does not fail to give account of. One day in the Sunday-school a little boy behind indulged in an occasional pull at his coat-tail, or a facetious poke at his back, to all of which demonstrations he preserved an appearance of utter unconsciousness. When the school was over, and they were waiting their turn to get out, he turned round and said, not with a very ferocious countenance, "Now, which of you young rascals was pulling at my tails?" Of course, this occasioned immense amusement, and one bright-eyed little fellow said it could not have been so.

"Oh, well," he said, "it is strange; I wonder if the forms could have done it." This was a very tickling idea, and immediately the little fellow said, "Sir, I gave you a poke." He said, "That is honest, now, and I suppose some other one took the tails." "Yes, sir, it was me," said another merry young monkey, with a comical look. He answered, "I know you are not good scholars. How do I know that? Oh, you never heard of good scholars pulling the teacher's tails!" This was a very striking view of things to them, and they did not know whether to be impressed or amused.

The quickness of the city children, and their readiness of sympathy, specially struck him. But the main issue of the work was practical. "I cannot help saying that I feel that this work will do me real good, and will give me an actual, and not a mere theoretical interest in the work I have before me. And that is a thing very much needed. One other thing I may mention here. We have been having worship once a day very regularly, and to me at least it has been very pleasant and very useful. And now good-night to both."

"I shall be very sorry to leave my poor little bairns, for I have come to like them exceedingly, especially of late; they have become so numerous that I have to put some of them on the floor—nearly fifty last night. I don't know how it is, but I have a strange sort of feeling, as if they were having a deeper interest in what I say than I ever saw before; perhaps it is because I think I have myself. Since Christmas-time I have told them every night about Jesus, and only stories that directly illustrated His love and work, and I feel a difference in the way they listen; some of them especially sit so very still and quiet, with such an earnest, solemn look on their faces. Some nights ago Donald English (who made the disturbance the first night I began), as I was beginning, took hold of my hand and said, 'Oh, tell's about Jesus again, the night!' I often end by asking them to pray Jesus, before they go to bed, to make them His little ones; and several times, as they went out, some of them have put their hand in mine and whispered, 'I'll ask Him the nicht.' Last Sabbath, when I was speaking of Jesus having died for our sakes, they were all sitting so very attentive, but three little boys in one corner began quarrelling about a bonnet, and disturbing me by the noise. I stopped twice and looked at them, but they always began again. Presently I stopped for the third time, and was going to speak to them, when one of the boys, who had been very attentive, rushed at them, and before I could interfere dragged one of them on to the floor, and commenced a furious onslaught of blows and abuse for interrupting me. I had hard work in persuading him to stop. Another very funny thing was the looks of reproachful indignation which some of the attentive ones had been casting at the disturbers, previous to the final outbreak. It was terribly annoying at the time, especially as I saw that many of them were very deeply interested. When I was ending I spoke of how Jesus deserved to be loved, and that they should ask to be made to love Him. One little girlie whispered, 'I will ask Him, for, oh, I do want to love Him!' and when I said it was time to go away they cried, 'Oh, dinna' send's away yet, tell's mair about Jesus;' and then they came round me, and made me promise to tell them 'bonnie stories about Jesus' next Sabbath. I have found that nothing interests them more than what is directly about Jesus. I could not help telling you all these little things, but I never had the same sort of *feeling* in teaching a class before, and I would like you to *remember* sometimes my poor little children down in the Canongate. I wish I could take them all into a better atmosphere, for it is sad to think of their chances of ever becoming good in such an evil, wretched place. Harper and I have been having many nice talks. I mean to preach often in the summer—I *want* to."

Here he describes an incident of open-air preaching. A friend was speaking, and Elmslie was managing the audience.

"EDINBURGH, *Jan.* 23rd, 1872.

"During this the man I had heard swearing at F—— came up to S——, who was standing a few yards off, and spoke to him. I went up just in time to hear him say, 'That fellow cannot even talk grammar.' I replied, 'We don't come here to teach grammar.' He was rather taken aback, but replied, 'Well, *I* could have said all your man said in half the time.' 'Then wait till he is done, and you shall have the next turn.' 'No, no, I don't want that; if I spoke I should oppose you.' 'I am ready for that; will you do it?' I said; 'We don't come here to argue.' 'No; you are wise to decline to argue with me.' I answered, 'Pooh! are you so conceited as to suppose that our arguing would make any difference to Christianity? Why, it has been argued hundreds of times over by men a deal wiser than you or me, and you see Christianity has not gone to the wall.' By that time I saw I was going to win, and got very cool and at my ease, while he got excited and put out; then he started on a new tack by saying, 'And what good do you expect to do to humanity by preaching here, and disturbing us?' I said, 'Well, perhaps, for one thing, we will get some drunken characters like those' (pointing to some) 'to give up the drink, and be decent, and keep their wives and children from starving.' 'Well, that may be, but speaking like yours will never do it.' I answered, 'No, you are quite right, but we are young, you see, and some of us have not much voice, and some have not much sense; but we are just trying to find out who of us can do the thing, and so, you see, we are just doing as well as we can.' He looked rather amazed at my frankness, and said, 'Well, I'm sure I have not any ill-will to you, but I don't believe in religion, and there are such a lot of hypocrites.' I said, 'Yes, there are a great lot, but that's just a reason why you should believe in the goodness of religion.' 'How do you make that out?' 'Why, you never heard of people making imitation of the stones and stuff like that' (pointing to the gutter), 'but it is sovereigns and things like that they make counterfeits of.' 'Ay, but I hate hypocrites, and say, Down with them.' 'So do I; and if you could down with all the religious hypocrites you would do more for Christianity than we can by preaching here.' 'Ah!' he said, 'if that's your opinion you should not take to street preaching; they are all hypocrites.' 'Oh, nonsense!' I replied. He exclaimed, very bitterly, 'Look at —— (mentioning a recent scandal); 'what good has that man done?' I answered, 'More than ever you or I have.' 'I would like to hear how,' he sneered. 'Why, you know, for one thing, he did manage, whether his preaching was sense or nonsense, to persuade a lot of drunken working men to give up drink and go to the kirk, and not waste their money in the public-house; and now you go and ask their wives and bairns whether R—— has done any good in the world.' 'Ay, but what do you say to,' etc.? 'That it was a great sin and shame to him; but that is no reason for refusing to own that he has done a vast deal of good before he did that piece of ill; and besides, I doubt if you or I are so good as to throw stones at him, etc., etc. Now I've listened to your criticisms on us, and pretty hard some of them were, so you will come up with me now, and hear what we've got to say.' He said, 'Well, I must say I like your way of taking things; I never heard them put in the way you have done; but I have not time now to come up; I have to take tea in half an hour with a mate.' I said, 'Still, you'll promise to come back next Sunday and hear us, and I may tell you, in secret, we shall have better speakers next time, and if you like, after the meeting is over, I'll have a talk with you. I never did meet one of your side before, but I've read some of your books. We won't call it a discussion, for I've not had any experience at arguing, and I suppose you are an old hand.' He gave a queer laugh, and said, 'Any way I never came across anybody on your side with half your sharpness and common sense; and besides, I must say *you* are honest about it.' And then we shook hands, and he promised to come along next Sunday. ... By the way, in my talk with the Deist my 'heretical' reading came in useful to me; for if I had not come through all that, I could not have heard his attacks on religion and kept my coolness, or taken them up the way I did; so it is *some good;* it will give me confidence in myself for the future—*another* good thing."

Pleasant interludes in his New College life were a session spent at Aberdeen University, as assistant to the Professor of Natural Philosophy, Mr. David Thomson, and two sessions spent at Berlin in the study of theology. At Aberdeen he had in his class Mr. Chrystal, now the celebrated Professor of Mathematics in the University of Edinburgh, whose abilities he repeatedly refers to in his letters. His work was enjoyable, and his relations with Professor Thomson of the most cordial kind. He was tempted in various ways to alter his life purpose, was offered a professorship of Natural Philosophy with a large salary in the Colonies, and was specially tempted to enter the medical profession. His closest friend at the University, Mr. James Shepherd, now a medical missionary of the United Presbyterian Church in India, was pursuing his professional studies, and with him he frequently visited hospital patients, finding a double interest in the work. Thus he writes:—

"ABERDEEN, *March* 14*th*, 1870.

"As to Medicine, I have read up most of the textbooks prescribed here, so that I am really very well up on the subject, and Jim Shepherd says I would make a capital doctor. I went along with him to the 'Dissecting-room,' 'Anatomical Museum,' 'Infirmary,' and 'Incurable Hospital,' and he did his best to sicken me (as you remember befell me three years ago), but I was all right, so he says I am now 'hardened'! It was very interesting seeing all the poor ill folk, and it was a real pleasure to speak to them, and joke with them, and leave them cheery."

In Germany it is evident even from his meagre notebooks that he thoroughly enjoyed life, and entered into it with his usual zest and brightness. But everything was subordinated to study. He made himself master of the language, and did his best to profit from the lectures he attended.

His good parents were naturally alarmed at the effects which German practice and thought (more dreaded then, perhaps, than now) might have upon their son. He warns them against uncharitableness. "There is nothing so difficult," he says, "as to convey a true and fair picture of the religious state of a people. Just as one's opinion of a person's character is often wholly changed on coming in contact with him, so actual life in a country alters one's estimate of it, and differences of circumstances and training condition the development of thought." He comes to the conclusion that it is not a breach of charity to say that the Germans are in a lower state religiously than Scotland, but asserts that at the same time there are many good and spiritual men among them, and that Germany is not so much more irreligious than, for example, London. He quotes Dorner as saying of missionary work, "You send more money, but we send more men." At that time he was beginning to understand Dorner's lectures, and says they are very good and very useful, especially for Germany. "For instance, he has been defending the doctrine of the Trinity, the personality of the Holy Ghost, the Divinity of Christ, and eternal punishment. He is very practical and thorough."

His attachment to Dorner grew as is witnessed by the following letter:—

"Dorner is a thoroughly good and very able man, and I have found your remark true, for I have already got a great deal of good from his lectures on Romans. He is at present lecturing on the 4th chapter, and since I began to understand him I have enjoyed his lectures very much; formerly the first few chapters of Romans seemed to me almost unintelligible, but I now see not only the meaning of the separate verses, but the grand line of thought and argument running through the whole, and I have a far clearer conception of many of the grandest Gospel doctrines than I had before, and especially of the nature of Christ's sacrifice for sin, and the necessity lying on God to punish sin. I wish I could send you some extracts from the lectures to show you how very good they are, but I can only give you one illustration. On iii. 28—which Luther translates, 'We conclude, then, that a man is justified by faith *alone*, without the deeds of the law'—he remarked that the Romanists misrepresent the meaning of this, and accuse Luther of Antinomianism, but (he added) Luther's position is simply this: 'The fruit does *not* make the tree, but a good tree cannot be without fruit.' When he was lecturing on iii. 25, where the question comes up whether Christ was merely the Altar for the propitiatory sacrifice or Himself the Sacrifice, he quoted Dr. Chalmers and another Scotch theologian with *extreme* approval, viz., Morison—do you know who he is? (Dorner took strongly the view that Christ was Himself the Sacrifice.) It is a great pleasure to hear him reading the verses of the passage he is to examine, for he does it with such earnestness and impressiveness that they seem to have double the meaning that they have ordinarily; he has a great deal of eloquence in him, and I like him very much."

"I always read Meyer's Commentary on Romans before going to the class, so that I am studying Romans very thoroughly, and as the other Professor I attend is lecturing on Paul's Teaching, and has been lecturing on his Life, I shall know a good deal more of Paul before I come back."

"On Wednesday, the 9th, I bought two Commentaries—De Wette on Psalms, and Meyer on Romans; they were rolled up in a sheet of paper taken out of an old book, containing some sixteen pages. I happened to glance at it in unfolding it, and my attention was caught by these words, in German, of which the following is a translation: 'Look upon your children as just so many flowers, which have been lent to you out of God's garden; the flowers may wither or die, yet thank God that He has lent them to you for one summer.' I thought at once that I had surely known the style long ago, and on glancing down the pages I was not at all surprised to find where the letter broke off—'S. R.—Aberdeen, March 7th, 1637.' Was it not strange to come in that odd way on a German translation of Samuel Rutherford's Letters? (See it you can find the passage.) I also notice, in the bookseller's catalogue, that Bunyan's works are all translated, also Spurgeon's, 'Schonberg-Cotta Family,' Mrs. Henry Wood's novels, etc."

In the autumn of 1873 Mr. Elmslie came to London. Four years previously Dr. Dykes had assumed the pastorate of the church at Regent Square. His health made it necessary for him to receive, from the commencement, assistance in his work. He was always anxious to secure the services of young men who might be trained under him for high achievements in later years. He heard of Mr. Elmslie's brilliant promise and invited him to fill the position, then vacant, of assistant to himself. The invitation was accepted, and Mr. Elmslie settled in London.

At Regent Square he flung himself into the work of the congregation with eager sympathy. He rapidly became popular and was made welcome in every home. In Dr. Dykes he found a wise and kind helper, to whom he became warmly attached. He appreciated his methods of working and his power as a preacher; but most of all he was struck by that grace of devotional fervour which gave Dr. Dykes' prayers so constraining a power to draw the souls of his people into communion with God. Nothing could have been brighter and happier than the life of the young preacher in his new surroundings, and his contagious enthusiasm and energy reacted on all who knew him. Here in London, at the busy centre of so much of the world's activity, his eager, questioning spirit found material for its restless enquiries; whilst that knowledge of human nature and its needs, which lay at the back of his most powerful spiritual work in later years, was slowly moulded by the opportunities of this time.

He describes in a letter to his mother the opening of his pulpit work at Regent Square. His chief fear was for his voice: "It looked such a distance," he writes, "to the faces in the end gallery." He got a friend to sit at the far end of the church, just over the clock, with a handkerchief which he was to wave if the speaker were inaudible. The subject of his sermon was, "The blood of Jesus Christ cleanseth us from all sin."

It is curious that the only despondent note that sounds through his correspondence at this time is the lamentation that he is unfitted for the pulpit. Repeatedly he expresses the fear that he will never make a preacher. He feels stiff and ill at ease. Official trappings of any kind he always disliked; and the pulpit robes, which he afterwards, as far as possible, discarded, he even then, as he told Dr. Dykes, detested. "I find it," he writes, "most hopeless to get anything I much care to say, and even then it is a perplexity generally to see what really is the reason. I am at the very point of giving over preaching altogether." Again, "I am more sure than ever that I am not a preacher," "Romps with Mr. Turnbull's children's singing-class are, on the whole, the most satisfactory occupation I know of."

These doubts and discouragements are not surprising. From the very first Dr. Elmslie conceived of the Christian Faith in a deep, comprehensive way, and its ideals of purity and holiness touched and warmed his nature at many points. Just because the outline was so large the filling-in took years to accomplish. It was only by continuous and patient self-analysis, by long observation and study of his fellow-men, that he was able to meet the needs of humanity, at all points, with a message which no one interpreted more largely. His sermons at Regent Square are sketches and outlines which experience alone could embody and complete. I have been much struck, in preparing a selection of his sermons for the press, with the growth of their composition. The sermon, for example, which stands first in this volume is, I think, the earliest he ever wrote. But the sermon, as it was last preached and is now printed, is not the sermon as he wrote it. The latter, though in outline identical, has been emptied of its original contents and re-filled out of the abundance of a heart which had grown in deeper knowledge of human needs and the approaches of Divine compassion.

His greatest satisfaction he found in his intercourse with the young men in the congregation.

"At the Young Men's Society," he writes, "I have been chairman for some time, and have to sum up: it costs me no preparation, and yet how they listen, and how I feel I can sway them as I please! I enjoy *that* kind of speaking."

It was at the close of these weekly discussions that Mr. Elmslie and I used often to meet. Our homeward paths were not identical, but we used to imagine that we were alternately escorting one another home as we spent a measurable portion of many a night upon the pavement, heedless of the thinning traffic, in keen debate over some of those deep insoluble problems which, I am glad to think, trouble his eager heart no longer. "I have long believed," he writes, "*thinking* to be more unhealthy than fever, cholera, bad drains, etc. I would give a good deal to be only an animal now and then."

Almost the first hopeful word about his preaching in Regent Square occurs in the following passage; it is interesting otherwise:—

"On Monday evening I was at Mr. Bell's. He pressed me to stay; thought I should not be a Professor; meant for a preacher; would have great power; something quite peculiar about my sermons; made Christ and everything so real, and near, and helpful; and my prayers always did him good, etc., etc.

"Curious, *that* in my sermons tells with everybody, for it comes from my line of reading and thinking at college, especially from the *German books on Christ, such as Strauss;* they made me trust Him as a Person rather than a doctrine; besides, I know I have come to regard Him all round differently in consequence. I have had to pay dearly for the reading, and have often wished I had not, so it is a little comfort to find that my coming through it makes me more helpful now."

The following is worth quoting as an instance of his ready resource:—

"48, REGENT SQUARE, *Tuesday.*

"MY DEAR FOLKS,—On Saturday morning a shabby man called, said he was a cousin of Dykes, needing money too, etc., just come from America—awkward Dykes on Continent. I saw he was an impostor, so resolved to get rid of him. I answered, 'It *is* awkward.' Then he said, 'What is to become of me? I look to you, sir.' 'Nothing will come of that, I fear.' 'But are you not Dr. Dykes's assistant?' 'Yes, I assist *him*, but not his relatives.' 'Well, but, sir, what would you advise me to do?' 'To say "Good morning," and not lose more of your time here.' As he got up he rubbed his stomach and said, 'I have had no breakfast to-day.' 'Very hard that mine is over, and my landlady does not like to have to make a second; do you often go without food?' 'Many and many a time, sir.' 'Ah, the doctor says it is good for the health! I wish I looked as well-fed as you do, going without breakfast. It must be economical. Good morning.' And we parted with mutual grins."

Among the congregation at Regent Square Mr. Elmslie formed many friendships. He conceived a warm regard for Professor Burdon-Sanderson (now of Oxford) and his wife; and other names might be mentioned of those who became lifelong friends. Among men who have since become well known, he saw something of Professor G. J. Romanes, who was then an occasional visitor at Regent Square. About this time he describes a meeting with Macdonell of the *Times*, whom he speaks of as "full of light." On the same occasion he met Dr. Marcus Dods for, I think, the first time. "*Dods, I like very much,*" is his brief comment.

Two years after his first arrival in London Mr. Elmslie settled in Willesden as minister of the Presbyterian Congregation there. When he left Scotland in 1873 he had formed no resolve to sever his ecclesiastical connection with that country. Circumstances and inclination, however, kept him in the south. He was much impressed with the type of congregation which represented English Presbyterianism at Regent Square. For many members of the session he had a warm respect and friendly admiration. He was interested in the experimental position of a Church, such as the Presbyterian one in England, comparatively young and small. The appeal that came to him from Willesden was direct and urgent. It is not to be wondered at that he yielded, at first rather reluctantly, to its pleading. The next eight years of his life were spent in active ministry in this little metropolitan suburb.

When Mr. Elmslie came to Willesden the place was much less populous than it has since become. The streets were only partially lighted. The road from the Junction Station to the little village of Harlesden, which is now a continuous row of shops and houses, passed then between ragged hedges, under a canopy of elms. The Presbyterian Church was not built, but services were held in a hall, which was the first building the Scotch residents put up. Mr. Elmslie took rooms near the site of the prospective church, but shortly after moved to the little house in Manor Villas which belonged to the chapel-keeper and his wife—Mr. and Mrs. Oxlade—a worthy couple, who returned the respect with which he regarded them by a loving admiration for the best man, as they phrased it, whom they ever knew.

On November 23rd, 1875, Mr. Elmslie was duly ordained. His dear mother was present at the service, and many friends. I had been with him during the earlier part of the day. Among other subjects of conversation we had been anticipating an episcopal discussion on the ethics of betting. He recognized the difficulty of the subject, and as he got more hopelessly perplexed in his effort to justify an absolute prohibition of the practice on grounds which could be intellectually defended, he turned, I remember, to his mother with a look of comical helplessness: "Here am I going to be ordained, and I don't even know why it's wrong to bet."

The congregation under his watchful care grew and prospered. A more united body of people never kept together in corporate life, and this happy result was due in chief measure to the unwearied tact and resource of the young minister.

In the spring of the following year the new church was completed and opened for public worship. Mr. Elmslie seemed to be able to draw into it men of all shades of religious opinion, and some even whose family traditions were at variance with evangelical orthodoxy. One of the distinguished sons of a famous Unitarian household was a fellow-worshipper with Ned Wright the evangelist. Throughout the whole of the little community which he ruled, for young and old alike, there was life, energy, and kindly charity. He felt that the path of Christian living was not to be trodden without ardent effort; and his example was at once a stimulus to the strong and an encouragement to the weak. "Your prayers," said a lady to him at this time, "always make me feel that it is a terribly difficult thing to be a Christian—but you can't think what a lot of good they do me."

The year after (1877) Mr. Elmslie commenced mission work. The London and North Western Railway Company had just built an Institute for their employés who are housed in large numbers in what is known as the Railway Village, at Willesden Junction. Above the recreation rooms in the new building was a large hall, which was placed at the disposal of Mr. Elmslie, by the directors, for Sunday services. He willingly took advantage of this kindness to gain a further hold on men whose hearts, in many cases, he had already reached. An engine-driver, who had been long ill, remarked to a friend about him: "He comes here, has a long chat, and tells me about many things; but never lets me feel he knows more than I do." The services then commenced are still continued under the oversight of Mr. Elmslie's successor.

Four years later another mission was started from Willesden which has since grown into an independent charge. The district of College Park came into being beneath Mr. Elmslie's eyes, and its spiritual needs attracted his attention. He applied to the London School Board for use of a schoolroom in which to hold Sunday services. The application having failed he bought, in the following year, along with his office-bearers, the site for a hall and church. The hall was at once built, and by the kindness of Mr. Andrew Wark, and other friends to whom Mr. Elmslie made a personal appeal, the money to meet the cost was subscribed. The church has been more recently completed.

One noticeable feature in his work at Willesden was his power to attract the young. I remember his saying on one occasion, half jestingly, that he liked to make children happy, as he knew how miserable they would be when they grew up. He meant that the strain of living was bound to tell, and that children should have all the happiness which can be enjoyed in the elasticity of youth. I do not know which were more attractive to the young people of Willesden—his children's sermons, or the sweets which he used to produce from mysterious stores when they came to visit him. Both were excellent and both did good.

The following contains an interesting account of his pastoral work, and is worth quoting at length:—

"Though it is late, and the text for Sunday (Communion) has not been fixed yet, I am going to tell you a very sad story, that has made me think of many things. Over a year ago Mrs. X——, on my recommendation, engaged as governess a Miss Y——, a great friend of Mrs. Z——, who asked that she might be very kindly treated, because she had had a deal to bear, and was all but disgusted with religion. She was a bright young girl, very pretty and graceful, clever in talk and repartee. Often I wished to find a way of showing her some kindness, but naturally that was hardly possible. However, I knew that both Mr. and Mrs. G—— were good to her. She was to have left last Saturday, but took suddenly unwell—had to go to bed. On the same day I called in at Mrs. G——'s on my way to say good-bye to Miss Y——; learning of her attack, I did not go on. ... Mrs. G—— had given her some eau-de-Cologne, and she had liked it much, so I took with me my little spray bottle. Her mother was with her; she looked wretchedly ill in face, eyes, and hands, but spoke in a very firm voice, and that made me think there was certainly no immediate danger.

"I at once told her about the spray bottle, and making her shut her eyes, applied it on her temples. She said it was delicious, and took it in her hands.

"I cannot try to describe her talk, for it was broken by moments of wandering, when she said very odd things, and in the midst she grew sick, and I had to go outside; she was too ill then to say much. I deemed it kind not to remain, but had a short, simple prayer. She said, very earnestly, 'Thank you so much for that!' I told her I would come again, and she must not fear to say to me all she wished. She answered, 'Yes, come again.' Thursday was a very busy day, for I had many engagements in London. Though I tried hard, I could not get home early, but it would have made no difference. She had been delirious night and day, with occasional intervals, and died at a quarter to three in the afternoon. She was only twenty-three.

"... J—— G—— went up and held her hands. She struggled for a moment or two, and then let her head down, and while he spoke to her, quieting her, she said she was going to be good and sleep now. Her wild eyes shut at last, and she was in a sleep, such as she had not had since Saturday.

"The mother and Mrs. G—— stole out, leaving only a sister, thinking it was recovery; but it was death. In ten minutes, with a little sigh, she ceased to breathe. Mr. G—— was her great friend, and she died in his arms. You can hardly think how sad her death has made me. So many forlorn things are about it that I have no time to write. Those lonely nights of agony and death-like sickness, that she had said nothing about at the time, believing herself dying, a governess among strangers, etc.

"Two things I am glad of—that Mrs. G—— was with her one night, and that I thought of the spray bottle. She said to me, '*You* had Mrs. G—— to nurse *you;* is not she an *angel?*' and I said, 'Yes, as much as if she had wings,' and I meant it.

Then her sisters told me that all that last night and day, till close on the end, my little bottle was never out of her hand; the coolness of the air and the softness of the spray relieved her sickness so much. Once, when in a spasm she jerked the bottle on the floor, she cried, for fear it was broken. The mother has sent a message asking if she may keep it, since it was the last thing in her child's hand, and the last that gave her any pleasure. It seems, too, that she spoke more than once of my prayer for her. Before the mother left last night to go home, she said to Mrs. G——, 'I shall always love you and your husband for what you have done for my child. Your kindness to her and the preaching she heard in your church did her so much good. She came to you with her life embittered, and with her religious beliefs nearly gone. Only a month ago she told me they had all come back again, and she understood Christ better, and believed in Him more, because of the way Mr. Elmslie preached of him, and we all have seen that this last year at Willesden has been the happiest in all her life. If she had been taken a year ago our recollections would have been very, very sad; now it is different,' and then the poor lady burst out crying. To-day I tried hard to get some white roses to lay on her ere the body is taken home, but I could only get some smaller white flowers, and maiden-hair ferns. Mrs. G—— had also got a basket of flowers, and I think the sight of them will comfort the old folks at home a little, as also a letter I have sent the poor mammy, saying some kind things about her lassie.

"Many other touching things the poor girl said and did come to my mind, and I could tell you more, but there is not time. I called it a sad story, but in some ways it is not sad. Indeed, I almost think that it is death alone that makes life at all sacred.

"All these things have made me think that Christ's account of the judgment must be quite real. I mean the 'Inasmuch as ye did it to one of these,' etc., for that is just how we would feel, that is just how the poor mother of the dead girl felt. There is nothing to thank God for more than to have been able to do a kindness to a dying soul. To think that a poor troubled soul has gone out of the pain and tiredness of life straight into the arms of God from yours, with the touch of pitying hands fresh on it; to feel God sees that, and knows those hands were yours, seems to me to bring you and God very near to each other. If it be true that He loves 'the souls that He hath made,' surely He must love you for loving them. I do not think it would matter very much about other things, if you had loved a good deal. If a little child said, as you were being turned away, 'He made me so happy!' and another, 'He fed and clothed me;' and another, 'He held me so gently in the agony of death,' even if he were a very sinful man, what could God do to him who had been good to the 'little ones'? The Apostle John had thought of it, and said, 'He that dwelleth in love dwelleth in God,' and Paul must have been in the same mind when he wrote 1 Cor. xiii."

They were very bright and happy, those Willesden days with their expanding usefulness; and before Mr. Elmslie left the district his life had been crowned by the commencement of that heart-union with another which seemed to more than double the separate influence of each for good. He worked unremittingly, and even his holidays were not given to idleness or rest. When he came to London he knew little of French, and one of his first holidays was spent in Paris, where he worked at the language with conscientious thoroughness, and obtained an adequate mastery over its difficulties. He returned to Paris on another occasion for further study, and one late summer he spent in Rome studying Italian.

His second visit to Paris was very helpful to him in more ways than one, especially in the influence exercised upon him by Bersier.

"I find that the £30 I spent on going to Paris is going to pay me far more than I thought of, not merely in French, though I rejoice in that daily, but in preaching. Perhaps you remember me saying that I had got several hints from the style of Bersier, who spoke, not read—mainly in letting out, adopting a free, direct style, variation, etc. Since coming back I have had constantly to preach very badly prepared; but I knew that (partly in consequence) I was much more free, bold, and roused. On Sunday I was very ill-prepared, nothing written, even order of thoughts not fixed; and I did not stick, even, to the line intended; but feeling this, I let out tremendously in vehemence and language. I saw how it took, and several spoke. Yesterday two old folks were on the sermon, and then they said, 'But ever since you came back from Paris you have been so much improved,' etc., etc. And indeed, I have heard more of my sermons during the last few weeks than ever before. So I owe a debt to M. Bersier. Another item, however, is, I fancy, that Paris made some things a little more real to me than they were before."

During all these years Mr. Elmslie's reading was wide and various. At the same time it was not difficult to see that the subject that interested him most was the study of man, and the books that attracted him were those that threw light upon the actions and passions of men. When he returned from Paris for the first time, for example, the author of whom he was most full was Rousseau—not Rousseau the philosopher and speculative thinker—but the Rousseau of the "Confessions"—with their strange candour and unblushing avowals. He read little of the works of the great imaginative masters of English prose or verse. If he did read a volume of Tennyson or Ruskin, for example, his criticisms were always brilliant and penetrating; but he never nourished his spirit upon their loftier utterances, nor was his style moulded by the melody or theirs. One exception I should perhaps make. His study of George Eliot was frequent and appreciative. One of his students has told us how, shortly before his own death, he referred to the scene in which Mr. Tulliver's is described to point a characteristic lesson in theology and charity. The passage was a favourite one, from the day when a friend first gave him the "Mill on the Floss" to read. I remember another remark of his about George Eliot which is worth quoting, but to appreciate its point I must introduce a word of explanation. I had, just at that time, drawn up a memorial on a subject in which we were both interested. Avoiding the conventional "wharfoes" which "Uncle Remus" has satirized in such documents, I had worded the appeal with perhaps exaggerated directness. Each sentence contained a distinct proposition, and the whole was expressed with something of that oracular emphasis with which, in those days, Victor Hugo used, from time to time, to address the citizens of Paris. After talking of this composition, and the subject of which it formed part, the conversation turned on George Eliot. I referred to "Romola"—especially to the closing scenes in the life of Savonarola, which, as it has always seemed to me, touch the highest point that has been reached in analysis of the drama of spiritual conflict. As I recalled the passage in which the disciplined imagination of the writer shows us the great Florentine stripped, one after another, of all those dazzling evidences of divine favour with which he used to feed his soul in pride, till there is nothing left to tell him of the unforsaking love of God save the lowly witness of his own bowed and penitent heart, the eyes of my companion grew bright with a large approval. After a pause he said, "If we find George Eliot is not in heaven when we get there, I think you and I will have to draw up a memorial—in the style of Victor Hugo."

When one thinks of the versatility of Dr. Elmslie's mind, and of the keenness of his intelligence, one feels that he might have won laurels in any domain of intellectual effort. And yet theology was the one subject on which his heart was set. He conceived of it grandly and nobly. He believed in it in that deep, derivative sense in which it is referred to by Carlyle in the opening to his story of the Puritan revolt, as a knowledge of God, the Maker, and of His laws. And for him Christ was the Divine Lawgiver—sole Lord of his conscience as well as Saviour of his spirit. For me at least, the facts of Christianity seemed always to grow larger and more solemn as he pressed their spiritual significance; its doctrines seemed to grow more real as he pierced beneath the forms in which they are encased to explore their ethical contents. God and man, and the relations between them, were the absorbing subjects of his study. It was his constant brooding over human nature as seen in the light of Divine pity, which gave its largeness to his measurement alike of the deadly hatefulness of sin and of the atoning charity of Christ. Sin was for him a thing far more terrible than any punishment which could possibly await it; and his sense of its dread, though still expiable, terror gave to him his Christlike eagerness to watch for the faintest signs of contrition and amendment. The following passage in a letter written to his mother some years earlier contains, it seems to me, the heart and soul of all his preaching.

"Am very much touched to hear about the poor Doctor. No matter what he may have done, with his disordered brain and troubled home life, I had rather go into the next world like him than like most of those who have condemned, though there were even nothing more than that near the end he tried a little to do right, and had a pitiful wish in his heart to be at rest, and go back to his old mother, and live a Christian life. And if it is really true that there is a heavenly Father who pities sinful men, and a Christ who died to save them, then I think my mammy, in helping him only but a little to better thoughts and hopes, did a greater thing than most deeds men call great. Any way, she has the satisfaction of having done kindly by an unfortunate man, and of knowing that it is all well with him—unless, indeed, Christ was altogether mistaken. It is not the first time, either, that she has done that sort of thing."

In 1880 he was appointed tutor of Hebrew in the Presbyterian College, London, and carried on the work along with that of his congregation in Willesden. He made himself very popular with the students, and when a permanent appointment came to be made in 1883, he was unanimously elected Professor of Hebrew. He writes: "It seems that the speeches of Walton, Fraser, and Watson were just perfect, so earnest and generous, and loving and hopeful. That put the Synod into a melting and happy mood. All yesterday I felt very grave, and almost afraid. I see that a very great thing, of good or evil, has happened in my life. God grant that it may be for good."

Almost immediately after his appointment to the Professorship, he married Kate, daughter of Mr. Alexander Ross, formerly Rector of the Grammar School, Campbeltown. The home which he made first at Upper Roundwood, Willesden, then at 31, Blomfield Road, Maida Vale, will ever have the brightest associations for his friends. He had all the qualities that fit a man to bless and grace married life. When his son and only child was born it seemed as if he were drinking the richest happiness of life in its fulness. I shrink from quoting words so sacred and tender as these which I take from a letter to his wife, but I cannot otherwise convey the full truth:—

"It makes me so glad, dear, every time I think of it, to know that we chose each other for no base worldly motives, but out of pure love and esteem for what (with all faults and defects) *was* good, and tender, and true, in one another. It was not for the mean things that the world and fashion make much of and worship that we two came together, meaning to go hand in hand through life with mutual help and kindness. We knew quite well the world's ways, and we could feel the pressure of its lower estimates and aims. But this act at least was done not with shallow hearts and for mean ends, but in honest friendship out of true affection, and with a very earnest wish to do only what was good and right, and to help each other to live a happy and a noble life." Such a life it was, though its years were few; and when the news of his death came, amid all the absorbing and confounding regrets which filled many minds, the thought was ever uppermost of the wife and child left desolate in the home that had been so full of sunshine.

Dr. Elmslie gave himself unsparingly to the work of his chair. He declined preaching engagements, and made zealous preparation for his classes. Apart from his own high standard of duty, he greatly respected the opinion of students. He thought Professors could have no fairer judges. The diligent study of the Old Testament, with the aid of the best German commentaries, was of course the main part of his preparatory work. But he did more with dictionaries than with commentaries, and made up his mind for himself. He always kept pace with the progress of research, and followed with deep attention the absorbing discussions of recent years on the structure of the Old Testament. As he was himself so chary in expressing publicly the conclusions he had arrived at on these subjects, it would not be right for me to say much. Of this, at least, he was sure, that the worth and message of the Old Testament were unimpaired by criticism, and would be so whatever the ultimate conclusion might be. He was also exceedingly sceptical as to the finality of the critical verdicts generally accepted at present: he believed that the analysis would be carried much farther. But although he diligently studied these things, and was an accurate and exact grammarian, he had his own theory of the duties of a Professor, which cannot be better described than in his own words, in an anonymous article contributed to the *British Weekly* for September 16th, 1887. There he says—

"Theological colleges are not in the first instance shrines of culture or high places of abstract erudition, but factories of preachers and pastors. They are not so much fountains of pure scholarship, but are rather to be classed with schools of medicine and institutes of technical education. Their function is not to produce great theologians, but to train efficient ministers—though they will hardly do that without possessing all that is essential to do the other. The ideal Professor is not your dungeon of learning, in whose depths he and his pupils are buried away from all practical life and usefulness. Information is good, in large measure indispensable, but the rarer gift of the heaven-born teacher is infinitely more. The old institution of the "lecture"—pretentious, laborious, in every sense exhaustive—must vanish. What was spun out into an hour of dry-as-dust detail must be struck off in ten minutes of bright, sharp, suggestive sketching. It is the difference between the heavy leading article of our newspapers and the crisp incisiveness of the French press. There must be much more teaching from text-books, and direct instruction from the Bible and human life. Dogmatic must deal less with theories and mouldy controversies, and more with the actual forces of sin and salvation. Exegetic cannot be allowed to fool away a whole session in a wearisome analysis of a few chapters of an epistle or a prophecy, fumbling and mumbling over verbal trivialities, blind to the Divine grandeurs that are enshrined within, while the students are left without even a bird's-eye view of the contents of the Bible as a whole, and destitute of any adequate conception of its vital majesty and meaning. Above all, a new scope and purpose must be given to the teaching of Practical Theology. Instead of a few lectures on the doctrine of the Church, and the ideal construction of a sermon, and the theoretical discharge of pastoral duty, this ought to constitute the crowning and chief study in the curriculum. And it should be in the form, not of teaching, but of actual training. Montaigne complained of his physicians that they "knew much of Galen, and little about me." They manage better in medical education now. Fancy the souls of tempted and sick men, women, and children handed over to the unpractised mercies of our book-taught young ministers. Colleges cannot quite mend this difficulty; but they might do much. And still more would be done if each student could be secured a year of travel abroad, and after that be required to serve an apprenticeship as curate or evangelist in connection with our larger congregations."

Through the kindness of my friend Mr. W. D. Wright, B.A., a student in the English Presbyterian College, I have received some very interesting reminiscences from his students. Space does not permit me to give them fully, but they show that Elmslie acted up to his own conception of a Professor's duties. One gentleman says—

"In recalling my impressions of Professor Elmslie, nothing strikes me so forcibly as his unfailing gentleness towards his students. It was very seldom indeed that any student was inattentive or troublesome in class, but when anything of the kind did occur Elmslie never spoke a word to the offender, and but for the pained flush on his face, one would have thought he had not noticed the occurrence. Again, when a student had not prepared his Hebrew lesson, and was unable to read it, Elmslie always appeared more ashamed than the student himself, but never said a word in blame or warning. Only he was afterwards chary of asking the same student to read.

"Elmslie was always ready to answer questions or meet any difficulties raised by the students, and he was often more eloquent on these occasions than when engaged in the ordinary routine of the class. He had rather a dislike for the schoolmaster's work that he was compelled to do with junior students, and hurried the class on until they were able to read passages in Hebrew. He did not aim so much at turning out Hebrew scholars as at making preachers, with a deep interest in Hebrew literature, and imbued with its spirit. If he could only secure our interest in a Hebrew author, and enlist our sympathies, he was willing to excuse any ignorance of ours in regard to grammar or syntax."

Another says—

"Perhaps my most vivid remembrances of Dr. Elmslie collect round his criticisms upon his students' trial discourses. Always kind, invariably conciliatory, in his criticism, yet he pointed out very plainly the defects, and indicated what was lacking with unfailing clearness of judgment. Even in the midst of his rebukes he would frequently take the bitterness away by some half-playful remark or reference to his own experiences. ... But better than any criticisms were his own concluding remarks on the text. Compressed, as they had to be, into a very few minutes, the whole intensity of his nature was seen in them. We often left the lecture-hall with our brains all astir and our hearts glowing with the inspiration of his words.

"I rather think some of his first-year students generally thought him occasionally heretical in his remarks at the close of his criticism. The one thing he could not bear was dulness, a uniformity of mediocre unreproachableness about a sermon. So he loved to give with startling effect a single side of a truth, and thus to send us away with our minds in a state of rather anxious activity. Once he half-humorously gave us the advice to begin our sermons with a truth stated in an unusual, half-heretical way, if one liked; for there is nothing makes people listen so attentively as a suspicion of heresy. But these early doubts of our Professor's soundness soon vanished, and we found him, as one has said, 'not so much *broad*, as *big*.'"

"He read to us a letter from a young man in much doubt as to whether he should enter the Wesleyan pulpit or no. His correspondent had read with relish Dr. Elmslie's article on Genesis. Could the Professor tell him of any books in which points of Christian faith were dealt with in an intelligent and convincing way? He, the correspondent, knew of no such books. Dr. Elmslie asked our opinion. I ventured to suggest that everybody had to hammer out these points of faith for himself. The Doctor was rather pleased with this remark, and at once said, 'Oh, yes! indeed he has, and to live them out too.'"

In his old students who had become ministers he took an earnest interest, and their letters show sufficiently how they prized him. "I feel," says one, "that you have inspired me with a something quite apart from the detailed work of the class—with spirit and enthusiasm for preaching."

He himself was soon drawn back to the pulpit, and as he preached in the various Nonconformist churches of the Metropolis it was almost immediately felt that a new force of the first rank had appeared. He preached frequently in Brixton Independent Church, then under the brilliant and devout ministry of James Baldwin Brown. Mr. Brown's health was very infirm when Dr. Elmslie began to preach there, and on his death the congregation looked to the Professor as his natural successor. Ultimately a cordial invitation was given. The inducements offered were great, and the position was among the most influential London Nonconformity can bestow. That a change of ecclesiastical relations would have been necessitated by his acceptance would have been no difficulty to Dr. Elmslie. But he feared to face the physical strain involved, and preferred to continue his work as Professor.

The disappointment felt at his declinature of the invitation to Brixton Independent Church was very deep, although the members construed his refusal in the right way, and understood that no difference of opinion on ecclesiastical polity and no doubt of their fidelity had anything to do with it. Some of the letters written to him were very touching. Among these I may quote the following:—

"DEAR SIR,—We are, with the exception of my husband (who is somewhat of an invalid), closely occupied all the week, sometimes even the strain becoming excessive. On Sundays, when you come, your teaching and influence lift us above all our difficulties, and we start for the next week full of hope, and feeling nothing too hard to be accomplished. With regard to my sons, it is an especial boon, because, though they are thoughtful and good, it has been almost impossible to get them to attend church during the last two or three years. They did not meet, perhaps, with a single service for many weeks into which they could enter with the slightest interest, so they stayed away. We have all found our Sundays very wearisome, but on those you have visited us all is changed. All are deeply interested, one competing with the other in bringing forward the ideas that have interested them." The writer goes on reluctantly to acquiesce in a declinature which had evidently gone to the heart of the whole household.

His sphere as a preacher steadily widened, and he became, in addition, a most popular platform speaker at the May meetings in Exeter Hall and elsewhere. There is no room to recount his triumphs, and no need to do so. All who heard him bore the same testimony. If he was preaching in one of the suburbs the trains towards the time of service brought a company of admirers from all parts of London. The chapel would be crowded to the doors. When he stood up in the pulpit strangers felt surprise. Youthful in appearance, unpretending in manner to the last degree, and in the early part of the service generally nervous and restrained, it was not till the sermon began that he showed his full powers. He usually read the first prayer, and was always glad if he could get some one to help him with the lessons and the giving out of hymns. But in preaching all his powers were displayed at their highest. He did not read his sermons, but his language was as abundant and felicitous as his thought, and his audience was always riveted. Alike in manner and matter he was quite original. He imitated no preacher; he did not care to listen to sermons, and was rarely much impressed by them when he did. I doubt if he ever read a volume of sermons unless it was to review them. His knowledge of the Bible and his knowledge of life gave him inexhaustible stores; he had always matter in advance, and never felt that sterility of mind which so often afflicts the preacher. He would retell the stories of the Old Testament, and make them live in the light of to-day. The reality and firmness with which he grasped life—the life of toiling, struggling, suffering men and women—was his chief power. His sympathetic imagination helped him to divine the feelings of various classes of the young men in business, for example, with a small salary, and little prospect of rising, forbidden the hope of honourable love, and tempted to baseness from without and within. He had an intense concern for the happiness of home life, and much of his preaching was an amplification of the words—

> "To mak' a happy fireside clime
>   To weans and wife;
> That's the true pathos and sublime
>   Of human life."

Mothers' hearts he would win by praying for the "dear little children asleep in their beds at home." Young couples he would warn to keep fresh the tenderness and self-sacrifice of first love. But the sermons which follow speak for themselves, though nothing can transfer to the printed page the light and fire of which they were full as the preacher spoke them.

Of the helpfulness of his preaching he had from time to time many testimonies, of which he preserved a few. These were very welcome to him, far more so than any appreciation of the intellectual ability or the eloquence of his sermons. This, from one letter, is a specimen of many more: "I wandered past my own church in a heavy weight of business care, knowing that a mortgagee would this week likely take all I had, and caring little where I wandered when I went in to hear you, and was surprised at the text you preached from, and more so at the helpful words you spoke, which I hope, by God's grace, will enable me to see—

'Behind a frowning providence
He hides a smiling face.'"

He delivered courses of lectures to Sunday-school teachers under the auspices of the Sunday-school Union. These were very largely attended and highly appreciated. He received many letters of encouragement, among them one from the vicar of a London church, who wrote that although he could not attend them all, owing to the exacting nature of his own work, he listened to those he could be present at with the deepest attention and the greatest thankfulness. "That a great scholar should fearlessly approach these vexed questions, and with his grasp of them be able to make them popular and understood by the people, and above all attractive to the people, is to me a great joy. You make the Bible a living book, filled with people met with in workaday life. You show that the social problems which superficial minds imagine are utterly new are only old difficulties under new names, and that the Bible has a definite word to say upon them, and its 'Thus saith the Lord' is to be listened to still. I venture to think that this is the great need of this fevered age of ours, and I heartily thank you."

An attempt was made in 1888 by the Westminster Congregational Church, where he had often preached with great acceptance, to secure him as pastor. This invitation he was inclined to accept. The condition of the Theological College was not at the time satisfactory, and for that and other reasons it seemed not unlikely that the call would be closed with. To me, as to others of his friends, it seemed certain that his physical strength was wholly inadequate to the position, and I am glad to think of the urgency with which this view was pressed on him. He was reassured about the College, and gratefully declined the invitation. In connection with it he received the following letter, which reflects so much honour on all concerned that I venture to include it here:—

"LONDON, *March 8th*, 1888.

"To THE REV. PROFESSOR ELMSLIE, M.A., D.D.—We hear with sympathetic interest that the Westminster Church is calling you to its pastorate.

"The traditions of the Westminster Church are good, its ministry has always been highly spiritual and largely human, and its importance and influence have been second to none among the churches of our order in this great Metropolis.

"We feel special interest in this call from the fact that it will involve on your part the crossing of the denominational boundary between Presbyterianism and Congregationalism. Identical though the churches practically are in the foundation of their theological belief, we appreciate the strain upon early and sacred association which this may involve, with, however, this compensation, that, borne in answer to a call for service and furtherance of the kingdom of Christ, it is a practical and valuable evidence that the sister denominations are truly wings in the one great army of God.

"Should you accept this call to the highly honourable post which the Westminster Church offers you, we beg to assure you of the cordial welcome, brotherly sympathy, and, as the occasion may arise, the friendly co-operation of the ministers of our body.

"It is unusual for the representatives of other churches to intervene in cases of this kind, but understanding there may be questions in your mind as to the feelings with which you would be received into the ranks of the Congregational ministry, we have thought it right, on the suggestion of a representative of the Westminster Church, to give you this assurance.

"With best wishes for your future welfare and highest prosperity,

"Yours fraternally,

"Alexander Hannay, Robert F. Horton,
Henry Allon, John Kennedy,
J. C. Harrison, John Fredk. Stevenson,
J. Guinness Rogers, R. Vaughan Pryce,
Andrew Mearns, Alfred Cave,
Samuel Newth, John Stoughton,
Joseph Parker, Henry Robert Reynolds."

It is unnecessary to refer in detail to the numerous invitations to Presbyterian pulpits which reached him from time to time. Some of these were from Scotland, on which he looked back with mingled feelings. He did not willingly turn his face to the north, or think of it with much pleasure. "I worked too hard there," he would say. On the other hand, he writes from Edinburgh in 1880—"I had a splendid talk, fit to be printed, with Taylor Innes, Davidson, and Iverach. I think I might become a great divine with such stimulating society."

Elmslie's connection with the Congregationalists not only greatly heightened his estimate of the loyalty and piety still abiding in the Nonconformist churches of England; it also brought him more fully into the current of modern life. He began to be deeply interested in politics, which he had previously rather held aloof from, became a diligent reader of newspapers, and was led to an absorbing interest in Socialism, on which he delivered a memorable address in Exeter Hall in connection with the Pan-Presbyterian Council of 1888. In politics he was an ardent Liberal and a thoroughgoing Home Ruler.

Dr. Elmslie added to his other engagements some of a literary kind. He became adviser to the firm of Messrs. Hodder and Stoughton, of 27, Paternoster Row, and occupied this position for a few years with great satisfaction on both sides. His work was to write estimates of any manuscripts Messrs. Hodder and Stoughton submitted for his consideration, and that he did it incisively and honestly the following specimen, selected almost at random, will show:—

"Energetic, intelligent, earnest discourses on the lines of the old Evangelical Protestant school, not in any way original in exposition or fresh in presentation, but quite sensible, vigorous, and good. That they are not up to date appears in such a reference as this: 'The excitement caused in this country by the publication of "Essays and Reviews," and subsequently of Bishop Colenso's heretical works, is still fresh in our memories,' etc. Even if thoroughly rubbed up and revised, the sermons would only sell where writer's name would carry them, and to some extent to preachers in search of ready-made discourses."

He ceased to act in this capacity some time before his death, but continued to be a constant visitor to No. 27, where his appearance gave pleasure to every one in the place. His inaugural lecture on Ernest Renan was published in the excellent "Present-day Tracts" of the Religious Tract Society, and was very well received. He had often heard Renan lecture, and was thoroughly conversant with his books. To the *Expositor* he made some contributions, but in spite of pressure, delayed publishing extended articles. In *Good Words* and the *Sunday Magazine* some of his sermons were published from time to time. To the *British Weekly* he was a large contributor, mostly of short anonymous reviews and paragraphs; occasionally he would write an extended critique or a travel sketch. But he was making ready for work as an author. A remark made by Dr. Marcus Dods had sunk into his mind; it was to the effect that men should study till they were forty, and then publish the result of their studies. He had arranged to begin writing and to give up preaching, and had he lived this purpose would have been carried out. His schemes were numerous, but the chief was to write a book which should make the Old Testament intelligible—its contents and message—to the common people. He had made a careful study of the Minor Prophets, the result of which will shortly appear in a popular commentary.

So his life went on, useful, happy, honoured, and but too busy. In 1888 he received the degree of Doctor of Divinity from his Alma Mater. In the same year he preached the opening sermon at the Nottingham meeting of the Congregational Union. This high honour was never before conferred on a Presbyterian minister. He enjoyed social intercourse, and in recent years had much of it. He had many pleasant Continental holidays. But the claims upon him constantly increased, and alas! his strength did not. He had the happiness of being under the care of an accomplished and skilful physician, who was also an intimate friend—Dr. Montague Murray. I need not speak of the faithful care that never ceased its vigilance. But although often warned against overwork, and constantly paying the penalty in severe headaches, no serious danger was apprehended. I am anxious to make it clear that he did not wilfully throw his life away. He apprehended no danger, and thought he was taking sufficient precautions. The last summer of his life he took two Continental holidays. He loved life. His last years were his best—the brightest and the fullest of influence. If one had been asked to say who among his friends had the prospect of the surest happiness and the greatest influence, he would have named Elmslie without hesitation. It was in such a noon that his sun went down.

He spent September 1889 in the Engadine. Although he enjoyed the trip he benefited from it less than he had hoped, and began the work of his classes with a certain feeling of weariness. He did not, however, imagine that anything was seriously wrong, and accepted many engagements for the winter. He preached with wonderful eloquence to crowded audiences in St. John's Wood Presbyterian Church on the Sunday evenings of October, and had promised to take anniversary services on Sunday, November 3rd, for the Rev. John Watson, M.A., of Sefton Park Church, Liverpool. Although unable to go to College on the previous Friday, he was anxious not to disappoint his friend, and accordingly went to Liverpool. His medical adviser reluctantly allowed him to preach once. He officiated at the forenoon service, getting help from one of his students in the service. That afternoon he spent in bed, and he was too unwell to return to London till Wednesday. Dr. Murray saw he was seriously ill, and ordered that all his engagements should be postponed. On Thursday, however, he lectured at the College, but on Friday he was prostrated, and remained so till Tuesday, when unconsciousness set in. He suffered from agonizing headache. Symptoms of diphtheritic sore throat set in on Sunday, November 10th. On Tuesday the medical man in attendance pronounced the disease to be typhoid fever, and after the evening of that day he was never conscious. His busy brain worked on. The faithful friend and physician, who hardly left his side, says he never heard such intelligent unconscious talk. If his mind travelled to the scene of his recent journeys he would give directions in German about ordering rooms, arranging for dinner and the like, with perfect clearness. More often he would fancy himself in his class-room teaching Hebrew, and urging the students to put heart into their work. Over and over he spoke to his wife of what had been the master thought of his life. Lifting his hand he would say with great earnestness, "No man can deny that I always preached the love of God. That was right. I am glad I did not puzzle poor sorrowful humanity with abstruse doctrines, but always tried to win them to Christ by preaching a God of Love." Once he turned to her with wistful eyes and said, "Kate, God is Love. All Love. We will tell every one that, but specially our own boy—at least you will, for I seem to be so tired these days, and my one wonder and trouble is, that all these people (meaning the nurses) try to prevent me from going home, where we were always so happy." He was reassured for the moment, when some familiar object was pointed out, and asked that he should often be told that he was at home. He was soon to go home indeed. He recognised his wife on Friday, with the last signs of consciousness. Shortly after he became faint, closed his eyes, and never opened them again on earth. About four o'clock on the morning of November 16th, 1889, he quietly passed away.

Scarcely any death could have made a greater rent than this, and the tokens of sorrow—public and private—were almost unexampled in the case of one who held no high office in Church or State, who had not lived long enough to make his mark in literature, who had sought no fame or honour, but had been content with doing his duty as it called him day by day. The funeral service was conducted in Marylebone Presbyterian Church (Dr. Donald Fraser's), of which he was a member. Dr. Fraser and Dr. Allon delivered addresses, while Dr. Dykes and Dr. Monro Gibson offered up prayer. The great church was crowded with a deeply moved audience of two thousand persons, every one of whom probably represented some word spoken or some service rendered by the kind heart then cold. He was buried at Liverpool next day by the side of his mother, his attached friend and colleague the Rev. Dr. Gibb, being among those present at the interment. A service was conducted at the Presbyterian College, where Principal Dykes delivered a deeply moving address. "You may send us another Hebrew Professor," said he, "and we shall welcome him, but you cannot send us another Elmslie."

Tributes from the Presbyteries of the Church, from congregations of various denominations to which he had ministered, from well-known Church leaders, from old students, and, not least, from unknown men and women whom he had helped and comforted, poured in. They were too numerous to be quoted or further referred to, but the intensity and turmoil of feeling expressed in them, showed that the sorrow for him was as deep as its appointed signs were extensive. One for whom much sympathy was felt, his aged father, seemed to bear up bravely against the blow. He received with eager gratitude the abundant testimonies to the honour and love in which his son was held. But the grief had gone to his heart, he soon began to sink, and died a few months later.

What was said of Henri Perreyve is eminently true of Elmslie: he was gifted for friendship and for persuasion. During the last years of his life, the period when I knew him intimately, he came to what has been called the grand moral climacteric, and all his nobler qualities were manifest in their full strength. There was about him the indefinable charm of atmosphere, at once stimulating, elevating and composing. He had an inexplicable personal attraction that drew to it whatever loving-kindness there might be in the surroundings, as certain crystals absorb moisture from the air they breathe. In his company speech became of a sweeter and purer flavour. There was no austerity, no Pharisaism about him; he delighted in fun and gave himself a large liberty; but nothing he said or welcomed marred the moral beauty which he had reached through long self-discipline.

No one could know him long without perceiving that he was full of generous ardour for pure aims. His was not the coarse ambition for the glittering prizes of life, nor was his enthusiasm such as would have cooled with time. In that delicate and watchful consideration for others, which has been called the most endearing of human characteristics, he could hardly be surpassed. He concerned himself with the whole life of his friends, and especially with their trials and perplexities. Dr. Elmslie was, indeed, one of the very few men to whom one might go in an emergency, sure of a welcome more kindly if possible than would have been accorded in a time of prosperity. His whole energies were solicitously given to the task of comforting. If things could be set right he delighted in applying his singular nimbleness of mind to the situation. He was adroit in action, and almost amusingly fertile in schemes and suggestions. I think it is safe to say that all his friends felt it was better worth while talking over a difficulty with him than with any one else. Even in cases of moral failure—perhaps I should say specially in those cases—he was eager to do what was possible. He had a profound and compassionate sense of the frailty of men, their sore struggles and thick temptations. Wherever he saw true repentance he would do his utmost to secure a fresh opportunity for the erring. He thought the Christian Church sadly remiss in allowing so many lives to be ruined by one great fault. Out of an income which, for a man of his talents, was not great, he gave largely, secretly, and with the most careful discrimination.

His spirit in speaking of others, whether friends or foes was always charitable. But I must guard against the danger of mistake. He did not indulge in indiscriminate laudation. His perception of character was very keen, he was not a hero-worshipper, and he had always a certain impatience of extravagant and unmeasured speech. But he had learned the secret of not expecting from people more than they have to give, and this, along with the generosity of his nature, helped him to make large allowance for what seemed unhopeful and disappointing, and made him eager to do justice and more than justice to whatever was good. On occasion however, he would with grave kindness point out the limitations of a character, and sometimes, though very rarely, he would be moved to vehemence as he spoke of modern religious Pharisaism.

In conversation he was ready alike to listen and to speak. Nothing gave him greater delight than a long and animated talk. He loved individuality in whatever sphere it was manifested, and would often relate with delight the racy remarks made to him by poor people. Of decorous commonplace he was rather impatient, and complained once that a young man of promise, with whom he had spent a day, had said nothing during the whole of it but what he ought to have said.

Dr. Elmslie had abundantly that charity which "rejoiceth not in iniquity." It gave him real pain to hear of the mistakes and misfortunes of men. Without a trace of jealousy, he delighted in any success or happiness that came to his friends. Of all virtues he most admired magnanimity, and when he was told of generous actions, his face would glow with pleasure. To the spirit of malice and revenge he was always and utterly opposed. Like other public men he was occasionally attacked; the fancied breadth of his religious views excited animosity in certain quarters and was at times the subject of anonymous letters. He would regret that his critics did not know him better, and might show pain for the moment, but it was soon past. He never in any way retaliated.

Dr. Elmslie had no dæmonic passion for literature. For books as books he had no love, and this indifference disturbed some of his associates not a little. When he had got out of a book what he could he exchanged it for another. Hence his personal library was small, consisting mostly of Oriental literature, and some favourite French and German works. But his reading was wide, and he knew the best in everything. He was master of French, German, Italian, and Dutch, and had a working knowledge of other languages. Of his preferences in literature he did not often speak; when he did he would say that to George Eliot and Goethe he owed much and very much.

No one could be his friend without perceiving that he was through and through a Christian. In his later years his doubts seemed completely conquered. You saw nothing but the strength he had gained in overcoming them. He held his faith with a certain large simplicity, but with absolute conviction. Among all his attracting qualities the chief was his great hope in God. He was indeed "very sure of God." Latterly, he could hardly listen without impatience to gloomy forecasts of the future. He believed that all was right with the world; that Christ was busy saving it, and would see of the travail of His soul. Men prone to darker thoughts loved him very much for that. No sickness, no bodily suffering, ever altered this mood of trust and hope.

His dogmatic position is not easy to define. Although liberal in his views he disliked rashness; and avoided giving offence so far as he could. My impression is, that he held an attitude of suspense towards many debated questions. He did not feel the need of making up his mind. The truths of which he was sure gave him all the message he needed, and these were independent of the controversies of the hour. But he kept an open mind, and was ever ready to add to his working creed. He could not preach what did not thoroughly possess his own soul, but never dreamt that he had reached finality, and I think was increasingly disposed to respect the doctrines, which, as history proves, have stirred and commanded men. A thorough Liberal and Nonconformist, he knew comparatively little of the Church of England, and was repelled by its exclusive spirit, but when told of the great qualities of the younger High Church leaders, he listened with interest and pleasure. He was happy in being able to think more kindly and hopefully of men from whom he was divided in principle. As has been already said, he considered the spiritual life of Congregationalists very deep and true; he loved the warm old-fashioned piety he found among them, and heartily believed in their future. Of the differences among Nonconformists he made nothing, was a vehement advocate of union, and strongly opposed to whatever interrupted cordial relations between Churches.

Though never chary in speaking of his religious experiences he did not obtrude them. A real belief in immortality he thought could hardly exist without other faiths being right. Such a belief would give life its true shape and colour. He was very patient of honest doubts, but had to make himself sure that they were honest, not the cloak of moral laxness. What he loved best to speak of was the magnificence of Divine grace—the love of God commended in Christ's death.

But it is time to lay down the pen. We may apply to Dr. Elmslie words, used, I think, about an American writer: his charm was of the kind that we fail to reduce to its grounds. It was like that of the sweetness of a piece of music, or the softness of fine September weather. In a certain way it was vague, indefinable, inappreciable; but it is what we must point to, for nothing he has left behind gives any adequate idea of his powers. Friendship occupied an immense space in his life, and all who knew him are conscious that,

> Now the candid face is hid,
> The frank, sweet tongue has ceased to move,

something has gone from them never to be replaced till that daybreak which shall unite all who belong to one another. But over the sense of their own loss there rises and remains the feeling how much God indicates in this life of which only some small portion is fulfilled. The world of expectation and love thus suddenly closed for earth must be open somewhere. There must be ministries in other spheres for which he was prepared and summoned. His life must—we know not how—be complete in Him, Who alone of all who lived fully achieved His life's programme, Who came down from Heaven to do His Father's business, and having done it died.

I.
FROM THE REV. PROFESSOR MARCUS DODS, D. D.

"From my first acquaintance with the late Professor Elmslie, I availed myself of every opportunity of seeing him, for intercourse with him never failed to be inspiring. Our acquaintance may be said to have culminated in a five weeks' tramp through the Black Forest and the Tyrol, in company with Professor Drummond—to myself a never-to-be-forgotten holiday. Often compelled to sleep in one room, and always thrown upon one another from sunrise to sundown, we came to have a tolerably complete insight into one another's character. And for my own part, I never ceased to marvel at the unfailing good humour and gaiety with which Elmslie put up with the little inconveniences incident to such travel, at the brightness he diffused in four languages, at the sparkling wit with which he seasoned the most commonplace talk, and at the ease and felicity with which he turned his mind to the gravest problems of life and of theology, and penetrated to the very heart of them. His cleverness, his smartness of repartee, his nimbleness of mind, his universal sympathy and complete intelligence were each hour a fresh surprise, and were as exhilarating as the mountain air and the new scenes through which we were passing. I have often reproached myself with not treasuring the fine sayings with which he lifted us into a region in which former difficulties were scarcely discernible and not at all disturbing. But, indeed, one might as well have tried to bottle the atmosphere for home consumption, for into everything he said and did he carried a buoyancy and a light all his own.

"As a preacher Professor Elmslie was, in many of the highest qualities of a preacher, without a peer. No one, I think, appreciated more highly than he the opportunity the preacher of Christ has to apply balm to all the wounds of humanity, and no one exercised this function with a more intelligent or tender sympathy or with happier results. No human condition, physical, mental, or spiritual, seemed beyond his ken, and none but found in him the suitable treatment. His wealth of knowledge, his unerring spiritual insight, and his rare felicity of language gave him the ear of cultured and uncultured, of the believer and the sceptic alike. It has always seemed doubtful to some of his friends whether such exceptional aptitude for preaching should have been, even in any degree, sacrificed to professorial work. Yet he himself delighted in that work, and the very last time I saw him he was full of enthusiasm for Old Testament studies, and hopeful of what might be done by himself and his fellow-labourers in this field.

"When so energetic an individuality is withdrawn the world suffers an appreciable loss; and one cannot yet think of the place he filled, or of the place we all hoped he would yet fill, without a keen shoot of pain."

II.
From Professor Henry Drummond.

"DEAR MR. NICOLL,—It is futile to plead want of recollection as an excuse for what must be a too brief contribution to your little portrait, for no one who ever knew Elmslie could ever forget him. But the truth is, I never knew him well. At college he was too much my senior for me to have presumed to know him, and in after years we scarcely ever met, except on one occasion, for more than a passing moment.

"I never heard Elmslie preach, or lecture, or do anything public. I knew him chiefly as a human being. Elmslie off the chair was one of the most attractive spirits who ever graced this planet. It was not so much his simple character, or the bubbling and irresistible *bonhommie*, or even the amazing versatility of his gifts, but a certain radiance that he carried with him, a certain something that made you sun yourself in his presence, and open the pores of your soul, and be happy. I think I can recall no word that he ever spoke, or even any idea that he ever forged, but the *man* made an impression on you indelibly delightful and joyous.

"My first distinct impression of him was crossing the College quadrangle with 'Romola' under his arm. He was kind enough to stop and introduce me to the authoress, whom I forthwith proceeded to cultivate assiduously. Shortly after this Elmslie gave a supper-party, a function much too rare among Scotch students. I had the honour to be invited to represent the juniors—an act of pure mercy, for I then neither knew Elmslie nor his set. If I were now asked by a senior man at college how he could best influence his less-advanced colleagues, I should answer, 'Make him your debtor for life by asking him up to your rooms.' Of the entertainment itself—the literary entertainment, I mean—I remember little; it was the being there that helped me. And what I do remember I do not know that I ought to divulge, for the *pièce de resistance* was the Hans Breitman Ballads, which Elmslie carved and served himself, with extraordinary relish, throughout most of the evening.

"It was this same man, unchanged by the weight of years and work, whom I met several years after in the Black Forest, and accompanied for some weeks in a walking tour. The third member of the party was Dr. Marcus Dods, and we tramped with our knapsacks through the Tyrol, the dolomite country, and the Saltzkammergut. Elmslie at first was full of the Strasburg professors under whom he had been studying, but after a few days I saw no more of his wisdom, for he gave himself up like a schoolboy to the toys of St. Ulrich and the Glockner glaciers. But of this most perfect of all vacations nothing now remains with me but an impression of health, sunshine, and gentle friendship.

"Elmslie's graver side I can only dimly realise from the appearances he used to make in the Theological Society of the New College, Edinburgh. I do not remember even the theme of any debate in which he ever took part, but the figure and voice, and especially the look of the student as he stood up there amidst the almost awe-stricken hush of his classmates, lives most vividly in my mind. When Elmslie spoke every one felt that he at least had something to give, some message of his own. He never seemed to be merely saying things, *i.e.* 'making a speech,' but to be thinking aloud, and that with an intensity and originality most inspiring and impressive. His voice and tone had that conviction in them which was as impossible to define as to resist. I could with difficulty imagine any one moving the previous question after Elmslie. Another peculiarity, which added greatly to his power, was that he thought with his whole face. In fact, in listening to him one did not so much hear a man speaking as see a man thinking. His eyes on these occasions would become very large and full of light, not of fire or heat, but of a calm luminosity, expressive of a mingled glow of reason, conscience, and emotion.

"One of the last things I read of Elmslie saying was that what people needed most was *comfort*. Probably he never knew how much his mission, personally, was to give it. I presume he often preached it, but I think he must always have *been* it. For all who knew him will testify that to be in his presence was to leave care, and live where skies were blue.

"Yours very sincerely,
"HENRY DRUMMOND.

"BRINDISI, *March 17th*, 1890."

III.
FROM THE REV. JOHN SMITH, M. A.

"BROUGHTON PLACE UNITED PRESBYTERIAN CHURCH,
"EDINBURGH.

"It is very difficult, in a few sentences, to convey to another the impression which gradually grows up from frequent contact with a nature so sympathetic, clear-sighted, active, and many-sided in its activities as that of a fellow-student and friend like Elmslie. Acquaintance with him was mainly confined to two widely sundered periods, both of them anterior to the last, crowded, brilliant years.

"It was during the session of 1866-67, at King's College, Aberdeen, that I first met him. As every one who knew the Aberdeen of that time is aware, the third year was to most students peculiarly severe. Bain—a consummate teacher—made distinction in his class appear the blue ribbon of the college course, for which the best men earnestly contended. Fuller was merciless in his demands upon his senior mathematical class, who found, as the months went on, that it was less and less possible to keep him in sight. And with 'Davy' Thomson there was no trifling,—fear of his sarcasm greatly helping our thirst for natural philosophy. As the session advanced the chariots of most of us drave heavily. Elmslie, however, who studied everything, seemed to do his work with a masterful ease which impressed us all. He came up smiling to an examination as if it were a thing of nought. Study could not blanch the fresh bloom on his cheek, or damp the lively play of spirit which characterized him then as much as in after years. I have just been looking at his portrait in our class group, and at his clear bold signature in the lithographed autographs which accompanied it. To a singular extent his personal character was formed, and his peculiar excellencies were developed, at that early date. He was, when little more than a boy, a man whose words clung to you, whose ways lingered in your memory. Even then, too, he had something of that sweet hopeful Christian spirit which was to make his preaching so helpful. One student, whose opportunities had been few, whose struggle had been painful in the extreme, used to speak to me with enthusiasm of Elmslie's kindly notice and assistance. While other natures were but emerging from chaos, barely conscious to themselves, giving but the faintest indication to others what they were to be, he whose course was to be so soon run, was already girt up and disciplined for life's way.

"After our college course was completed, I did not meet him till 1878, when already he had been for some time minister in Willesden. On more than one occasion, I stayed with him for a day or two, and saw with my own eyes how full and many-sided a life he was living then, even before fame came. He was carrying on his studies, advising publishers with regard to learned and bulky MSS., superintending a railway mission, maintaining in briskest activity the work of his congregation, and in these and many other channels winning 'golden opinions from all sorts of people.' Especially did I admire his faculty of adapting himself to English ways of thinking and feeling. And amid this abounding life, and with the promise of all that came after bright before him, he was so unaffected and ingenuous and humble, never shrinking from his future, yet not feverishly anticipating it, that it was impossible not to love him. Here, too, he showed his skill in discovering elements of strength in men whom others would dismiss as incompetent. I remember a missionary who succeeded to the astonishment of everybody, and I verily believe of himself, under his kindly and stimulating superintendence. It is one of the pleasant memories of my life that I carried the motion in Synod which made it possible for him to be elected as permanent Professor. I remember how the Willesden flock were between smiles and tears all that day, and how when the second vote was carried which severed the tie between their minister and them, they did not know whether to be grieved or glad, so strong was their love, so eager was their desire for his advancement. No one could hear him speak that night and doubt his future. All that the great world has since seen in him, we knew to be there, and more, which would have been revealed had not death so soon sealed his lips.

"Of the later years, others will speak. Out of these earlier memories I have woven—all unskilfully I fear, yet with sincere affection—this modest wreath for his tomb."

IV.
FROM THE REV. JAMES STALKER, D.D.

"6 CLAIRMONT GARDENS, GLASGOW,
"*March* 24*th*, 1890.

"DEAR MR. NICOLL,—What a bright time it is to look back to! There is nothing else in life afterwards quite equal to it. Never again can one mingle day by day with so many picked men; never is thought so free; never are there such discoveries and surprises. Those years in the New College have in the retrospect almost a dazzling brightness, and Elmslie contributed more, perhaps, than any one else to make them what they were.

"I just missed being by his side all the four years, for we entered together; but after a week or so I left to go abroad with the Barbours, to whom I was tutor. I have no recollection of him that session, for I had not gone in for the bursary examination, where any one competing with him was pretty certain to be made aware of Elmslie to his cost. Next session, when I returned, I was of course separated from him by a year, which makes a great difference in college life. But for three sessions we must have met nearly every day, and I was thrown into the closest contact with him in the committees and societies where students of the different years come together.

"The Theological Society was at that time the centre of the life of the College. Under Robertson Smith, Lindsay and Black, whose last year was Elmslie's first, it had entered on a career of the most brilliant activity, in which, I suppose, it has never faltered since. We used to say, in our exaggerative way, that we got more good from it than from all the classes put together. And indeed it would be difficult to over-estimate the gain to be obtained from debates for which the leading men prepared carefully, being stimulated by audiences of fifty or a hundred to do their very utmost. Questions of Biblical Criticism were at that time the staple of the most important discussions; and then were fought out in secret the very battles which are now about to be fought out in the Church under the eyes of the world, with very much the same division of parties and amid the play of the same passions.

"It was here that Elmslie first unfolded his marvellous powers as a speaker. At the University I had been a member of the Dialectic, where there were one or two fine speakers. One of them was more fluent and agreeable to listen to than any one I have ever heard since; another—long ago, alas! gone over to the majority—spoke with a freer play of mere intellectual force than even Elmslie possessed. But I had never before, and have never since, heard speaking which, taken all in all, quite came up to that to which Elmslie treated us Friday after Friday. The combination of powers was the marvel of it—the knowledge, the clearness of exposition, the fecundity of ideas, the telling force with which he put his points, the play of fancy, the exuberant wit and humour, the tenderness and pathos into which he could glide for a moment if it invited him; there was no resource which he had not at perfect command. Yet it was entirely without display; he was always perfectly natural and familiar. He never won a triumph which humiliated any one; and, whilst others by expounding the same free views excited bitter feelings of opposition, he had the gift of saying the most revolutionary things in such a way that no one was hurt; his weapon, though it cut deep, having the marvellous property of diffusing an anæsthetic on the wound it made.

"If it is necessary to throw some shade into a picture so bright, I should say that in those days his speaking had one defect: while he had always complete mastery of his subject, he rarely made the impression that the subject had complete mastery of him. He could play with it so easily, and he could play so easily with his audience, that, as part of the audience, you felt that you were not quite sure whether he was giving you all his mind or only as much of it as he considered good for you. He had not yet been gripped so tightly by the realities of life as he was later, when his sense of the wrong and misery of the world transformed his eloquence into an irresistible stream of passion and made him the most earnest and whole-hearted of comforters. As yet the bantering, laughing element was in excess; and he did not always remember where to draw the line in the *abandon* of animal spirits. I used to wonder how it would do when he was settled as the moderator of a session of 'douce' Scotch elders.

"But to us at the time it was splendid. It was in one of our sessions that Dr. Blaikie founded the College dinner, which has since proved so valuable an institution, bringing all the students together daily in a social capacity; and any day you could have told where Elmslie was seated at the table by the explosions of laughter rising in that quarter all through the meal. Men strove to sit near him, and he diffused a glow up and down, his budget of stories never getting exhausted or his flow of spirits flagging. I well remember a speech he made at the close of the first session during which the dinner existed, to thank Professor Blaikie for his efforts on behalf of the students and congratulate him on the success of his experiment. It was, perhaps, the most remarkable of all Elmslie's speeches. Professors and students alike were simply convulsed with laughter, and one explosion followed another, till the assembly was literally dissolved; yet under all the nonsense there was capital sense, and the duty which he had undertaken could not have been more gracefully or completely discharged.

On the serious side of college life he was equally a leader. His enormous influence over his fellow-students was uniformly pure and elevating; and in confidential hours, when conversation went down to the depths of experience, it was easy to see that his life, which was so gay and exuberant on the surface, was deeply rooted in loyalty to Christ. He threw himself heartily into the work of the Missionary Society in the Cowgate and the High Street.

We began one winter to speak in the open air, but none of us were successful till we brought down Murray, who afterwards also went to the English Presbyterian Church and finished his career even sooner than Elmslie. Murray was no scholar, but in ten minutes he had a crowd round him extending halfway across the street, while we could never attract more than forty or fifty. It was a lesson which we often afterwards discussed with no small astonishment.

"I remember an incident of the Mission which Elmslie used to tell with great gusto. He was addressing the Children's Church on the story of Samson and the lion, when, observing that the children were not attending, he, instead of saying that the lion roared, emitted as near an approach to the roar itself as he could command. Instantly there was breathless attention; and when, after pausing long enough to allow for the full effect, he was about to proceed, a little girl cried out anxiously, 'O sir, do it again!' On another occasion he stopped to reprove rather sharply a boy who was very restless, when a companion, springing up, told him with great solemnity that he ought not to speak so to this boy, because he was deaf and dumb. Taken completely aback, Elmslie began humbly to apologise, when the whole class burst out into a shout of laughter at the skill with which he had been taken in. The boy could both hear and speak.

"After he went south I saw him very seldom. Once he caught me in London and took me out to preach at Willesden, where I was immensely impressed with his hold on the people and the extent of the field of influence he had opened up. Like his other friends, I was very impatient for some literary production worthy of his genius, and, when the brilliant tract on Renan appeared, I took the liberty of writing him urgently on the subject. It was always my hope that before very long we should be able to entice him back across the Border, to adorn a chair in one of our colleges. I did not hear of his illness till you wrote me that he was just dying. 'God moves in a mysterious way.' I have no hesitation in saying that Elmslie was by far the most brilliant man I have ever known, and there was never a human being more lovable. He seemed to be the man we needed most; but it is little we know; the Master must have had need of him elsewhere.

Believe me yours most truly,
"JAMES STALKER."

SERMONS.

I.

CHRIST AT THE DOOR.

"Behold, I stand at the door, and knock: if any man hear My voice, and open the door, I will come in to him, and will sup with him, and he with Me."—REV. iii. 20.

GOD is close to us. Every moment of our life He is doing countless things in us and around us. If a man were to do these things we should see him with our eyes, we could touch him with our hands; we should not fail to observe his presence. Because we cannot see God with our bodily eye, or grasp Him with our hand, we forget His working, we lose sight of His nearness.

When you were children, some time or other, I suppose, in your young lives, you got hold of a flower-seed, and planted it in a pot of moist earth, and set it in the sunniest corner of your room. Morning after morning, when you awoke, you ran to see if the flower had begun to grow. At last your eagerness was rewarded by the sight of some tiny leaves which had sprung up during one night. Then the stalk appeared, frail and tender, and then more leaves, and buds, and branchlets, till at length there stood, blooming before you, a fair and fragrant flower.

Who made it? Somebody worked to produce that flower. It could not make itself. The dead earth could not shape that lovely leaf; the bright sunshine could not paint those tendrils. A deep-thinking man, when he sees these wonderful things, must ask himself, Who fashioned them? Not the sunshine nor the air, but God, if there is a God, willed that that plant should grow. God toiled to make the plant—in your room, at your side.

At this moment, in your breast, your heart is beating. All your life it has gone on beating. It is not you who sustain its motion. Even when you forget it, when you are asleep, its pulsations do not cease. Somebody works to keep your heart beating. God, who is the foundation of all life, out of whose loving heart it streams, and back to whom it must return, has to remember your heart.

But God comes still nearer to you. Do you remember a time in your life when, in your inmost heart, that hidden, secret chamber where you dream your dreams, and love your loves, and pour out your sorrows all alone, you felt a strange influence? It was a vague unrest, a great self-weariness. It was as if all brightness, hope, and satisfaction had gone from your life, and had left behind them, in departing, a sick, wistful longing to find something new, something brighter, better, and more noble than you yet had known. It was as if you could hear voices calling, and your heart moved within you, as if some new friend might be there. Do you know what that was? It was God. It was the great Heart that made your heart, longing and pleading to have it for His own. "Behold, I stand at the door, and knock: if any man hear My voice, and open the door, I will come in to him, and will sup with him, and he with Me." Do you believe that? You, men and women, who love your Bible, and are angry if any man seems to speak against it, or throw doubt upon one jot or tittle of its letter, have you ever thought what that means if it is true? Ay! it stands written there, and you have read it a hundred times, and think you believe it; but do you indeed know what it means? It means that God, the Eternal, Infinite, Almighty God, who wields these worlds of shining stars, and keeps them in their mighty courses; that God, the Spotless, the Holy, the Stainless, cares with a great longing to have the heart and love of *you;* you, who are no saint; you, the most commonplace and lowly, the most insignificant and sinful of men. Is that easy to believe? Is it easy to believe that God would miss something if your heart never went out in tender affection and adoration towards Him; that He should take pains and trouble to get Himself into your poor, battered heart—that heart which is so filled with sordid cares as to how you may make a living, and the envyings and strivings which accompany; in which such sinful, base, and vicious thoughts too often dwell? Is it possible that the great, holy God wishes to get in there?

It is not easy to believe it. One of the greatest religious thinkers who ever lived, by the confession of believers and unbelievers alike; a man who laboured so much under the effort to find out God, and became so absorbed in the quest, that the name of "God-intoxicated" was applied to him; a man who conceived more than any one else of the grandeur and transcendency of God, till he found this poor world of ours and the whole universe fade into insignificance before the thought of Him; this man, this great philosopher, Spinoza, said, "A man should love God with his whole being, but he must not expect God to love him in return." And the Bible says, "We love Him, because He first loved us." Which is true?

There are two things, I think, which make it hard to believe that we can be of consequence to God—that God holds each one of us in a separate thought of knowledge, sympathy, and Fatherly affection. One of them is this: How is it possible for God to do it? Think of the myriads of men and women on this world of ours, and the possibility of this universe teeming with countless creatures of God's creative power and Fatherly love. How is it possible that God should know each one of us, and love us each one? God, so omnipotent, so transcendent, so almighty! But the very thing that makes the difficulty to our reason seems to me the very thing that should undo it. If God were not so great, then I could not have the hope that I was something to Him by *myself*.

Is it not a fact that it is precisely a weak, uncultured, low, and undeveloped intellect that finds it difficult to give attention to a great mass of details, holding each apart, and doing justice to each? Precisely as you rise in the scale of intellect and mental power, that capacity increases quite incalculably. It is the great genius of a general who not merely directs his army as a mass, but holds it at every point, knows the value of every unit of force at his command, follows the movement of each squadron, troop, and even of each single individual, and precisely by this faculty is able to overthrow the enemy and lead the army to victory.

You have listened to a beautiful oratorio, where scores of instruments and hundreds of voices were all blended together in one tide of magnificent harmony. How is it possible for a small intellect to keep them thus in unison? It requires a master-mind in music to do this—one that is fully conscious of the value of each string and voice, and who can therefore combine them all in glorious harmony. And God is almighty; it is nothing to Him that He is far away from you; you, a speck of dust upon this world. It is precisely because I believe in God's omnipotence that I can believe that He cares for each separate creature He has made.

But then there is another question. Even if God can love each one of us, apart from all the rest, with an individual, personal, watchful kindness, what right have we to think that He should care to do it? Once again, that difficulty need but be faced, and you discover that it is a delusive spectre and empty of reality.

Is it likely that God should miss the love of me, His creature?

Turn to the early chapters of Genesis, and read the story they have to tell you. They tell you how through measureless periods of time, in the fields of infinite space, the great God built up our world; first the stone foundations, layer upon layer; above that, the strata of mineral wealth, to be used hereafter, clothing the surface of it with a verdant soil. Out of the mineral world he evolved the nutritive, vegetable world, out of vegetable life the higher creation of animal life, and out of that emerges man, standing on the summit of God's great toil and building, with eyes that see, ears that hear, and mind that can understand, answering to the call of God, interpreting all the wisdom, patience, beauty, and love in that mighty labour of creation, and saying, "Father, I adore Thee." Do you think that man, then, His last crowning work of creation, is nothing to God? What should you say of one who spent years and years, and sank uncounted capital, upon a great mass of wonderfully contrived machinery, to produce some beautiful fabric of beneficence to mankind, and when it was produced turned away and left it all? You would call such a one a fool, and mad.

God made this world, and spent toil and industry in making the heart of man, and keeping it conscious of Him, capable of loving Him. And do you mean to tell me that God does not care for human love? It is impossible. There is no God at all, or the Gospel is true. He does miss it when your heart does not bend to Him. The supreme gladness we can give our Maker is the simple, sincere adoration of our poor human hearts.

There is a picture that paints the idea of my text. It says, to those who look at it, what I could not say in many paragraphs. A cottage neglected, falling into ruin, is shown in the picture. In front of the window tall thistles spring up, and long grass waves on the pathway, leading to the door overgrown with moss. In front of that fast-closed door a tall and stately figure stands, with a face that tells of toil and long, weary waiting, and with a hand uplifted to knock. It is Christ, the Son of God, seeking to get into our sinful hearts. Is it true that there can be a man or woman who refuses to admit so fair a guest, so great and good a friend? It must be true. "Behold, I stand at the door, and knock: if any man hear My voice, and open the door, I will come in to him, and will sup with him, and he with Me."

But you think you can justify yourself. You say to me, "I feel it were a mad, foolish thing to refuse to admit to my own, if it be true, the loving heart of God, and a thing altogether unjustifiable. You say He comes and knocks at our hearts—that He calls and asks us to let Him in. No; many have called at the door of my heart, but I never knew Christ to call or knock. If ever He had, I think I should have let Him in." I believe you speak the truth, but I am certain that Christ has been to your heart.

Let me speak plainly to you. There may be various reasons why you have failed to detect His presence. Perchance your life has not been so good as even common morality would have made it, and now your heart is a very dreary place, filled with painful memories. Perhaps you are always outside, gadding about, and do not like to dwell alone in your heart and think; and so when Christ knocks and calls He finds empty rooms; or if even you are there you are not there alone, but you have filled its chambers with a noisy, revelling company and din. The call has reached you as a dim, half-heard, strange sound, which moved you half pleasantly and half with pain. You turned in your heart and listened for an instant, but there was something in the sound too painful, and you plunged back again into revelry and mirth. You did not know that it was God, the very heart of God, that had knocked and called.

Again, your life may have been very respectable, but very light and frivolous, engrossed in earthly affairs; and Christ has come, and you did not know it. For He comes in such simple, human guise. You remember when He came on earth the poor Jews did not know Him for more than the carpenter's son. He comes like that to you and me. He takes a human hand, and with its fingers knocks, but all you see and recognise is the human touch. You do not see the heart Divine that touches you through it with an appealing thrill.

Thank God, there are so many good mothers in this world. Thank God for the little children, and the lads and maidens here, whom a mother's memory follows like a very angel, often after she herself has gone. You remember that Sabbath evening custom when you and the little ones knelt at your mother's knee, and she told you the stories of the Bible; and the last one was always about the gentle Jesus, meek and mild, who came to the world with such a great heart of love, who knew no sin at all, who was so good to women and children and the very worst of broken-hearted sinners, and whom men with hard hearts and cruel hands took and crucified; oh, such a death of pain for *you!* till you could almost see His face on the cross. And your mother's voice had got so low and reverent that it felt as if some one else was in the room, and your young child's heart grew so soft and loving to that Christ that died for you. Yes, He was there. Did you take Him quite inside? Or if you took Him in for a little while did you let Him go again, when your heart grew colder? Oh, young men and maidens who had a mother like that, remember her, and take that Christ into your hearts!

Some of you can remember a time when you had grown many years older, and perhaps had memories you would not like your mother to know of. And God struck you down with a great illness, and for a long time you were at the point of death. But at last the crisis was past, and you woke out of unconsciousness, brought back to life again, weak as a little child. All the din and turmoil of your manhood's life seemed to have faded in the distance, and once again you became as a little child. Do you remember how you felt when you turned that corner between life and death? Somehow, old memories came back to you—perhaps because your body was so weak—the memory of old days, of the father and mother, and the church in the country, and of all the things that were said and done. And then there came a wish that many things in your later life had never been done by you; a strange, solemn sense that there is a God; and into your heart a feeling of repentance for the past, and a wish to do better in the future. And you were so tired, and wished for a friend to speak to you in these words: "Come unto Me, all ye that labour and are heavy laden, and I will give you rest." Afterwards you got stronger and said, "Perhaps it was only weakness." But I tell you it was the living, loving Christ, seeking to get into your heart.

I cannot stop to enumerate the countless knocks and calls that come to all of us, in those strange aspirations that come with the secret, tender affections, the dreams of love and truth. For God's sake, never be ashamed of them, and be true to the dreams of your youth. Do not think that Christ is part of a creed only, or belongs only to church and Sunday. No, Christ is in everything holy, everything pure, everything loving, and everything that draws your heart. I would have you understand that Christ works to get into your heart, and not into your head. There is plenty of time for the latter after He has once secured possession of your heart and life. Into the homeliest chamber of your heart, too, not into a state apartment, opened only on occasions of ceremony, He seeks to come, that He may stay with you and sup with you, and be with you in your home. There are some people who think this would be treating Him with very scanty respect, and so they think they must take a nook of their heart, like a piece of consecrated ground, and keep Him there, and only visit it on Sunday. No; Christ wants to come into your life and mind. Take Him to your office, and consult Him about your business; your affairs will not be managed with less skill and wisdom, but perhaps more honourably. Take Him to the fireside, where you plan your plans and dream your dreams, and make out a future for your little boys. He loved little ones on earth, and do you think He has lost that love in heaven?

Take Him into your heart to overcome the evil passions and habits, the things you would be ashamed to own to the most loving earthly friend, which you are fighting in God's name and cannot conquer by yourself. You say, "Tell us how we can do it. He is so very good, we fain would have Christ in our heart, but it seems so difficult when our heart is so unworthy." No, it is so easy—and yet so difficult to describe in words. The moment you have done it you wonder that you ever asked how it must be done.

I can tell you some things like it. You know what it is for a great grief to come into your heart, the first great disappointment in love, in friendship or ambition. You did not see it enter with your eyes, but you knew it had got in, for it changed everything, throwing a dark, cold shadow over all your life. Some of you know what it is for a real, true joy to get into your heart. Some of you, fathers and mothers, know what it is for a very true friend to get there. You hardly know how it happened, but one came right in to the inmost being of your life, and ere you knew it, you would be nothing without him—without him loving you. Love was all joy and happiness, and has stayed there ever since. It has made you different; you have learned to love the things he loves, and the love and knowledge have brought peace.

It is just like that when you take Christ into your heart. Go to the Gospels, you who feel the want of a friend like that, and read what He said to poor weeping men and women, till you feel the breath of His love encircle you, till your heart goes out to Him, and you will be vexed to grieve Him, and want to please Him; and you will think as He thinks, and love men as He loves.

There are many, many things about the mysteries of our religion which I do not understand. But this I say to you, before God: Beyond all this world holds of pride, splendour, pleasure, and joy, to have taken that real, living, holy Jesus Christ into your heart, to be your Saviour, Counsellor, and Friend, your Divine Lord and Master, means blessedness both here and hereafter.

II.
THE DARK ENIGMA OF DEATH.

St. John xi.

THIS morning I ask your attention to the story that has been read in the eleventh chapter of the Gospel of St. John.

The rulers of the Jews at Jerusalem had resolved on Christ's death, and the mass of the people sympathised with them. The Master's life had been threatened by a popular outburst. His work on earth was not yet done, and so He withdrew into the country, to escape from the violence and danger of Jerusalem. He went away to the Jordan, to the point, not very far from Jerusalem, where John first began baptizing, and there He remained in comparative seclusion. But people knew where He was. Probably people in the surrounding districts gathered together to hear Him teach; and possibly, as a very ingenious commentator has suggested, Christ, reaping the harvest of John's prolonged teaching in this district, succeeded in winning the faith of a great many of His hearers; and so He was busy doing good and happy work, building up His kingdom on the banks of the Jordan.

Meanwhile, sickness came to the home at Bethany, where most He felt Himself at home during His wanderings in this world of ours. Lazarus was stricken with a very dangerous illness, grew worse and worse, and at last all hope was gone. Now, I should fancy that from the very first day that it became evident that their brother was seriously ill, the hearts of Mary and Martha longed to have Jesus come to them, if it was only to be with them in their anxiety, and suspense, and watching. And the heart of the sick man must have longed for that great Divine Friend of his to be by his sick bed. Why did they not send for Him at once? I think there is a very simple reason. They were not selfish, as we sometimes tend to be in our sickness or in our sorrow. They thought about others as well as about themselves. They remembered that for Jesus to come back to the vicinity of Jerusalem was to risk His own life, and not even for the safety of their brother could they bring themselves for a long time to ask the beloved Master to run such a risk as that, and so they delayed really till too late. In the extremity of their grief and despair they sent a messenger to Jesus—not to ask Him to come: there, again, I read that that was their meaning—they would not take it on themselves to ask Him to imperil His life, but they could not resist just letting Him know that their brother, whom Jesus so loved, was very sick. It is exceedingly touching, that simple message, "Lord, behold, he whom Thou lovest is sick." And they knew that it would say to Jesus, "Thou knowest how much we would like Thee to come and recover him, and Thou knowest, too, the last thing we would ask of Thee would be, out of favour and kindness to us, to risk that life on which so much hangs—the kingdom of God upon earth."

There was real danger in Christ's return to Jerusalem. He was conscious of it, for you find that when He did make His way to Bethany He seems to have taken care, as far as possible, to conceal the fact from the inhabitants of Jerusalem. He came very quietly. He did not at first enter into Bethany. He remained outside the precincts of the village. He sent word secretly to Martha, so that not even Mary or the other persons that were with them in the house knew of the fact. And then, again, He sent Martha back, or Martha went back, to Mary, and, with somewhat studied concealment, warned her of the Master's vicinity, so that when she went out those who were with her fancied she was going to the grave. I point all that out to you in order that you may see that it is not a mere imagination or fancy, but that one of the great elements in determining the conduct of the family at Bethany, and the action of Christ, was that real hazard of His life, which He dared not needlessly risk in perils at this time, since His time of toil on earth, His daylight of labour, was not yet over and done.

When Jesus received the message He behaved in a seemingly strange fashion. Apparently He just did nothing, but went on with His teaching and preaching for two long days. Did He think how often anxious faces would be at the door of that house in Bethany, peering along the road that led to the home, looking for the figure that had so often trodden that way, because His heart drew Him to that happy family circle? Did Jesus know that Lazarus was dying? Did Jesus think that the hearts of Mary and Martha were breaking? Oh, He had the most loving heart that ever man had on earth, and yet He delayed two days before He set out for that home of distress. Now, that fact is often presented in a somewhat revolting fashion, and I think it is worth while just to diverge from my main theme to remove the effect of such presentation if it weighs with any of you. It is said that Jesus deliberately hung back for two days in order to let Lazarus die. That is a mistake—a total mistake. Lazarus had been already buried four days before Christ arrived. Now, suppose He had lost no time; suppose He had set out at once, He would only have reached Bethany two days earlier, and so, you see, Lazarus would have then already been buried two days. The real fact is just this, that the message was sent too late, and the sick man had died; and even if Christ had gone at once, all the same He would have found him in the grave. But none the less the story is so told as to shut us up to this conviction, that it was planned, and purposed, and accepted in the will of God, and in the will of Jesus, that Lazarus should be sick, and grow worse and worse, and should sink and fail, and die and be buried. Indubitably Jesus, with His knowledge, could, of His own action, have returned earlier to have intervened and prevented the sickness ending fatally. He was absent that Lazarus might die. When He spoke of the thing He told His disciples, first of all, the perfect, complete truth. "This," said Jesus, "is not to end in death's darkness. Its real goal and termination is to be the glory of God, revealed in the glory of his Son, the Christ on earth." That is the end of it; nevertheless, Lazarus must die. God's glory is to find its consummation, not in rescuing Lazarus from the grave, but in restoring him from death, and bringing him back into life. It was part of the material Christ used in building up His kingdom—the sickness and the death of Lazarus. He did delay, not in that seeming revolting, cold-blooded fashion in which it is often portrayed. He did deliberately hold His hand and delay; ay, and He held His loving human heart too, and He let his friend sicken, and suffer pain, and die, and He let the hearts of those two women that loved Him well-nigh break. He did it.

Can we justify Him? Did the sisters divine truly when they sent that message, "He whom Thou lovest is sick"? If He loved him, why did He prolong the agony? Why did He not intervene? Why did He not at once cancel death? Why those terrible four days of mourning, and gloom, and darkness, and doubt? Now that is precisely the painful position of all of us in this world of sin, and pain, and sickness, and parting, and death. We think a good God made our world; we think a loving Father holds our lives in His hands; and then we turn and look at this world, we look at the terrible strifes and struggles, we look at the great entail of sin that lies on our race, we see the ravages of disease, and disaster, and violence, and cruelty, and see everywhere the last black enigma of death and the grave, and this in spite of all our Christian faith, learnt from the Bible; ay, learnt from God's Spirit speaking often in the instincts of our heart and natural—we, too, are forced to ask the question, "Lord, why art Thou not here? Why does our brother die? If Thou wert here Thou couldest save him. Dost Thou love him? and if Thou lovest, why are we sick? Why do we die?"

The inmates of that house at Bethany had received Jesus with a rare degree of sympathetic feeling and heartfelt welcome. They entered into the meaning of His teaching and preaching with a degree of fellowship and quick response that moved His heart and soul even beyond the best of His disciples. One of them at least—Mary, and almost certainly Lazarus too—had come very near to that Divine Lord, in full understanding of all His grandeur, His sinlessness, His mighty love. Though yet all ignorant of a great deal about His person, and about the fashion in which He was to make His kingdom, with a genuine purity and ardour of attachment and affection, they worshipped Him, they recognised the Divine within Him, they hailed Him as the world's Christ and Saviour. Listen to Martha's cry in her perplexity: "I cannot understand it all, but I know Thou art the Christ come from God, the world's King, the world's Saviour. That I know, that I hold to." It was that understanding, that sympathy in that home, that made it so sweet a place of rest to Jesus. More than that—manifestly the two sisters and brother lived a life of sweet human affection. There was an atmosphere of tender love in their home, broken by little storms of misunderstanding, as may be in the very best of our imperfect human homes, but in reality a great depth of tenderness, and clinging attachment, and loyal love to one another, bound the household together. Oh, thank God for every such home on earth! That is the real bulwark against all pessimism, the charter of our eternal birthrights. Given the grandeur, the reality of human love, as, thank God, most of us know it in our homes, that is the absolute guarantee that it came from the creating hands of grander Love Divine.

Jesus was not merely loved by the family where He came to spend the nights when He was working in Jerusalem, but He got to love them with a very wonderful tenderness. You remember that chivalrous, impassioned defence of Mary, when she was assailed by the coarse attacks of the disciples.

You catch it, too, in that message sent to Him—"He whom Thou lovest." Ah, many an act of affection, many a look that was a caress, many an appeal for sympathy that bespoke brotherhood, had passed between Jesus of Nazareth and that Lazarus, else the sisters would not have thought of saying, "He whom Thou lovest is sick."

And yet into that home so dear to the heart of Jesus, the Son of God, into that home that had for its Friend the Man that was master of life and of death, of calamity and prosperity, of all earthly powers and forces, into that home there penetrated cruel, painful, deadly sickness. The man Jesus loved lay there on his bed dying.

Now, I emphasize that, because there used to be a great deal of thinking about God's relation to those that love Him and whom He loves—a great deal of teaching in the Christian Church that counted itself most orthodox, and which was, indeed, deadly heresy, coarse, materialistic, despicable, misunderstanding the ideal grandeur of the Bible promises. Some of you know the sort of teaching that used to prevail—the idea that God's saints should be exceptionally favoured; the sun would shine on their plot of corn, and it would not shine on the plot of corn of the bad man; their ships would not sink at sea, their children would not catch infectious diseases; God would pamper them, exempt them from bearing their part in the world's great battle, with hardness and toil of labour, with struggle, and attainment, and achievement. It came of a very despicable conception of what a father can do for a child, as if the best thing for a father to do for his son was to pet and indulge him, and save him all bodily struggle and all difficulties, instead of giving him a life of discipline. As if a general in the army would, because of his faltering heart, refuse to let his son take the post of danger; as if he would not rather wish for that son—ay, with a great pang in his own soul—that he should be the bravest, the most daring, the one most exposed to the deadliest hazard.

Ah, we have got to recognise that we whom God loves may be sick and dying, and yet God does love us. Lazarus was loved by Jesus, yet he whom Jesus loved was sick and dying. Ah, and there is a still more poisonous difficulty in that materialistic, that worldly way of looking at God's love; that horrible, revolting misjudgment that Christ condemned, crushed with indignation when it confronted Him. "The men on whom the tower of Siloam fell must have been sinners worse than us on whom it did not fall."

Never, never! The great government of the world is not made up of patches and strokes of anger and outbursts of weak indulgence. The world is God's great workshop, God's great battle-field. These have their places. Here a storm of bullets falls, and brave and good men as well as cowards fall before it. You mistake if you try to forestall God's judgments, God's verdicts on the last great day of reckoning.

Still we have got the fact that Christ does not interpose to prevent death, that Christ does not hinder those dearest to Him from bearing their share of life's sicknesses and sufferings, that God Himself suffers death to go on, apparently wielding an undisputed sway over human existence.

What is the consequence of it? Well, the first consequences seem to be all evil. You might look on the surface of life, and when you read superficially the narrative of this chapter in St. John, it looks as if mischief and evil came of the strange delay of God and of His Christ. Look at the effect upon the disciples. Now here there is not enough told to justify me in putting more positively to you the picture of their inner hearts, but I am going to present—I dread that I may be guilty of a want of charity, at all events of disproportion—but as I read this chapter, and try to think myself into it, this is the conception I have: Had these men known that Lazarus was very sick, they would not have wished their Master to go back to try and save him. They were selfish enough to have been rather glad that He was at a distance, to wish that He should not know. When the message did come I think they were puzzled and perplexed. Selfishly, they were rather pleased that He did not set off to go. But, on the other hand—for, mind you, a selfish man understands the dictates of love—they said to themselves, "It is not quite like Him. Well, it is wise, it is prudent not to go, but it is a little cowardly. Does He love Lazarus so much as we used to think?" Oh, if I am right, what a painful thing, all these bad, poor, selfish thoughts of the Divine heart in Jesus! all created, mark you, because Jesus suffered the man whom He loved to be sick, and at last to die, and did not go and check death, and drive the dark King of Terrors back.

Then Jesus says to them that He has resolved to go and visit Lazarus. It is here I get the ground on which I stand in forecasting that selfishness in them. Then they thought He was wrong. They did venture to blurt out what was a censure: "He will go; He ought not to do it. What are we to do who see with clearer eyes the pathway of prudence? To let Him go and die? It was a total blunder, a mistake, but all the same we cannot let Him go and die alone. Let us go and die with Him."

Oh, what a dearth of understanding of their Master, His love, His power, His real character, created by the enigma of Christ's conduct, that He had held His hand, that He had suffered His friend to be sick, that He had permitted him to die!

Then come to the two sisters. Ah, what a struggle must have gone on in their hearts, as hour after hour passed after the point had come when Jesus should have been with them if He had listened to their message, if He pitied their brother, His own beloved friend. What could the Master mean? Did something hinder Him and prevent His coming? or was it the danger to His life? Was there a little selfishness? or had they any right to expect it? Either He is lacking in love, or else He is lacking in power. What could it mean? And then, when at last the poor sick eyes shut and their brother lay there dead, their hearts were like stones within them. And the burial, following swiftly after in the East, because decay begins so quickly there; and then the mourning and the hired mourners, professional mourners, all around them, and these poor women there saying in their hearts, "Surely, surely it need not have been; certainly if the Master, who healed so many sick, had been here, if He had come, if He knew, if He had been here all this horror, this agony, this pain, might have been escaped."

So when Jesus did come, look at them, how they met Him. Martha goes away out, and the first thing she says is just what they had said so often to one another and to their own hearts: "O Master, if Thou hadst only been here our brother had not died." And then the spirit of the woman told her that perhaps she had hurt Jesus' feelings, that perhaps He was not to blame, that perhaps there was some explanation, though she could not see it, and so, in her blundering way—for she had not the fine tact that was in Mary—she tried to mend it, and only made it worse by volunteering that she did believe in Him after all.

The soul of Christ felt the intended love, and shuddered at that tremendous distance of sympathy and understanding. "You believe in Me." He could not hold it in. "Thy brother shall rise again." And poor Martha was unable to rise to the height of Christ's meaning. "Oh, yes, Lord, I know, at the great resurrection. Yes, he will rise again." Then comes Jesus' declaration, "I am the Resurrection and the Life. The man that lives in Me, in whom I live, has in Me a deathless life. I am here to-day to prove that." That was what He meant, but He was far away above her. The poor heart in her had lost Him. She was dazed, and so she just fell back upon the one thing that she was quite sure of, even if He had not been quite kind to her, or even if His power was limited. "Yes, yes, Master, I know Thou art the Christ, the Son of God, come into this world to be its Saviour and its King." And then, perhaps, with a sort of sense that Mary could understand the Master better, could read His meaning and tell it to her, she slipped away, and she found her sister, and whispered in her ear, "The Master is come, and asks for thee." Then Mary went away to meet Him too.

It is much harder to read what was in that sweet heart of Mary. I have no doubt that she, too, had fought a battle with doubt. The story seems to show that she had attained to greater faith than Martha. She had been pained, but still there was a divining instinct in her, like the divining instinct that warned her, when all the disciples were blind to it, that He was going to die, and she went and anointed Him to His burial; a divining instinct in her that somehow the cloud was going to be rolled away. And she went out and said simply, "Lord, if Thou hadst been here our brother had not died." And then she was too wise to say one word more. With her finer tact, with her deeper understanding, she knew that was all she should say. But it was like saying, "There is perplexity in this visitation, in Thy delay, in my brother's death; Thou couldst have made it different if Thou hadst seen it well to be here. I cannot understand the right and the love of it." It was a question. It did say, "Master, what art Thou going to do?" And Christ felt it was. As she broke out and burst into tears, He lost control and wept with her.

But there were others—the Jews, the enemies of Christ; men who hated Him, men who disbelieved in Him, men who grudged Him all His glory and the love He had won on the earth. They had hurried out—some of them with a degree of human compassion—to that home of bereavement. It was known as the home of Christ, and I think some of them had come with greater pleasure that Lazarus had died. What they said when they saw Him weep betrays their mood. "This is He who professed to be able to open the eyes of the blind and heal all sicknesses. How, then, is it that He allows His dearest friend on earth to be sick, and die, and be buried? He has lost His power, if

He ever had it." They were rejoicing over His seeming defeat. They had no love for Him, and so had no faith in Him.

Is not that true of our world to-day? The best of you, Christians, when death comes to your own homes, do you manage to sing the songs of triumph right away? Well, you are very wonderful saints if you do. If you do not, perhaps you say, "If God is in this world, how comes that dark enigma of death?"

And others of you grip hold of your faith, but yet your heart cries out against it. You believe that God is good, but has He been quite good to you? Like Martha, you feel as if you had some doubt; you feel bound in your prayers; you say, "O God, I do not mean to reproach Thee;" weak, sinful if you will, yet the sign of a true follower of the Christ.

And then the enemies of Christ, the worldlings all about in this earth of ours, as they look upon death's ravages, they are saying, "If there were a God, if there were a Father, if there were a great heart that could love, why does not He show it?" Now, I said to you that at first it looks as if nothing but evil came of God's delay to interpose against death; but when you look a little deeper I think you begin to discover an infinitely greater good and benefit come out of that evil.

I must very briefly, very rapidly, trace to you in the story, and you can parallel it in the life of yourselves, that discipline of goodness there is in God's refraining from checking sickness and death. Christ said, the end of it is first of all death, but that is not the termination. Through death this sickness, this struggle of doubt and faith, should end in the glory of God. He meant this: In the preparation of His life and His death the death and resurrection of Lazarus held a central position. It was the turning-point, the thing that determined His crucifixion on Calvary. That tremendous miracle compelled the rulers of Jerusalem to resolve on and carry out His death. That miracle of Lazarus' resurrection gave to the faith of the disciples and of Christ's followers a strength of clinging attachment that carried them through the eclipse of their belief when they saw Him die on Calvary.

Now, what would you say? Was it cruel of Christ to allow His friend Lazarus, His dear friends Mary and Martha, to go through that period of suspense, of anxiety, of sickness, of death, and of the grave, that they might do one of the great deeds in bringing in the world's Redeemer? Oh, men and women, if God be wise, and if God be great, then must it not be that somehow or other the structure of this world is the best for God's end, and our tears, and partings, and calamities but incidents in the grand campaign that shall end in the resplendent glory of heaven? Yes, for the glory of God, and for the sake of others, for the sake of the disciples, for the sake of the world, says Christ, I have suffered My friend Lazarus to die.

"Ah," you say, "you have still got to show God's goodness and kindness to me individually. My death may be for God's glory, it may be for the good of others; but how about me and those who mourn?" Well, now, look at it. You must get to the end of the story before you venture to judge the measure, the worth, of God's goodness. After all, was that period of sickness and death unmitigated gloom, and horror, and agony? Oh, I put it to you, men and women, who have passed through it, watching by the death of dear father or mother that loved the Lord and loved you, and whom you loved—dark, and sore, and painful enough at the time; but oh, if I called you to speak out, would you not say it was one of the most sacred periods of your life—the unspeakable tenderness, the sweet clinging love, the untiring service, the grateful responses, the sacredness that came into life? Ay, and when the tie was snapped, the new tenderness that you gave to the friends that are left, the new pledge binding you to heaven, and to hope for it, and long for it—death is not all an evil to our eyes. Death cannot ultimately be an evil, since it is universal—the consummation, climax, crown of every human life. Ah, if we had the grander majesty of soul to look at it from God's altitude, we should call death, not a defeat, but a victory, a triumph. I think sometimes that if death did not end these lives of ours, how weary they would get. Think of it—to live on for ever in the sordidness, in the littleness, in the struggle, the pain, the sin of this life of ours. Oh, we need that angel of death to come in, and now and then stir the pool of our family life, that there may be healing in it, that there may be blessing in it! Death, holding the hand of God through it, to those that stand by and see the sweetness of human love, the triumph of faith celestial, has a grandeur in it, like Christ's death on the cross; it hides out of sight of the people the ghastly, the doubt-creating features and elements of its external impediment—death becomes God's minister. It is going home to one's Father.

Yes, but you want the guarantee that death is not the end, and that day it was right and lawful for Christ to give it, to anticipate the last great day, when in one unbroken army, radiant and resplendent, shining like jewels in a crown, He shall bring from the dark grave all that loved Him, fought for Him, and were loyal to Him on the road, and went down into the dark waters singly, one by one, in circumstances of ignominy often, and yet dying with Christ within them, the Resurrection and the Life.

Ah, that great, grand vindication of God, and interpretation of this world's enigma was made clear that day when Christ called Lazarus back, and gave him alive to his sisters in the sight of His doubting disciples, in the sight of those sneering enemies. And what I like to think as best of all and most comforting of all is this, that Christ did that deed of love and goodness to hearts that so misunderstood Him, were so ignorant of His glory, denied and disbelieved so much of His claims, were then and there so despairing, so hopeless, that perhaps it was only in one heart, the heart of Mary, there was hope or faith like a grain of mustard-seed. Yet He did it. Why? He whom He loved died, and they whom He loved mourned. It was not that they loved Him; it was that He loved them.

Ah, when I read sneers at the simple Evangelical Gospel that says, "Put away all thoughts of earning heaven; your good works are rags"—true enough, true enough—the sneers are mistaken. It is a very grand Gospel that, for what it says is this, "There is hope, salvation from sin, life eternal, for you and for me, not for anything in us, nor for anything we can do, even if we did the best we could. We hold the hope and confidence of redemption, resurrection, in our hearts, because the God that made us loves us;" and so—as I read lately in a recently published book, amid much that I think is foolish, what yet struck me as singularly tender and true—"When in the hour of death we cry, 'Good Lord, deliver us,' we might stop and leave out the 'deliver us.' It is quite enough if we are dying in the arms of a God that is good."

III.
THE STORY OF DORCAS.

Acts ix. 36-43.

TO a man who believes in a living, personal God the world's history is the record of God's actions. The Bible story is an account of an exceptional period in the Divine activity, during which God's dealings with men are peculiarly significant; as it were more immediate, frank, and expressive, more true to His inmost character. Then, traits found utterance that in general are mute. Repression gave way to expression. The incidents in this expression are out of the common, look marvellous; we call them miracles. Such things do not happen to us, but we hold they happened for us. They are, so to say, a personal explanation on God's part, at once a disclaimer and a declaration. He is not altogether to be judged by the normal course of events. His feelings do not quite answer to appearances. His heart does not correspond entirely to His hand. He is more than His deeds. Measure Him by these, and you mistake Him, because for the most part He acts under restraint. His love may be much greater than His language, His kindness warmer than His conduct. Reticence is often imposed on affection. You do not always tell your child all the praise you might express, and admiration you feel. When he has entered the struggle of school-life you look on while he battles with a hard task, till his weariness pains you, but you hold back and do not help him. It may be my lot to know of a friend contending against unjust accusation, well-nigh crushed, and I may not stand by him, knowing my aid would harm, not help, though at the risk of his misunderstanding me. God would have us know, as we with perplexity look to His silent heaven out of our sin and sorrow, that spite of strange seeming, His heart is love. We do not fare as our Father fain would have us fare. Things are not as He would wish them. There is a discrepancy between the desires of His heart and the doings of His hand. He cannot quite trust us as He would. There is an obstacle; we should be better off but for that. We do right to say, with Martha, "Lord, if Thou hadst been here my brother had not died." And that we may be sure it is so, once He broke through His reticence; He *was* here; He gave His heart full play, and treated men as He always feels towards them. Their sicknesses were healed, their sins forgiven; the Infinite Love laid soft hands on their pain; the Eternal Pity whispered peace in their souls. Now we can look on Christ and say we know what God is. But for hindrances, we can say, He would always act so. Spite of our fortunes, that is how He feels. At length the barrier will be over-thrown, and He will treat me so likewise.

This is the practical use we are to make of such stories of Scripture as Dorcas's restoration from death. It is a marvel—what, precisely, we know not. But, for this woman God did a splendid and wonderful act of love, that dispelled the eclipse of death in a sunshine of endless security. What happened to her happens not to us. But God's heart is unchanged. If you be life and in death is as tender and strong as it was about her.

In the important seaport town of Joppa there were gathered together some believers in Jesus. Among them was a woman named Tabitha (Heb.), or Dorcas (Gr.). The name signifies Gazelle, or Fawn. It was one of those pet names given to woman, a name of beauty, though the bearer of it may have been plain enough. Not much is told about her, but what is told is of such a kind that we may conjecture more. Little things have a significance in combination. Thus we can fill in the meagre outline that is given us, till the picture grows into completeness.

Dorcas was a lone woman. Of husband or of children we hear nothing. Unlike those others with whom she is linked in Bible story as fellow-sharers in the miracle of restoration to life—unlike Lazarus, unlike the daughter of Jairus or the widow's son at Nain—we read in her case of no loving relatives who soothed her dying bed and wept when she was gone. She stands alone in the world—one of those women of whom we speak as of persons to be pitied, unhappy; with a woman's natural hopes and occupations, in which she finds rest for her instincts, denied or blighted.

Dorcas is a forlorn figure, stricken by grief and woe. We feel inclined to turn away from such. The bleak, cold winds that blow across the lonely spaces where they find their planting seem to chill our joy. We forget that it is not thorns alone which grow in spots that we deem waste; not seldom God's fairest flowers and fruits spring up on what we count barren and forsaken ground. In Dorcas, we may well believe, there was nothing woe-begone or repellent; it is as pleasant, amiable, and beloved that we think of her. The tree of her life had been stricken by the lightning; its own leaves and branches stripped; but it did not remain a bare and unsightly stump, naked and alone. Lichens and clinging plants had gathered at its roots, and twined about its stem, and clothed it with a new verdure and beauty.

All this might have been so different. Dorcas might have succumbed to sorrow, and amid the ruins of her shattered home she might have flung herself on the ground in despair. She might have been moping and repining, selfishly nursing her grief, embittered, envious, and grudging to others their joy. God pity those who are; it is often that the milk of human kindness has turned sour: the fault is of misfortune. She might have made herself a burden to all around, held the world a debtor, and herself a wronged creditor. She might have insisted on being miserable—as if a long face made a lighter heart. Some in her position act so. They resent the smiles of others, and hold that if weeping is their portion, then all should weep. Others hide under a smiling face a sad heart, and laugh with you. Dorcas did none of these things. She set herself to be of use, to give aid and help to others. Ah! I think it sometimes happens that God removes the home of a woman's love, breaks down its walls, and unroofs it before the storm, in order that the love may go out to embrace a larger family. The hearts of some women are made to shelter and console all homeless ones. Their love takes wings, and flies through the earth in search for the desolate and afflicted. It does not need the ties of home, of husband and children, to form a loving, useful, warm-hearted woman.

How long had Dorcas been such a woman as the story tells of? We cannot say. Perhaps she was humbly good and sensible, and had borne her sorrows bravely from the first, an unconscious follower of Jesus. Perhaps she was once soured, bitter, and woe-begone, till she heard of the great Sorrow-bearer, and learnt from Him to make her sorrow an offering, and to use her knowledge of sadness to lighten others' woe. For she was "a disciple." That means just one who looks how Christ went about the world, and sets to go likewise.

Having made up her mind to do good, what could she do? Nothing much. She could not preach; she could not be an apostle, and do great deeds of healing. She was too poor, too stupid, too uninfluential to start a mission or build a hospital. But she could darn, and stitch, and plan garments for widows—and how many such does not the life of a seafaring town create! She could speak kind words and do good turns, go to meeting, and be a quiet, gentle, sweet, helpful woman. That she could be, nothing more; and that she was. Why should she be more? That is what God means a good woman to be.

A homely, unromantic, dull, unattractive life, you say; good, but uninteresting. So, perhaps, the neighbours said. So we all go on thinking and saying, while the angels laugh at our folly. As if God did not often conceal under the hardest, coarsest shells and husks the silkiest of downy lining and the very sweetest of fruit-kernels. Yes, outside it looked a stripped, bare, monotonous life. But within there was a whole world of beauty and pathos. God knew the tender thoughts of the dead; the rising of old cravings that woke and called once more for buried loves; the silent, speechless prayers in lonely eventides. He knew of memories that were tears to her, but turned to warmth and cheer for others; of very kindly thoughts and gentle love woven and sown into those garments. No, the neighbours did not see all this. But God's eyes looked, and saw a very garden of the Lord for beauty and fragrance. I know it must have been so, from the love her way of doing kindness won. Merely to do good is not enough to get love; one must be good. It is wonderful how some people do endless good, and yet none cares for them. Dorcas was not a machine, actively good because actively wound up. People do not weep such tears as fell when she died for the loss of a sewing-machine, useful though such might be, and working for nothing. Nor was she a woman with a mission, bustling, important, loud-voiced; useful and needed such may be, respected, but not quite loved. Nor was she a lady patroness, looking down on those upon whom she showered her benefits. Those who work like Dorcas do not work of mechanical duty, nor for fuss of fame, nor for thanks. It is but little likely that thanks were given her. People would say, "She has nothing else to do;" "She has no family to look after;" "She has plenty of time on her hands;" "It's almost a kindness to take her sewing;" "She had sooner work than not." Exactly, that was it. She was nothing more than a kindly, humble-hearted, womanly soul, that feared God and loved men, and did good in solid ways; one whose life made other women glad that she was born. What more would you have her be? Are you sure you understand what that was?

She became ill. She did not tell how ill she felt, but lay lone and sick. She would not burden others with her pain, and to die she did not fear. Her neighbours found it out and nursed her tenderly, but she died. Then there was nothing to do but reverently to lay her out, to put flowers on her breast and in her hands; it was all the kindness they could do now; how they wished they had done more when she was alive! Then they thought what to do next. When one is dead there is so little you can do, and yet you want to do so much. Then some one thought of Peter. The Apostle was only twelve miles off. He will surely come to see poor Dorcas once again, and show honour to her memory. And so the little groups of busy, tearful talkers united in one resolve to send for Peter. They would like him to be with them, to tell him all their trouble and sorrow, and pour into his sympathetic ears an eager chronicle of Dorcas's holy deeds. It is wonderful how much good your neighbours know to tell of you when you are dead, and how much evil while you are still alive.

This was the reason why they sent for Peter; not that they expected him to restore the dead to life. Had they not laid the dead body of their benefactress out, and washed and prepared it for burial? Why should they expect a miracle on her behalf? Stephen and James had trodden their martyr path, and no voice from heaven had called them back to leadership and witness-bearing in the Church. What should they expect for Dorcas from the Apostle beyond his sorrowful compassion?

Peter came. He found the room full of weeping women, telling of her goodness, of her clever fingers; showing him *on them* (*middle voice*) the dresses and petticoats she had made. How many they seemed when gathered together in that little room! All the results of the toil of her busy hands, scattered through the town, now gathered in the chamber of death to tell of her goodness after she was gone. Herself, she did not know the whole. "Blessed are the dead who die in the Lord; for their works do follow them."

We die and are not much missed. The world rolls on. Yet none is quite unwept, unnoticed. There are two sets of people who will mourn. There are those who loved you and found their joy in ministering to you; a mother, a lover: good or bad you may have been, but they will weep over your grave. Or, in heaven, they smile; in smiles or tears they love. And there are those you loved, on whose souls are the marks of your kindness, warmth, help, and cheer; they will miss you.

How came Peter to conceive the hope of recovering Dorcas to life? It was not through the message of an angel, or the narrative would tell us of it; nor was it through a special communication of the Spirit, or the sacred history would record it, as the habit of the Bible is. It seems to have been in an ordinary way, though under the Spirit's guidance. A little thing in Peter's doings suggests that he followed the train of an old memory, that he was dominated and inspired by a bygone incident. Amid those weeping women his heart was moved: he recalled an unforgotten scene. He remembered an old man coming to the Master with a white, anxious face and quivering lips, to plead for his sick child. He remembered their hurrying steps, and the eager impatience of the stricken father as they turned their faces to his house; the messenger bringing the sad tidings "dead;" the Master's face lighting up with a quiet, strange resolution as He said, "She is not dead;" and then how He put them all out and restored the maiden to her parents. Why should he not ask the Master now? He put them all out. He prayed. Confidence filled his heart. He summoned the dead woman from the shadow-land. She opened her eyes. To the weeping, mourning, loving women he gave her again—alive from the dead!

It was a tremendous deed of wonder and glory. It was done on a lonely, simple, humble woman. Why on her? Why not on James or Stephen? I cannot tell, for certain. God knows. His reasons are other than our thoughts. But I see this as possibly a cause: You observe that two narratives are conjoined. Dorcas, for her alms-deeds, receives this miracle of resurrection; while, for alms-deeds, Cornelius is acknowledged in a miracle also. Nowhere else in the Acts of the Apostles are alms-deeds made so prominent. In each story, and in the conjunction, I see design. God meant to set a mark of honour on the love that was displayed. I think He would guard the Church against undue estimation of preaching, apostles, miracle-working, deeds of show, gifts; and teach us that beyond all is love. So He singles out not an apostle, not a martyr, but this gentle, kind, womanly life, and crowns it with grandeur and glory, makes it conqueror of death, encircles it with a halo of most wonderful, Divine, loving care. Not preaching, not angel speech, not mountain-removing faith, but love is the centre. God judges differently from us. We worship the great leaders, orators, reformers, creed-makers; our statistics are of Churches, prayers, and preachers. God reckons all love for Himself and man as vaster, wider, and grander. Ah! while we think not of it, in unseen corners, in hidden nooks, He sees and garners a harvest of love and lowly service that shall be the beauty and glory of heaven. Let us think as God thinks. Let us learn to worship not gifts, but graces, not greatness, but goodness only. Bend your knee to such a woman with a reverence you will yield to no king, to no genius, however Godlike; and bend it, for you bend it to Christ. Humble, lonely, simple Christian souls, God cares for you as for her, if you are like her. Patiently toil on; God feels towards you as towards her. Go forward to death, sure that He will gather your life with equal care, not back into earth's struggle, but up into heaven's glory.

IV.
Unfulfilled Christian Work.

"And unto the angel of the Church in Sardis write; These things saith He that hath the seven Spirits of God, and the seven stars; I know thy works, that thou hast a name that thou livest, and art dead. Be watchful, and strengthen the things which remain, that are ready to die: for I have not found thy works perfect before God."—Rev. iii. 1, 2.

Reading the last clause a little more literally will more fully bring out the meaning: "For I have found no works of thine fulfilled before My God."—R.V.

THE passage forms a picture—God on His throne, Christ by His side, the work of the Churches on earth travelling up to God, and presenting itself before the throne Divine, and Christ, as the Churches pass in procession, judging them. The religious activity of the Church in Sardis swept by before God's throne, under Christ's eyes, and as it passed He saw that not one single task undertaken by that Church was done fully; everything was half done, and therefore worthless. It was not that the Church was doing nothing, but it was doing nothing worth doing. These were the facts. Christ's judgment on the facts is this: "Thou hast a name that thou livest, and art dead." A Church all whose labours are but half done is dead. Yet there were good men and women in the congregation at Sardis. If you read on you find this said by Christ: "Thou hast a few names even in Sardis which have not defiled their garments."

So, then, a Church may be dead though it contains living members. How can that be? A Church is not a mere number of individuals added to one another; something results from that combination of separate individuals; something very different, with fresh powers and added responsibilities, rises out of grouping together a number of individual Christians, that is a Church. A Church, a congregation (it is in that sense I use the word "Church" all through this discourse), has an individuality of its own; a Church has a character of its own; a Church has a spirit of its own; a Church has capacities of its own; a Church can do what no individual nor any mere number of individuals added together can do; a Church, as soon as it is constituted, creates a new kind of life, a new kind of being, a new kind of activities. No individual Christian, however good he may be, can out of himself make Christian fellowship, Christian devotion, Christian labour and co-operation, all that social life which springs from the union of severed individuals; no separate Christian, nor any number of separate Christians, can produce that. A Church, therefore, is something distinct from the individual members of whom it is built. A house is not a thousand bricks; it is something quite different, something made not merely by the presence of the bricks, but by their being built together. Each separate element of the building, when united, is able to do its share in the great work that none of them, or any member of them, could do without that combination which forms the edifice. A Church, a congregation, has its own character. Each provincial town in England has a character of its own; and an intelligent man, with quick sympathies, recognises the difference of spirit when he enters a town from that which was prevalent in the town he left. One is Radical, one is very Materialistic; one is full of poetry, and imagination, and literature; and the individual residing in the town is affected by the general spirit of that town. Every school has a character of its own, a spirit of its own; not that each boy in the school is just modelled on that type, but to a large extent each individual pupil is affected by the spirit of the school. The spirit of the school exists in the boys that dominate it. It is the same with Churches. In one congregation you are conscious of warmth, and enthusiasm, and friendliness, and love; in another congregation you are conscious of stiffness, and a rigid propriety, and distance, and coldness, and artificiality. In one Church you are conscious of a large, and liberal, and generous spirit; in another Church you are conscious of factions, fighting, and meanness and stinginess. That is a fact; you have felt it. A mere stranger entering the building on a Sunday morning feels it; it is there, there in the very faces of the people as they sit in their pews, there in the minister as he stands in the pulpit. A public speaker said to me this last week, "I may come with my address to a weekday meeting, but it all depends upon the spirit and mood of the meeting; it is one thing in one place, and another in another;" and if you have ever tried to speak in a Church or at a meeting you will have found it to be so. There may be a dozen men present in that meeting whose spirit is all that you may want, but they cannot make the result; the general result of it is determined by the mass. So it may come to pass that in a congregation there may be not a few individual members who are warm, living, earnest servants of Jesus Christ; but their goodness is not of the dominating kind; they have piety, but they lack manly power; they have good feeling and good intentions, but they have not character; they cannot command the whole; they cannot give their spirit to the mass of men; they just survive, but they cannot take the offensive; they have need of protection. They live themselves, but do not live half so strongly or half so healthily as they would in a congregation which was warm to the very tips of its fingers and the fringes of its garments, they are living, but the Church is dead.

What is the life of a Church? The life of a Church is loving loyalty to Jesus Christ, present more or less in the actual human heart of all the members; an inner, hidden thing, that you cannot weigh in a balance, that you cannot set down in figure in an annual report, that you cannot exhibit to a non-believer or a worldling, but the greatest, the most powerful force in all our world.

The life of a Church is a living, real presence of Jesus Christ, as a daily influence on the conduct, the thoughts, the words, the deeds of all the members of that Church. The life of a Church is the living presence of Jesus Christ in every committee of management, in every meeting of Sunday-school teachers, in every social gathering of the congregation; a living loyalty and devotion to the Lord Jesus Christ, born out of a grateful certainty that He died to save us, born out of a grand sympathy with Him, and under the belief that He is willing to save all the men and women and all the little children who are round about us. That is the living life of a Church, and nothing else is. You may have a perfect orthodoxy, and death; you may have great activity, and yet you may have death. Nothing is the life of a Church but actual living loyalty and love to the real living Lord of the Church, Jesus Christ.

Christ stands at the right hand of God, judging the Churches. He judges them by their works. But the life of a Church is not a thing of the hands or of the tongue; it is a thing of the heart. At the same time Christ has to make His judgment just; He has to go upon visible facts, and He can safely proceed upon the Church's work. Wherever there is life it cannot be still; it works, it moves, it beats, it becomes warmed; it must come out. If a Church has no works it has no life. What are those works which are the visible signs of a living Church? They are these: No dry, spasmodic zeal for orthodoxy when some heresy crops up which makes a public sensation; no straight, rigid propriety, and fineness of outward form, and æsthetic culture of ceremonial. The life that is loving loyalty to Christ, present in the heart of every individual member of a congregation, comes out in this way: it makes hearty singing on a Sunday. Even a man who has no musical voice, and who is a little weary, cannot help singing when his heart is stirred, even if he stops short in case he should make discord to his neighbours. It is all nonsense to say that people have grateful hearts to Christ when they sit with shut mouths to Christ's praise. I know well that habit has a great deal to do with it. It is the way of some Churches to sing heartily, and it is the way of some other Churches to let the choir do the singing; and I know, therefore, that you must not too absolutely take such a test as a standard by which you will judge whether or not there is a living warmth, and enjoyment, and cheering in the service and in the congregation. I believe all that, nevertheless I have seen the most stiff and silent congregation roused to sing when their hearts were aroused. Such silence is a bad habit. And how about the prayers? Men will not merely listen to the words, and will not criticise a man when he prays; men will be reverent; men will, by their very attitude, make it felt that souls are face to face with God. Men will not be sitting finding fault with all the blurs and blemishes that there are in the services (which there must be in every human service) when their hearts are being fed, and when their souls are going out to God. There will be no lack of Sunday-school teachers; and the Sunday-school teachers in such a Church will not do their work in a listless and negligent way, and fail in keeping their appointments and engagements, but will do it as if it were a pleasure. It is not the blame of Sunday-school teachers in a dead Church if they are teachers of that sort; it is the blame of the dead Church. How can they keep alive? Shall we put the penalty upon those who are partially living? No; it is the great mass of death, and decay, and coldness which is to blame. Let us visit the sins on the guilty parties.

A living Church will show its life in hearty, generous liberality to every good cause. A living Church will show its life by bravery and courage in taking up new responsibilities that may offer themselves, and working them most heartily. A living Church is living, not because it does one or all of these things, but because it loves loyalty to the Lord Jesus, who died for it, and feels that goodness and holiness are the grandest things in the world, and is eager to have all the children taught to love the Lord Jesus, and all the young people who are going out amid the temptations of life strengthened and helped to withstand them, and old people whose lives are embittered when a disaster comes upon them made tender, and soft, and submissive, by the life of Christ in that Church and among their Christian neighbours. Yes, the life of a Church is not a mere liking for what Christ loves, and a wish to please Him, but real life and real love to Christ will come out, not in correctness of creed, but in life and in work. It is an awful thing when a Church is dead, with all the children in it gathering to go to a Church which is cold, and to a dragging service, and to spiritless singing, and to melancholy prayer, and to a dry preaching. Ay, I have seen children who hated religion, because their parents, as I believe, were living in a dead Church. I have often said, "Cut your connection with such a Church; go rather to another denomination, which has life." I venture to say that a father who loves his child will sacrifice anything in order that that child may have pleasant and attractive views of religion. But shall the child's first idea of religion come to him in the shape of a crippled and broken-down failure? Fathers and mothers are absolutely bound thus to promote the spiritual interests of their children; it is worth more than anything else that is done for them; and I say that a Church which is gathering those young people around it, and keeping them from more dangerous places, and leading them to have it in their hearts to come and sit down with Christian people, is doing more than all the world will ever do. It is worth taking a great deal of trouble to belong to a living Church, and it is the absolute duty of every member of every Church to do all he can not merely to make himself alive, but to make the whole Church full of warm, living life.

When a Church is dead, or only half alive, the defect shows itself specifically and certainly in this manner: The Church's work is only half done, and can only half be fulfilled, when only a portion of its members fulfil their allotted task to their Master. If, in a Church which numbers five hundred, only fifty are doing the utmost they can do, the Church's measure of work will not be fulfilled before the judgment-seat of God. Fifty individuals cannot do what it takes five hundred to do. A half-done work, how it is spoiled! The army were defending the frontier bravely and successfully; but one cowardly regiment gave way, and the ranks were broken, and all the bravery, and the blood, and the death of the brave men were lost—lost by the cowardice. The work of a Church that is wearily done, in its life and extent, by a few living men and women in it, is poorly done; they do it with such a struggle; they are so weary and worn out; they have not pleasure, they have not enthusiasm, in doing it. How can they have? Oh, it is hard when a few men and women have to do all the teaching, and all the visiting, and all the work at the meetings! it spoils their work; it is not fair play. I appeal to you to determine whether I speak truly or not. One man cannot do another man's work. One link of a chain cannot do duty for another link, and if the one goes, sometimes the chain is worth nothing at all. The work of a dead or half-dead Church stands before God's judgment-seat unfulfilled. How can it tell on the careless? how can it tell on the worldly? Do you think that they will be just, and say, "Ah, look at what the fifty are doing"? No, you may be quite sure that they will look at the deficiency of the four hundred and fifty, and say, "Is this a Church of Christ?" Who blames them?

A living Church must work, and it must work on, and it must send life through every part and fragment of its whole frame, or else it has begun to die. It is not a small thing, of no concern, if some members of a Church are doing nothing by being idle. The work that a Church has to do is the creation of living Christian character, and of the conviction that being in Church on Sunday and belonging to a congregation make a man a kinder brother, or a more loving father or husband, and make a woman a better mother or a more kindly neighbour. That is the best work a Church can do, and that does not come to a man through a dead Church. A living Church must be making itself felt all around in the world outside by work of that kind; and I say that it is not a matter of no consequence if some members of a Church are not receiving and not transmitting that warmth and activity. It is not a small matter if one organ of my body be dying, be passing into mortification; it means death to the whole body, and I must cut it off unless life can be brought back again into it. It is the very law of life, as God has made it, that everything which has life in it must be working; it cannot stop. If your heart stops it is death; nothing else can make it stop but death. If any organ in your body is always receiving, but giving nothing, and not sending out what it gets, improved, to the rest, it means diseased life, it means death. Does the stomach receive its daily food to keep it to itself, as we so often receive the prayers and sermons in a Church? No; as soon as the feeding is done the hard work begins; the stomach gives it to the blood, and what does the blood do? As the great carrier of the system, it delivers it here and there—here a little to this muscle, there to that bone, there to the brain, and all through the body. And what the muscles and the other parts have received do they keep? No; if the various portions of the body did not give out what they receive they would get choked; it would be death by surfeit; they must work. And so the circle of life goes round; stop it at any one point, and you spoil the whole circle. If the blood-vessels do not do their work, if the muscles do not do their work, and so on throughout the entire system, it means this, that that body is not healthy; it means death to the whole frame. A business man said to me yesterday, "As soon as a man ceases pushing his business, and does not endeavour to extend it, it falls off." He does not want actually to increase it, but he must adopt that plan to keep it up to its present mark. The Church, alas! has not been willing to increase its work, desiring to take on other responsibilities; it does not say, "I cannot rest while people are cold and not interested in doing the Church's work, not bent upon bringing in sinners, and bringing children into the Sunday-schools to be taught to love and reverence religion, and causing people whose life is sour and bitter to be soothed and comforted."

What I have been pressing upon you is the law of life. Is it a hard law? No, it is a kind law. That is how God rewards you for what you have done; He gives you more work to do. In reading the parable of the men to whom it was assigned to rule over the cities did you ever mark how they were rewarded? Here is a man who has actively and effectively used ten talents. How does his lord reward him—by giving him a sinecure? No; he says, "You shall be ruler over ten cities;" and in the same way the man who has been successful with five talents is made ruler over five cities. Did you ever know a man who had served his country well, and benefited it, wish to withdraw into a drawing-room, and spend the remainder of his life in luxury and ease? Did you ever know a successful general who wanted to get a big fortune and to retire? No; successful men cannot be rewarded better than by giving them a deal more to do—larger responsibilities, larger powers, a larger sense of strength successfully exerted. That is the blessing and the joy which shall go with larger toil, and grander accomplishment, and brighter goodness. The few who are used to work shall have plenty of work. I take it as a sign that God is pleased with the results of a Church when He gives them new work to do, and the heart to take it up. It is not extra work; it is the reward of the past, and it is a step that shall lead you to a higher throne. Nay, more; work is indispensable to the enjoyment of a Church's good. No Church can heartily enjoy what we call religious privileges unless it is working hard; and no individual member of that Church will get the good of it unless he is taking a part in the Church's work. He does not need to be an office-bearer or anything of that sort; his work may be just friendliness to others in the house of God, showing a kind spirit to them or taking an interest in them, showing neighbourliness by his Church character. Do not think that it is a high array of talents that is required; no, it is the Church's function of being "all of one mind," and knit together and helping one another, and sympathising with one another, being bound up in the common lot of disasters and trials. I say that no individual member, unless he is taking his part, is a living member of that Church. If people are very fastidious about the doctrines which are preached, if people are searching into the sense of every hymn or prayer, if people are finding fault with the way in which everything is done, then it may be that the Church is to blame; but if the Church is doing its work as well as any poor human Church can do it, I advise such a one to say to himself, "May not I be to blame?" If you think that the daily food which is provided for you is not properly cooked, and it is not of the proper sort, and does not taste well, is it not your doctor you want to go to, to ask him to cure you of dyspepsia? And in all probability he will recommend to you exercise and hard work. A hard-working man does not complain even of dry bread; he is not particular; he has an appetite. I have known, in the Church to which I belonged before I began to preach, how pleased I was even with sermons which had no originality in them if I saw that they were part of the common work. It was my home, and you do not criticise your own home; and you do not criticise your father and mother; you believe in the power which you get from your father, because he is yours. Throw yourself into the Church, become a part of it, take an interest in everything, and it is wonderful how little you will have of criticism about you. Take plenty of spiritual exercise, and you may be sure that even a bare and poor spiritual diet will agree wonderfully with you.

Christ reckons with Churches—Christ at God's right hand, what is He about? When He was down here on earth He went hither and thither, seeking the lost; He forgave the woman that wept at His feet; He saved the dying thief. Oh, gentle, loving Saviour Jesus, "the same yesterday, and to-day, and for ever"! And at God's right hand He is loving, and pitying, and forgiving my sins, and pleased with my tears of repentance—forbearing, tender, saving Jesus! We preach that; we should not be men, we should not be Christians, if we did not preach that; we could not live without that thought of Jesus. But let us be true; do not let us hide facts. That same Jesus stands at God's right hand, judging the Churches, reckoning with them. Oh, to a penitent sinner He is all heart, but to a slothful servant He is a faithful Master! He reckons with Churches; He reckons with individuals. It would not be kind if He did not reckon with you. Would you wish Him not to reckon? Would you like to say, "I do not care whether He does anything with me or not"? Ah, I should begin to think that Christ did not love you at all if He did not reckon with you, if he were not grieved and angry when you did not do your duty to Him and to your neighbour! Where would be the dignity of life if we did not believe in a great last judgment, with a stern reckoning with sin? We should sink to the level of the animals if there were no judgment. It proves that man has an immortal spirit. What does it matter, with the animals, what they do? But God must reckon with man, and He would not be reigning if man had not to reckon on an awful judgment-day for every spirit. It is a proof to me that I am of moment, and that my human spirit has dignity; it makes clear to me my place in the universe, and my claim to immortality; it shows me that I am of sufficient importance to necessitate God's reckoning with me. Churches, too, must be reckoned with. It would argue that they were mere nurseries, were hospitals for people to be convalescent in, mere nonentities, counting for nothing in the great work of the world and the mighty purpose of God, if we did not know that Christ was to reckon with them. They have great powers given to them, they have great capabilities, they have tremendous responsibilities; they can fulfil God's purposes in the world, and nothing but their supineness and listlessness hinders them; and God and Christ must reckon with Churches. I would not have it different. Let Them reckon with them, and let me remember that They will reckon with me and my Church; and let me be full of good works. Christ must reckon with it, for the Church's sake. How could He but care? Oh, if we did but believe what we preach and what we read in our Gospels! It is that Jesus lost all things which men look for; that He turned aside from every joy of life; that He gathered sorrows around Him; that His great heart was broken upon the cross; that He spent all His life—for what? That He might save men from eternal banishment from God;

that He might put happiness instead of misery into every house where there are unholiness and evil; that He might make men brighter and better. His great heart was all warm and eager for it. Oh, what He has sacrificed! He is a disappointed, lost man if He fails, and if He succeeds it must be done through His congregations, through His Churches, through men and women here. How can He but care? how can He but watch? As all the Church's activity goes by before God's throne, the recording angel takes it down. Does He see a Church whose members have taught the little children on the Sunday afternoon to love Him better; a Church which has made men whose faith in Him was nearly crushed out by sinful practices think again of Christ and heaven; a Church which has put a man once more on his feet, and given him to his wife and children, and they have been glad because the father and husband has loved them again? How can it but be that those who fight for Him should rejoice when a Church is thus acting for God, as compared with a Church that does nothing? Oh, if we could but believe and feel, when we come into church on a Sunday morning, that Jesus is watching all that is going on—watching to see if our hearts are made more soft and tender, more reverent and gentle, more full of kind thoughts to those who sit round about us—watching to see if we speak a kind word—watching to see if we resolve to do more for Him—watching to see if we can give liberally to help in what is being done for Him, and to support those who have special gifts for special work! The Lord Jesus has His eyes upon us in this spiritual Church framework. It does bind us together, and, thank God! I will say of ourselves has bound us together for much good work, and I believe will bind us more closely together. If every Sunday morning we only felt and believed it, and came and knelt and praised, and listened with light in our hearts, we should do our work well and have the reward of very faithful servants.

V.
A Lesson in Christian Help.

"Wherefore lift up the hands which hang down, and the [en]feeble[d] knees; and make straight [smooth] paths for [with] your feet, lest that which is lame be turned out of the way; but let it rather be healed [or, in order that that which is lame may not be caused to go astray, but may rather be healed]."—HEB. xii. 12, 13.

SUBJECTED to severe and harassing persecution on account of their Christian faith, and plied by subtle arguments and doubts, which had all the more seductive powers from the immunity from suffering which would be gained by yielding to them, the members of the Church to whom this letter was addressed had become discouraged, depressed, perplexed, and some, staggered and tempted, were even in danger of renouncing their allegiance to Jesus of Nazareth. After warning them of the doom and misery of deserting the cross of Christ, inciting them to endurance by the long and shining roll of patriarchs, prophets, martyrs, and by the example of the dying Saviour, the Apostle explains to them how all this trial and suffering is the chastening of Fatherly love, destined to bring forth the peaceable fruit of righteousness, and finally exhorts them to rise above their despondency and enfeeblement, to advance with strong, unwavering faith in the right path, in order that thereby those who were crippled by doubt or temptation might be saved from straying quite away, helped over their difficulties, and in the end restored to firm and abiding faith.

The command in the text assumes the existence of two classes in the Church—those that need help, that must lean on others, and those who are able and ought to give help and support. Just as in a flock of sheep, so in the Church, there will be some strong, vigorous, active, and others weak, feeble-kneed, lame. Let us recognise this fact honestly, and be prepared to face it. Differences and degrees of faith, assurance, consistency, there are and must be. When the Church of Christ is oppressed by persecution, seduced by temptation, assailed by unbelief, do not be amazed to find that some spirits will be crippled, drawn away into wrong, just on the very point of being altogether perverted, and remember that there ought to be others who, by their indomitable perseverance, their immovable faith, the unbroken solidarity and persistence of their march, shall support and carry forward in safety those who, but for such environment and protection, if left to combat solitary and unaided, had stumbled and fallen in the storm of persecution and seduction, or been clean swept away by the waves of doubt and unbelief.

There are ever these two classes among the followers of Jesus—the strong, the brave, the helpful, the steadfast; the weak, the timorous, the dependent, the wavering. Brother, to which of these do you belong? Answer that question honestly, and then think what you should reply to this other question: To which class ought you to belong?

I am confident if Christian men and women would but enrol themselves not according to their meaner and unworthier inclinations, but in accordance with the voice of duty and the promptings of all that is most noble and generous in them, we should not have (as we do now) in the army of Christ the vast majority ranking as incapable and non-efficient, while only a small minority do the fighting and defending. Clearly my text supposes that the mass will be strong and helpful, with only one or two feeble, incompetent; just as in a flock of sheep the greater number are healthy, whole, and able-bodied, while only a few are disabled and lamed. It should be so in all our congregations. Perhaps in some the ideal is fairly realised. But looking at the Church as a whole, do I exaggerate in thinking that there are many, very many, who ought to be able-bodied and aidful, but who regard themselves as exonerated from active service, as incompetent to take part in any way in the warfare of the Cross, as person to be defended, not to help in the defence?

How is it with each of you? What is your habitual attitude when goodness, truth, righteousness, Christ are assailed? In some social or intellectual company where the followers of Christ are in the minority, or it may be where you stand quite alone, you hear virtue or purity sneered at, contemned; or justice and mercy ridiculed, discredited; or the faith in things unseen rudely mocked and denied. Do you then always bravely speak out for the glory and majesty of purity and goodness, for the reality and grandeur of God and Christ? or do you yield to the craven cowardice that lurks even in regenerate men, and, saying it is for ministers, or apologists, or the strong and clever to defend Christ, meanly hold your peace? So far from dreaming that you are bound to defend the truth, you perhaps pity yourself for being subjected to such trial, and admire your own fidelity, that can survive such assaults. Instead of feeling yourself a coward, you rather regard yourself as a martyr, a person much to be commiserated and admired, and wonder how the Lord should so heartlessly expose your faith to such trials, while all the time you are in reality a weak, ignoble recreant. But you may say, "What! am I to speak when I know that I should only be ridiculed, laughed at, beaten in argument, when I am certain my effort would be defeated, rejected with ignominy?" But there is no necessity you should argue; nay, if your arguments will be foolish or weak it is your duty to keep them to yourself. But you are not bidden to argue, prove, demonstrate anything; only you are to confess, to protest against evil, and loyally side with the truth. And if you are not to do that except when you know you will be applauded and triumphant, what of your Master's conduct? He was laughed at, scorned, despised, rejected, defeated, and He knew it all from the first. Brother, you are to "follow Him" in all He did, and so you are to stand by the truth even when you know it will only bring scorn, scoffs, defeat, failure on you. Nevertheless be sure in such a defeat and failure only you shall suffer. As in Christ's death, though He dies, the truth triumphs, and the crown of thorns becomes a crown of glory.

This sin of selfish indolence, of weak-minded inaction, carries its own penalty with it. Who of us has not learned the terrible retribution by bitter experience? If you who ought to have been strong, who ought to have defended your Lord, were guilty of timidly shirking your duty, of feebly failing to declare your faith, then your faith will seem to you a poor, weakly thing, and Christianity itself feeble and infirm. In these days of outspoken unbelief, of staggering attack, and of widespread defection, if you think only of yourself, feel no obligation of defence, yield aggrievedly to terror and alarm, regarding yourself as wronged in being exposed thus, and reproaching others who, you think, ought to have been able to silence such foes and quite shelter you from seduction, then your faith will be shaken, your hands hang down, and your knees tremble. But if you felt yourself bound to be considerate of others, to be one of the strong, not one of the feeble, to defend the infirm and the timid, how different it would be with yourself! you would have courage, faith, strength; in this fashion doing the will of God, you would learn that the doctrine was of God.

In the case of Christianity men act as they would be ashamed to act in other situations. You who are so given over to alarms, so hopeless of the faith, suppose you were in a ship that has sprung a leak, how should you act? Should we find you among the timid and the hysterical, who lose head and heart, refuse to help at the pumps, fling themselves in despair on the deck, and do their best to dishearten and impede the brave men who, keeping their misgivings to themselves, toil on with bravery to try and save the lives of all? There are some constituted with such despondent, enfeebled nerves as to be excusable for such conduct, but in the Christian Church there are many with no such justification, who shake their heads gloomily, cry despairingly that the Church is in danger, the faith abandoned, do their utmost to weaken and dispirit their brethren, all the time never dreaming how weak and cowardly is their conduct, or that they ought rather to be comforters, helper, defenders.

The cause of this ignoble conduct seems to me to consist in the fact that many Christians have got to see only one side of Christianity, and that the selfish or personal side. They have learned that by becoming Christ's He undertakes to save them, but they have failed to apprehend that, on the other hand, this relation involves that they are to serve Him. Again, their notion of what is implied in entering the membership of the Church is quite as one-sided. They consider that the purpose of this tie is that you may be cared for, guarded, developed by the Church—all which is true; but then they quite fail to see that also you are bound to aid, defend, and protect the Church. How many Christians are there who never dream of owing any duty to the Church, but consider it to be simply constructed for the purpose of doing everything for them needful for salvation. Within it they are to be surrounded by sanctifying influences, fed by ordinances, guarded in its holy atmosphere from the world's miasma; in a word, they are to be fostered, preached to, prayed for, visited, tended, and all the time they have nothing whatever to do for the Church. But while all this is done by the Church, that is not the only nor the cardinal conception of either the Church or its members. Brethren, the Church of Christ is a great army of valiant and able-bodied soldiers, sent out to battle with evil, led on by officers who ought indeed to encourage and care for the men, but whose main duty, nevertheless, is to lead them to conflict and conquest. According to this modern notion, that Church members are to do nothing but be cared for and protected, the Church is made to be more a sort of great nursery or convalescent hospital, provided with a staff of doctors, and nurses, and visitors, and the Church members are not soldiers, but rather a sect of weaklings, invalids, and infirm, who are just kept in life by ceaseless care and nursing.

From this mistaken and perverted notion of what it means to belong to Jesus Christ, from the miserable failure to recognise the public and primary obligations resting on all the Lord's followers, from forgetting that the kingdom of God is founded not merely to foster and ripen those in it for heaven, but that they may extend its conquering boundaries over all the world; from these unhappy errors spring the impotency, the half-heartedness, the dispirited timidity of so large a part of the Church in the present day. This is the origin of that general sort of notion as if we should be thankful if Christians just survived; as if it were natural and changeless that the Church should be despised and scorned; as if against unbelief Christianity should not venture to raise her voice very assuredly, but stand on the defensive, and be thankful if she can just hold her own; as if it were natural and normal that Christians should find their faith hard pressed, hardly able to stand its ground, and they themselves feel weak, timid, alarmed, and helpless.

But perchance you may be inclined to defend this state of mind and this selfish notion of Christianity; nay, you may think that you have Scripture on your side. In opposition to the assertion that in place of being merely cared for, you are to fight, and in place of being timid, you are to be brave, you may recall the fact that Christ compares His people to sheep whom He shelters safely and tends in a snug fold, free from struggle and terror; and urge that sheep are not suggestive of combativeness, and that it is natural for them to tremble when a lion roars outside, and to count on the shepherd driving the evil beast away, while nobody expects them to face the ravager. But do you not see that our Lord meant that comparison to illustrate only His relationship to them and His treatment of them? while if you are to infer from it also that He meant them, in their attitude to the world and unbelief, to be timid and helpless as sheep, then how do you explain that elsewhere they are compared to soldiers, commanded to be valiant, fearless, daring? If they are to do no fighting, then why are they told to put on the whole armour of God, to be faithful unto death, to endure hardness as good soldiers of Jesus Christ? Ah, we are very fond of these pleasant, comfortable comparisons, and are constantly perverting them by misapplying them to positions they have nothing to do with. But you may reply, "Did not our Lord say Himself, to His disciples, that He sent them out as sheep among wolves?" Yes, indeed, but only to inform them of what treatment they might expect from the world, not surely with the intention of indicating that they were to meet the world's hostility as a sheep meets a wolf's, cowering, trembling, fleeing. If He meant that they were to be timid, helpless, sheeplike, why did He say also, "I give you power to tread on serpents and scorpions and over all the power of the enemy"? why did He send them out to conquer the world? How was it that the disciples so thoroughly misunderstood the command? When Peter, facing the hostile judges, avowed that he would obey God, and not them, that was not timid, that was not sheeplike. When Paul fought with wild beasts at Ephesus, that, too, was not at all in the manner of a sheep among its foes. When the Apostle, in the same Epistle, bids the readers resist unto blood, when you remember how so many of our Lord's followers have indeed sealed their witness with their lives, surely it is plain that we have forgotten one side of our Christian duty. We ought to be "wise as serpents" in dealing with the foe, "harmless as doves" to our brethren and friends; but that is very much inverted now, and the chief characteristic of many a soldier of the Cross is just his perfect harmlessness in the combat. Brethren, you look for the crown of righteousness that sparkled before Paul's closing eyes, bright amid the gathering shades of his martyr death. But that crown was not gained without hazard, not won by slothful ease, but earned on many a bloody, painful field, while he "fought the good fight." Believe me, there shall be no crown for you unless, like Paul, you too have fought that fight, and kept that faith, for which he bravely lived and bravely died.

Nevertheless there will always be among Christ's disciples those that are weak-handed, feeble-kneed, and lame; some permanently and constitutionally affected with feebleness and infirmity; and now and again a strong one maimed, injured by extreme and undue exposure, or crippled by some untoward accident. It was so among these Hebrew Christians. Intimidated by persecution, disheartened by the spoiling of their goods, shaken by the arguments of unbelief, several grew less steadfast in their confession of Christ, others were perplexed and confused, and some were just on the verge of deserting and abandoning the faith. Among us there is no more imprisoning, goods spoiling and persecution to stagger our faith in Christ, but there are instead a whole world of seductions, of discouragements, of mockeries, and of unbelieving sneers. Still, too, there are with us the weak, the maimed, the misled; many who never have attained to much spirituality or consistency; others who for a time went well, but became entangled in the mazes of the world's sinful attractions, or were overtaken by sudden temptation, enfeebled by persistent opposition and ridicule, paralysed by difficulties, disappointments, doubts, or unbelief.

I wish we did more fully realise and constantly remember that there are to be among Christ's own ones really such as these, weaklings, cripples, tempted, fallen; brethren overtaken by snares, seductions, unbelief, whom we ought to pity, whom we ought to help. Only it is needful to bear in mind that we are not to conclude that every one who gives himself out as such is really a wounded brother, to be sympathised with and aided. For there are many who only imagine themselves distressed, who give themselves out as greatly tried and buffeted, more from a kind of mental hypochondriasis or foolish fondness for being talked of and fussed over. This is especially so in the matter of doubt and religious difficulty. For just as it happens that in the fashionable world it is sometimes proper to have a lisp or limp, in imitation of some dignitary, so, unfortunately, at the present day it has become fashionable to go halt of one foot in faith; and there are persons, thoroughly excellent and orthodox in reality, who are impelled to let all their acquaintances know what dark struggles of soul they pass through, and of how much it costs them to face the unbelieving spectres of their minds. Brethren, when a man has a real skeleton in his closet he does not go round the circle of his friends, flaunting that unpleasant fact in their faces. When a man tells you, with a smile of complacent superiority on his face, of his conflicts with doubt, you need not expend much sympathy or anxiety on him; like all other affectations, this one may be left to die a natural death. No, the man to whom doubt is a real spectre, a veritable agony, does not blazon his pain abroad; like Jacob's wrestle with his dread midnight foe, the real soul-struggles are fought out in darkness and alone. It is these who are truly stricken, wounded, well-nigh carried away—these, and these alone, whom you are asked to pity and to help.

But as a matter of fact, how do we Christian men and women who have not fallen treat such weaker brethren, I mean persons who have really been crippled, really erred? The text very plainly implies that we are not to cast them off, but to compassionate them and seek to recover them. Nay, mere human kindness would require the same. As soldiers seek to rescue, not to slay, a comrade well-nigh carried off by the foe, so surely we Christians should not attack, but strive to regain a brother captured in the meshes of temptation or unbelief. And no doubt to a very large extent true Christians do act so, though I fear not with that unvarying pitifulness that ought to extend the same charity to all. Do we not make unrighteous differences, leaving room for restoration to some of the erring, and closing heart and door against others? Partly from thoughtlessness, partly from prejudice, partly from contempt of what is weakness or cowardice, there are some falling, straying souls whom we treat too much like those evil animals that whenever one of the herd is wounded or crippled fall upon the victim and tear him in pieces. When we hear of a brother falling, doubting, denying, have we not all sometimes felt only anger, reprobation—nay, uttered sharp, cruel, merciless words of final condemnation and irretrievable doom? Do we not often treat erring ones so? It is very natural, for these feeble-handed, weak-kneed, crippled ones are an eye-sore, unpleasant to have to do with, a discredit to the Church and the most convenient plan is to cast them off. Nevertheless, it is most inhuman, most unchristian, and can only spring from one of two errors. Either you do not have that fraternal love for all your brethren in Christ which you ought to have. When your brother after the flesh, or your son, catches a deadly complaint (it may be through his own recklessness and disobedience), or is wounded by some hostile assault, you do not in anger cast him out to die, for you love him. Would God we had more love among Christians! Or it may be the reason of your harsh treatment is that you mistake your straying, doubting brother for an enemy, and fail to see that he is a victim. Of course there is a great distinction between one of Christ's little ones swept into doubt, and a hostile, malignant unbeliever, seeking to harm the flock. This last you must indeed oppose, and seek to drive out of the fold, though even then you will feel for him as our Lord did when He wept over Jerusalem, and on the cross prayed, "Father, forgive them." But it is not of such we speak now, only of those who are themselves not wolves, but wounded, wandered sheep. Remember, therefore, that they are your brethren, and pity and help them.

Perhaps you say, "What! can it be right to feel pity, kindness, compassion, love for men who have gone astray from Christ, rebelled against the Master, forsaken and denied the Saviour?" Remember how Jesus treated the eleven, who deserted Him, Peter, who denied Him, Thomas, who would not believe. Nay, more, can you for one moment doubt the rightfulness of feeling so to sinning brethren, be they as bad as they may, and of treating them so, you who do believe that from all eternity God set His love, compassion, saving purpose on sinners—rebellious, hateful sinners—without one spark of merit or goodness in them to deserve it? Brethren, it is not wrong, it is not weak, it is noble, Christlike, Godlike to pity, to love, to tenderly seek and save the lost, the sinning, the erring, the fallen.

Finally, remark how the text suggests that you are to render them assistance and support. Suppose it is a brother becoming involved in worldly or dangerous entanglements, lapsing into doubtful courses, or yielding to the freezing influence of ungodly or sceptical companions. Now, direct interference, immediate intervention, is not always possible, is often difficult, sometimes impossible. Besides, often the mischief is already done ere you perceive it. Or again, it is intellectual difficulty or doubt that you have to deal with. To meet the objections, to remove the doubts, would be well, but perchance you are not skilled, competent to do that; or it may be they are such as cannot be removed. Here, again, direct remedies may be impracticable. Are you, then, powerless, helpless to aid? Far from it. A method better than all immediate and special action lies open for you, for all Christian men and women. "Make straight, smooth paths with your feet." It may be you cannot personally do anything to support the maimed or arrest the erring, but you can nevertheless render most important service. As a flock of sheep, by all moving on regularly in one united mass, with their feet smooth down the roughnesses and entanglements of the way, breaking down the entrapping brambles, clearing away the furze and tripping briers, leaving behind them a plain and open track, trodden down and freed of obstructions, stones, and stumbling-blocks, so that the weak and crippled are not turned aside or overthrown; so if the strong and whole body of Christian men and women will but move steadfastly on amid the mazes of temptation and over the stumbling-stones of evil, the feeble, tempted, erring will be helped forward, and, borne along in the united, combined advance, will not fall behind or be baffled, overthrown, or led astray by difficulties and impediments. Yes, infinitely more powerful than any isolated rebuke, or warning, or intervention, is the force of united Christian example and protecting aid, to keep in the right path the halt, the maimed, the blind. What the tempted, the world-seduced, the doubting, the unbelieving need is not rebukes, cautions, exhortations, refutations of objections, but it is to be drawn out of the cold, freezing world of evil and doubt into the warm, living, breathing atmosphere of loving, real Christian fellowship; to be surrounded by the resistless progression in rectitude, in faith and love, of Christlike, God-fearing souls. With blows of reprimand and logical argument you may pound and break the ice of sin and unbelief, but though broken, it remains cold, winter ice, freezing still. Bring it into the summer radiance, the golden sunshine of warm Christian life; then it will be melted away, and the hard heart grow soft and tender in the breath of the all-quickening Spirit.

Brethren, it is for this that the Master has gathered us into families and homes, friendly circles and fellowships, congregations and churches. It is because some of His own will be very weak, timid, facile to fall, lukewarm, tempted, erring, doubting. Have you settled it with yourself, strong, high-principled, undoubting Christian, that the Church is not a club of stainless, perfect souls, but that there are to be in it such foolish, feeble, ignoble ones, real doubters, backsliders, wanderers, and that yet they are your brethren, little ones of the common Lord? And it is just for their sake, that they may be saved, that He has caused us to be knit together into one flock, that they may be kept from falling, restored when they err, strengthened, cheered, loved, and helped. Ah, we know not for the most part how much there is of strength and comfort for us in this! For all of us there is, for even the very strong, they that have comforted most, sometimes will be very weak themselves, and long for sympathy and support. Once even the blessed Master Himself in broken-hearted agony besought that help, and prayed His followers, "Tarry ye here, and watch with Me." My brother, if you can remember a time when you were enabled to endure, to conquer, because Christian friends stood around you and watched with you, then be pitiful to your tempted brother now. It may be that his limping, stumbling gait is very unpleasant to you, and you do not care to be known as of his company; his halt, ungainly walk does not look well beside your high, triumphal march. Perchance in heaven there is more good pleasure over his paltry pace than over your proud progress. Ah, friends, we see too little now to judge, who know not one another's hurts and trials! We who have the sunshine on our path, and bounding vigour in our tread, forget, I fear, how to many struggling souls the path is very flinty, rough, and hard, swept by wild storms of passion and rushing floods of fierce temptation; while the thick darkness and awful solitude, haunted by mocking spectres of deathlike doubts and fears, wrap them round with a chill, paralysing shroud of despair. You who have never been so tempted, give God thanks and be humble, very humble, and lowly, and merciful. Have infinite forbearance and compassion. Remember that one harsh word, one hopeless look from you may numb a last feeble grasp on goodness, and sink a brother despairing in the black abyss; while a kindly look, a helping hand, a loving, free, generous pardon and word of hope from you may be to him the voice of eternal forgiveness in heaven, and power of restoration even now.

Brethren, when, against some brother who has fallen, sinned or gone astray, quick anger flames in your heart, and to your lips sharp, cutting words of reprobation leap, let this word of Christ ring in your ears: "Whoso shall offend one of these little ones which believe in Me, it were better for him that a millstone were hanged about his neck, and that he were drowned in the depth of the sea." And as that word of dreadful condemnation awes each lurid spark of hasty anger from your soul, let these words of endless peace, and joy, and mercy steal in, and soften all your spirit into gentlest pity, tenderness, and love: "Brethren, if any of you do err from the truth, and one convert him; let him know, that he which converteth the sinner from the error of his way shall save a soul from death, and shall hide a multitude of sins." "Wherefore let us lift up the hands which hang down, and the feeble knees; and let us make straight paths with our feet, lest that which is lame be turned out of the way; but let it rather be healed."

VI.
JOSEPH'S FAITH.[1]

"By faith Joseph, when he died, made mention of the departing of the children of Israel; and gave commandment concerning his bones."—HEB. xi. 22.

FAITH is a word that we hear a great deal of in theological exposition and in religious teaching. It is a good thing constantly to remind ourselves of what its actual meaning is. The 11th chapter of this Epistle begins with a definition of faith, and then gives examples of it. The definition is a little hard to understand; nobody can misunderstand the illustrations. According to the inspired writer, faith is recognising the will of God, taking it and doing it; that is faith, and nothing else is—no theories about God, no rules, and laws, and definitions about God's government of the world, no intellectual adherence to any explanation of theology. Faith, real and living, means that the God who comes into contact with you in your life and your world has a will, and shows it to you. If you bow down before that actual will of God, that it may save you from your real sins, and that He may use you in saving the dead around you; if you adore it, and worship it, and account it the best thing in your life, and give yourself up to it, as the one thing worth doing, though there be many a forsaking and many a return to God, if you hold on through your life, doing the will of God, then you are a man of faith.

Joseph was a man of faith, in the olden times, all his life long. From his very boyhood he had possessed faith. In the dreams that came to him as a lad he welcomed God's face, not quite understanding all He meant, and a little misusing the high vocation that came to him, accepting it in the pride of his heart. In his trials and his prosperity, in his public career, in his private home life, on his death-bed, he lived with God, reckoned with God, and loved God, and tried to do God's will on the earth. One deed stands out supreme and stupendous. Joseph on his dying bed looked forward into the future, and there, amidst the mists, discerned the promise of the world's redemption,

---

[1] Preached on Sunday evening, October 20th, 1889, in St. John' Wood Presbyterian Church.

forecast the coming of God's kingdom on earth, and chose what to him was the greatest and grandest thing in his dying, and so gave commandment for the burying of his bones away in distant Canaan.

I am going to ask you to follow me as I rapidly sketch the great outstanding elements of struggle and triumph in Joseph's career, in order that I may show you the splendid feature of faith, and that in dying he was still loyal to the dreams of his youth. Joseph was a younger son. He had the misfortune to be his father's favourite; he was exempted from hard toil; he was kept near his old father; his brethren hated him for it; probably he misbehaved himself; he was no saint, else there would be no good in my preaching about him. He had the misfortune to be spoiled by his father. He had intelligence, and he was wide awake; but there was nothing in the early years of the lad to give evidence of any extraordinary ability, or to forecast any splendid career for him, with the exception of one thing: Joseph was a great dreamer in his sleep; and as a boy he woke up from his sleep, and saw visions, glorious castles in the air; and they were not all floating away in cloudland, high up above him, but he saw *himself* in them; they had an intense personal interest for him. Perhaps he was very injudicious, and probably disagreeable, in the tone and fashion of telling these dreams to his brothers. Their sheaves in the harvest gathered round and made obeisance to his sheaf; the meaning plainly being that he was to rise to great power, that he would hold them in his hand, and be lord and master over them. They might not have much interest for us; but Joseph belonged to a family that believed that they held a unique position in the world's history, and that they were to bring a great blessing into this world. They had not grasped exactly what it was, nor understood the significance of the spiritual kingdom of heaven; but none the less they heard God's voice around them, so that this world became to them a place in which He lived and moved: thus they rose to the grandeur of the conception that they were to have a master hand in carving the fortunes of the world. Out of many of his brethren, God had selected Joseph to be an inheritor and administrator of the Divine purpose of blessing to the world, and to do unique deeds of valour for the kingdom of God.

Now I have said that the one remarkable thing about Joseph's boyhood, the one thing that might excite your expectation about his future, was that he dreamt dreams; he was a great dreamer in his youth. I can understand many a shrewd, practical man saying that that was not much to his credit: "A lad that is always dreaming dreams will not do much." Quite true, if the one, the only purpose of life is to eat and drink and to gather all the dirt together with the muck-rake; but if man has a Divine destiny in him, if man lives in two worlds—a world that you see with your eyes, a world where money is current, and another world where your sovereigns are worth nothing, a world of truth and honour, generosity, love, goodness, self-denial, moral achievement and victory, then it comes to a great deal; it means very much for a boy's future if he has dreams that are not of earth, but of heaven. There are dreams and dreams. There are dreams that come of laziness, idleness, selfishness, and over-feeding, gross nightmares, fit for swine; dreams coming of self-indulgence and worldliness, poor grovelling things; a man's mind is not much better for *them*. There are dreams that are born of a back-boneless sentimentality, of sweet mock chivalry, that loves to represent itself in pretty pictures; not much good comes of them. But there are other dreams, that come out of a man's wide-awake activity; dreams that are the vapours rising from a fervent spirit, from the cooling of the machinery. They work out the character that God is weaving in that lad or in that young girl. These dreams are prophetic; they have something of heaven in them; they are something higher than the common: from God they come; they are the threads and fibres by which He would lead us on to do great deeds on earth, and at last receive us as faithful and good servants of our Master. I do believe in the dreams of youth, that come in at that window which is open heavenward in every young soul, until the dust and dirt of earth cloud it over; the dreams of romance, that stupid old people try to crush and drive out, and that the world puts its heel upon; those dreams of friendship and honour, of truth and purity, to be chosen rather than worldly gain; those dreams of love, generous and tender, that shall make two lives knit together into one of exceptional tenderness and goodness. There is the breath of heaven here; these are the golden glows in the mists of life's morning, that come from God, and are the guarantees of a splendid sunset on earth, and beyond, a brighter dawn in heaven. Would to God that all of us, when we are old men and women, may be able to think without shame and remorse about the dreams of our youth; that the woman has been true to her dreams, and has fulfilled the sweet, unselfish ideals of her girlhood, and been a noble, loving wife and mother; that the lad has come through this world, at least comparatively unspotted, with a heart fresh and tender, not eaten up by selfishness and greed, with a clean conscience, with the benediction in his old age of having made other men happy and good. Oh, the worst enemies of your dying bed, that will come to mock you, will be the dreams of your youth, of your boyhood and girlhood, should they be unfulfilled! But if you can only in part realise them in your life they will be angels that will come to comfort you.

There is a great deal more dreaming done in this world than we dull, prosaic, old people will allow. It is not merely the lads and girls that dream, for the fact is that we do not know how much we ourselves dream; both young and old do it, but with a difference: the young folks mostly dream about themselves, and the old folks are tired of dreaming about themselves; but there are the wonderful dreams in the hearts of fathers and mothers, to keep their children pure and good, and to make them happy. What would the world be without those sweet, loving dreams? Thank God for them! How much it means for the boy and the girl that their mother dreamt noble things for them when they were young! There never was a man yet that came to be a very great or good man in God's world but his mother dreamt how he was to be brave, true, generous, loving, helpful to others; and because her dreams came from God, she prayed for that son that he might be good, and brave, and noble, and the lad grew great because his mother dreamt great things for him.

There is a sad experience that almost all young folks must come to: the day which breaks so shiningly, with such sweet promise of goodness, nearly always clouds over and grows dark and stormy; the dreams get broken, the dreams that hover over you and seem so easy to reach, recede farther and farther, like one of those Alpine peaks when you are trying to climb it. From the village you start from, you see a peak which you think must be the summit, but when you reach it, it is only to find yourself separated from a far higher ridge by a valley, which you have to descend in order to reach it, and you have no sooner climbed up again than you realise that this, again, is but an intermediate peak. How toilsome, how weary it is! but in the same way dreams would be worth nothing if you had not to win them by struggle and battle. It is the tedium of the contest, I suppose, that disheartens most. It is not easy for young hearts to wait for the fulfilment of life's promise till it can be achieved honestly. Joseph is trapped in a pit, betrayed by his brethren, sold to slave-merchants, settled in an Egyptian house, becomes the bond-slave of Potiphar, torn from father, from his own country, from his God, Who had not interfered to protect him, a bond-slave, his dignity gone, all the pride of life gone! Would it have been wonderful if all the heart had gone out of him too—if he had said that God had forgotten him—"My dreams were a delusion; there is nothing worth living for"? Are there young men and women here whose hearts are aching very bitterly, and who are tempted to think that there is no outlet to this slavery of life? How did Joseph look at it? He might have broken down, and got wild with despair, and said to himself, "I will become demoralised;" but though he lay down at night tired, yet he was cheerful, and still dreamt his old dreams, and God was over him. If a man is true to himself and to his God he will come through anything; if he will be man enough, if he will not be beaten, if he will make the best of things, he *must* conquer. So presently Joseph reached a better position, things began to look up a little, his master marked his spirit, and made him his chief slave.

A lad who had dreamt of being a ruler and king of men, so that his father would bow before him for what he could do for him, how terrible it must have been for the boy to be sold as a slave! How terribly he must have been tempted to say, "God has deceived me; He made me to dream dreams, and here I am left in a dungeon, a slave: I cannot get what I want honourably; I will get it dishonourably; I will snatch the fruit of life, even if it be in defiance of what God and good men call right"! That is the temptation that drives many a lad to dishonesty and treachery, and many a girl to bitterness and sin. It came to Joseph in the deadliest form. The mistress of the household made overtures to him which, had he accepted them, would have meant immediate promotion, perhaps to the court; for her husband was the chief of Pharaoh's body-guard. Could there have been devised a deadlier temptation for that poor, homeless boy, so treacherously treated by those who should have loved him—who had dreamt such dreams, and had such proud ambitions, and withal no danger of discovery if he would but take the path that opened up the way of promotion? I think that was the crisis in Joseph's life; that was the supreme deed which determined his destiny. Then it was that he had to stand, and stand for ever, for God and good, or to fall and sink for ever into ruin. And what saved him? I will tell you what saved him. When Fortune tells a clerk that he has but to take a little of his master's money, which he can repay very soon, and she will smile on him, what he will do all depends upon his past. Those dreams of Joseph's meant everything to him at that great moment. If his dreams had been of the flesh, if his dreams had been base, and selfish, and sordid, and of grasping the world's gains, honourably if possible, but anyway grasping them, he could not have stood. But that boy had dreamt of being a prince, a king among men; he had dreamt of a noble, stainless manhood, of self-respect, and honour, and truth; and he had dreamt of God caring about him, of God choosing him to be His instrument in this world; he was a lad in whose soul the whispers of childhood's prayers and of morning devotions murmured, with sweet echoes of heaven. A lad on whose head still rests the soft pressure of the blessing of his Father in heaven is no game for the devil. Joseph turned from that temptation without a moment's faltering; he said to himself, "Be a traitor and a knave! stain my soul and my manhood with this foul lust!"—and in the presence and the sight of God he conquered; he was loyal to the dreams of his youth, and the result was that he went to prison.

Young men and women, do you sigh? You would fight the battles of life bravely enough, and resist its temptations, if there were a fair field and no favour; but treachery and dishonesty are saturating everything. It is not the best men who get the best wages. The whole city is full of cheating. I am afraid it is so, for many good men have told me they could hardly keep their hands clean. When you hear of a lad going to the bad, for God's sake be just; be not hard on him; it is but the common immorality tolerated everywhere. But what of that? Are you going to lose your life, and stain your conscience, because another has injured you? So long as you do not injure yourself, never mind; be a man in the image of God.

If you come nearer and nearer to that standard it will be a grander work to do in your lifetime, if you live in a poor lodging-room till your death, than to become a millionaire by injustice or cruelty. In prison Joseph played the man; he was not broken nor dispirited. And remember what I said about dreams. Those dreams of his did not allow him to lie down idly in the prison; he wanted to do everybody's work. Joseph was industrious, and kept working on because of his dreams. The keeper of the prison was evidently a man who was glad to have things managed for him; and Joseph got promoted in a wonderful way till he reached the royal court, and aided by perseverance and intelligence and an untarnished character, he became the premier, the first prince in the land. And now followed—what, do you think? Prosperity, peace, ease? No; immense responsibility, discharged nobly by Joseph, and perilous temptations. When a man has overcome the temptations of adversity I can tell him that he has fought a splendid battle, but the deadliest are those that come in the days of prosperity. The generous deeds that you thought you would do, when you were a poor clerk, if you were only wealthy—the help to churches, to missions, to the poor, where are they? You know the story told in all the collection sermons about a man who gave liberally when he was poor, but did not give in the same proportion when he grew rich, and explained it by saying that when he was poor he had a guinea heart, but now it was a penny heart! But Joseph conquers once more. He loves his cruel brothers tenderly, and he brings them, with the old father, to the land of plenty, and tends them. What was his temptation? It comes out later on, and with it the reason why he triumphed over it. While the old man lived the brothers that had betrayed Joseph were safe, because of his love to his father; but when he dies the brothers are fearful lest Joseph should wreak his vengeance on them, and so they come with their whining lie to him; the old father had told them, they say, to implore Joseph to be still generous to them. Joseph burst into tears to think that his brethren had judged so meanly of him. But to do these men justice, we must confess that the average man would act as they did. How came it that Joseph had preserved the heart of his boyhood amid his Egyptian prosperity? Men and women, do you want to know the secret of a pure and loving life? Do you want to know the magic formula that will lift you up and ennoble your character, so that it will not occur to you to pay off old wrongs when you get the chance, the formula that will make you a blessing to others? It is to open your heart wide to the sight, and the touch, and the presence of God in your life and in your world. When I hear wise men, and men that mean the world good, telling us that we shall be able to preserve morality when we have ceased to believe that Jesus had a Father in heaven, when we believe that we live our little day, and then die and vanish, and the world goes on as well without us, my heart sickens within me. Tell men and women that they are the highest race of beasts, and what motives have they for being generous and doing noble deeds? Take away the good Jesus, take away the great high heaven with its sunshine, crush down a low roof over our earth, and you crush out life's grandeur. Tell men that every human spirit has in it something mysterious, that death means something awful, that their souls are born for eternity; then life becomes great and solemn, and the great thought arises that we are born to be the sons of God.

And now the last thing in Joseph's life. I think that when he died all men and women in Egypt were talking about him, and I am pretty sure they talked about him as much in a mistaken fashion and with as many blunders as people will talk about you and me when we die. There is no man that ever lived yet that was known to the world; God only knows what we are; so when we die they are bound to speak of us better or worse than we deserve, for they will not know you nor me as we are known to God, as we have lived, and what has been our purpose in life, how earnestly we have striven for it; these are known to God, and to Him only. Thank God, there are more merciful judgments up there in heaven about us than the kindest on earth will deliver. I am pretty sure that the Egyptians all said that Joseph would be proud to be buried in Egypt. He had lived very nearly all his life there. Had he not brought his relatives there? Was he not engrossed, heart and soul, in Egypt, with not a particle of interest left for the old land, the old home, and the old life? We may imagine what would have been the exclamations of astonishment if the Egyptians could have listened at the dying bed of the prince and statesman, and have heard that while all the time he had been a loyal servant to his royal master, his heart was nevertheless away in the land of his boyhood, and that the future he was looking for was not a future of immortality among the Egyptian dead. "Promise me this one thing," he says, "that when God takes you back to the sweet dear land, back to make God's kingdom there, you will take all that is left of me, that you will take my bones out of this Egypt, where I have been in body, but never in spirit." Oh, the grandeur of such an utterance! All the Egyptian greatness, power in one of the mightiest empires the world has ever seen, is as nothing to him compared with the power that his dreams of sweetness, and goodness, and the service of God had over him. That is a life that is not broken in two when death comes.

Men and women here, who have said your prayers when you were young, and have stopped praying now; who have gone into society and given yourselves up to the world, stop and look at your poor broken life, and before it is too late come back to where in your childhood you knelt at God's throne.

Oh, young men and women that have dreamed Joseph's dreams, pray to God that you may dream the dreams of your childhood once more, if you have let the lust and greed of the world into your heart! Old men and women, for whom this world is not long, go back to your childhood, and end your life as you began it.

This is the supreme thought (and I like to end with it, for it is a comforting thought too) in the story of Joseph's life; because I know that there are so many lives crippled and broken through their own fault, as well as through the wrongs and injuries of others; lives dark, and poor, and disappointing; lives that have no triumph in this world, and find it very hard to keep up heart, to keep true to hope, and faith, and God. Listen to the lesson of Joseph's life. No true life of goodness to man and God can ever be a failure. In a pit, in a dungeon in far-off Egypt, you may seem to be shut out of all splendid achievements; wronged and smitten by the storms of life, it may seem as if God had left you; but if you can only keep your heart sweet, and good, and pure; if you can but keep yourself honourable, and generous, and loving, then, though God may give you no ties of home-life, and all may appear dark and cheerless; if you can only keep yourself a good, sweet, loving woman, a brave, true, honourable man, if you can but hold fast to your faith, there is a great God over you, there is a Christ who came to die to save you, there is a holiness which God will give you. If you will but hold fast to the end—to *His* end,—then your life cannot be a failure; its roots are in God, and its end shall be with God; from heaven you came, and to God you shall return.

VII.
THE BRAZEN SERPENT.

"He [Hezekiah] removed the high places, and brake the images, and cut down the groves, and brake in pieces the brasen serpent that Moses had made: for unto those days the children of Israel did burn incense to it: and he called it Nehushtan."—2 KINGS xviii. 4.

IN that verse we hear the last of the brazen serpent; this morning I am going to put before you some practical thoughts that spring from the whole story. What has the brazen serpent got to do with our modern life? The children of Israel, with their cattle and sheep, wandering about the wilderness, get sick of it, complain against God and against Moses, and are ready to break into active rebellion. They are punished by a sudden attack of venomous serpents that sting them, and they, in dread of death, lose that sham courage of theirs and independence, and they appeal to God to save them. He bids Moses manufacture a mysterious brazen serpent, put it upon a pole, and then, if any dying Israelite looks at that serpent it heals him. The brazen image is regarded ever after as clothed with great sanctity. It was once the supernatural channel of life direct from God to dying men, and so, in course of time, men came to it, and in its vicinity offered up their prayers, and finally burned incense to it, and surrounded it with a false worship. Then comes a reforming king, who regards that symbol of wonderful old power Divine and goodness, that has been turned into an idolatrous and superstitious instrument of human degradation; and, divided between his respect for it and his consciousness of the mischief it is doing, he finally decides to break it into pieces, scatters it into the dust, and there is an end of it. Now, what has all that got to do with your life and mine? The Hebrew history does not have its meaning lying just on the face of it. If you take the bare letter you will not get much out of it; if you stick to the bare letter you will find yourself landed in a great many difficulties that are puzzling good people and bad people at the present day, and all the time, whether you attack those difficulties with a profound faith or with a doubting, critical, sceptical spirit, you may be missing the very heart of the story. Because Hebrew history is manifestly history written with a purpose. It was never intended that it should be taken as an exact reporter's chronicle of external things that happen. The real interest of the writers is something different; it is to get down below the surface, in behind the scenes, to come upon the great hands of God fashioning this world's story. They felt that beneath all the events, common and secular, that befell them, the battles they had to fight, the journeys they had to make, the famines that destroyed their crops, the outbursts of prosperity, the victories that were won by them, the lives they lived in homes like ours—behind and beneath all that they felt that God held the reins in His hand, that He Himself was thinking of them, had designs in them, was shaping and fashioning their fortunes, controlling all that befell them, and they comprehended that the greatest thing in this world is to get to know God.

The people at this point in their story had been wandering about in the wilderness for nearly forty years; at last they had been led by Moses to the very edge of the territory of Edom. Nothing lay between them and the land God had promised them except the country belonging to their kinsmen, the Edomites. You can understand how the hearts and faces of the people were flushed with eager expectation. Oh! they were so sick of that restless, weary life in the barren desert, and the pictures were called up before their eyes in their dreams at night, and in their day visions through the bright sunny hours, of those smiling vineyards, those oliveyards, and those waving cornfields in that land flowing with milk and honey, existing somewhat in fact, but very much in the imagination of those who were to be its possessors. Nothing lay between them and the actual possession and enjoyment but the country of Edom, so they sent an eager message to the king, their kinsman, asking leave to pass through the territory so that they might get at their enemies and his. The king of Edom doubted them, or he was churlish, and refused to give them passage. No doubt every brave young Hebrew warrior went to Moses at once and said, "Let us force our way through; if they will not yield us passage we shall make it for ourselves—we are able, we have the weapons, we have the spirit; let us get at the homes that are waiting for us." But then that would have been to enter into the land of promise with a bloodstain on their conscience, with a bitter, bad memory, spoiling all the joy of it; for those Edomites were their blood relations, and blood meant a vast deal in those old days—even if your brother treated you ill you must not stain your hands with his blood. To have your very living and money-making all corroded with that colour of blood of a near kinsman shed, was to get what your heart longed for, but to get it spoiled. So Moses, under Divine guidance, told them, "We must go back into the wilderness, we must make a big, roundabout march, and reach the land at some other point." Unwillingly the people agreed; they packed up all their baggage once again, put their weapons into their sheaths, turned their backs on the smiling land of Canaan, and their faces to the arid stretch of the sandy, scorched wilderness, and set out. But before they had gone very far their spirit ran short—that is what the old Hebraist says literally—their spirit ran down, they could not stand it. Man turned to man, and said, "This is too hard; more than man can endure; the thing is intolerable; Moses is blundering; let us depose our leader and choose generals of our own, and force our way across Edom into the Promised Land. What is the use of this God—this Moses who brought us out of Egypt and kept us in the wilderness all these weary years—at every new camp leaving a graveyard behind us, dying man after man, with no prospect before, no progress made, no goal reached, no land of rest attained?"

Now I wonder how many of my hearers to-day are wandering in the desert just like these Hebrews, and have been wandering in a wilderness for years and years. I am pretty sure that that is so with some of you old folks with white hair on your heads. Ah! it is so very far away in the Eastern world and in Old Testament times, this story of these wanderers, never living in a comfortable house, never owning any land, packing up, and on again, wondering where they are going to die, with nothing much to look forward to. Yes, but here in London, living in your own house, in your own workshop, there are men and women wandering in the wilderness. Ah! what a deal of weary waiting there is for young men and maidens, in this artificially bad society of ours at the present day—which has been made by selfishness much more than by the love of God and the love of man—waiting with divine instincts that God has put into their hearts; dreaming of a land of promise, a land of rest, a land flowing with milk and honey.

Ay, it is wandering in a wilderness. Our hearts were not made to live in a wilderness; our hearts were made to live in homes; we were all meant to be in a promised land. There is no need to ask who is to blame. There the wildernesses are, and they have to be got through. It is not easy. Many a time the bravest heart breaks down. The last straw breaks the camel's back. Some little extra worry or care adds itself on, and then the gentle woman or the courageous, uncomplaining man is broken in heart and spirit—oh! so weary—ay, and if they have a tender conscience, upbraiding themselves, counting it sin to feel so tired. Why have they not been doing good? Have they not been following the steps of Jesus? And there they are worn out in being good as He was. Do you remember how sometimes He sighed a great sigh? how sometimes He was so sick of men and their waywardness and selfishness and wilfulness, that for His soul's sake He fled from them and hurried off to the mountain-top to get away above the world, up beneath the blue sky into the purer air, up where God was direct above Him, and He all alone; then came back next morning all the braver and able to bear the battle once again? No, do not blame yourself if you are often very weary. Do not try to pretend that you like your wilderness, that you do not wish anything different. You may have got so used to your wilderness as to be like those people in the old Bastille. Some of the prisoners, we are told, were not willing to go into the world again; they did not know it. So there are hearts that get so wedded to sorrow that they are almost afraid to have done with it. Still, as a general rule, hearts do long for joy, for sunlight, for success. It is human nature, and there is no harm in being weary when the clouds are always over the heavens. Christ was weary, and He understands you and your heart.

Now, I have willingly allowed myself to run the risk even of exaggeration in sympathising with the men and women whose lives are a wilderness, and who are exposed to these dangers in their weariness, in the hardness of their battle. But now, precisely because of that danger, to steel your heart against its temptations, I am bound to speak about the other side; I am bound to ask you men and women, whose lives are not so good and rich as they ought to be, "Is not the blame, at least somewhat, your own?"

Why had these Israelites been wandering forty years in the wilderness? God had led them to the edge of the Promised Land, and bidden them go in and take it, and they had not the manhood to do it, they were such cowards that they trembled, they were craven-hearted; and so they could not enter because of their unbelief. Ah! it was no good to turn round on God and blame Him; it was no good to attack the brave-hearted Moses; it was their own fault that their life was spent in the wilderness. But, more than that, we must not make too much of the hardship, and the pain, and the weariness of wilderness wandering. It is human nature to want always sunshine and to hate storms; to love hours of play and shirk hours of toil; but, after all, does not the rain do as much for the corn as the sunshine? Does not darkness do as much on earth as light? Do we not need hardness as well as lightness in our inner lives if we are to make ourselves men and women? It was years of wandering in the wilderness that turned those Egyptian slaves into the dauntless warriors that carried Canaan by storm. Ah! men and women sitting in the church to-day with your children round you, do not spoil their lives, but lead them to live nobly. Was it not when you were kept to your tasks and toil, when you got your share of the world's burdens and the world's pain—was it not in the things least agreeable to you that there were formed within you elements of character that are doing most to make your joy to-day? Oh, do not grudge them to your children, do not grudge them to yourself! God gives them. Surely it is supreme wisdom to take our life in its entirety from God, to sing through the whole gamut of life, the low wailing note of sorrow as well as the bright, dancing, radiant notes of joy, rejoicing in God so that the music of our life when it is done shall be filled with the fulness of that great Heart Divine that planned and fashioned it.

There was deadly danger in that murmuring of the children of Israel. You must not imagine that God resented it because of the insult to His dignity. God is above such a feeling as that, He does not resent the ignorance, with the mixture of superstition, that goes into the lives, ay, of good men and women, Protestant or Roman Catholic. He takes men's hearts and their real life. It was not the insult to Him in their murmurs that made Him deal with them so strongly. Oh, it was not sternness at all that dealt with them, it was love unutterable! They were ready to spoil their lives, to rush away on their own plans to make their fortunes, and so to bring themselves to ruin. Do you know how God checked them? They were complaining of the food that they had, and of their long weary marches, and the heartlessness of their toil in the wilderness, instead of having comfortable homes and rich farms, and God cured them by sending among them fiery serpents that bit them, filled their veins with venom, agony, and death, and as they lay there writhing in pain with death looking into their eyes they said, "What fools we were to repine and complain because of the bread that was tasteless and the life that was void of interest." That was God's way of curing men who were about to spoil their lives by discontent. Is it not God's way still? You men sitting there, do you remember that for years you had been bad-hearted, bitter, discontented, because your life was not great or famous, till God sent that deadly illness and you lay in bed like to die, and then you would have given all you had to get back to that life that you thought so little of? I have seen the father who made the foolish mistake of harping too much on the faults and failings of those who dwelt in his home, not acknowledging the large amount of good and obedience, but ever making misery and bitterness there, and thinking himself justified in doing it, accounting himself an unappreciated, unrewarded man, till a day came when God sent a fiery serpent into his heart, when the blinds were drawn down in that house, and a life lay still and silent that had had faults, but had been sweet, and loving, and lovable. Or, a real disgrace has come to a home, and a child has done a deed that might break a father's heart. Oh, the misery and the pity of it, to see that man sitting there all alone with his head bent and his face buried in his hands, thinking of the years that might have been bright with joy, and love, and cheer, and that he in his madness had made bad and bitter! Ay, it was a fiery serpent, but it was effective.

Yet God's heart shrinks from those sharp penalties that come to cure us of our sins. See, what happened the instant those Israelites returned to Him, ignominiously crying to the very Moses, and the very God, they had cast off and grumbled at, to come and save them.

Ay, but God is more eager than they. Make the brazen serpent, lose not a moment. Set it up on high, and tell them that one look is enough, and they shall live. That is Godlike; that is how God forgives. Why did God bid Moses make the brazen serpent and set it up on that pole? God could have healed these men by telling them to look up even in any way. Why precisely the brazen serpent should be the instrument of their cure I do not know; the Bible does not tell me. I can only tell you a thought that has come to me about it. Perhaps it was for this reason: It would be surely the thought of every dying Hebrew who looked at that serpent and felt a new life pulsing through all his veins, and the pain of death vanishing away, that that serpent came from God, and was a very token and proof of the warm heart-love of God to him. But it would not be so easy for the man that had been bitten and lay there dying to think of that fiery serpent that bit him as a messenger of God's love. He would be more likely to think that the fiery serpent, that came with death in his bite, was from the devil. And yet the serpent that bit him to death came from God, and came from God's love as absolutely as the serpent that healed. Is not that it? Could they but put two and two together, would not the thought flash into their heart, "A serpent God gave to heal; a serpent it was that hurt"? Is it then so, that the serpent that harmed came from God's love, as much as the serpent that healed? Is not that just God's way with you? Do not many of you sitting in the church to-day remember great sorrows or sharp blows of disaster that came into your life, and at first you writhed against them and were in great pain? You could not think there was any love of God in them; but they have lain there and they have made your heart more gentle, they have made your faith more strong, they have brought God nearer to you, they have made you kinder in your own home, and you look at them now with the glow of a goodness that has grown from them, and you say to yourself that not merely the goodness that has followed since, but the pain that came and hurt was from God—from God who is love.

How did the healing come to the dying Hebrew who looked at the brazen serpent? Not from any efficacy in the serpent, not from any magical virtue in the look; the new life that came to him came direct from God. Why, then, did God interpose the looking at the serpent? Why did God make the cure dependent on a gaze at a serpent erected there by Moses? I will tell you why. It was not the look; it was the change of heart that was in the look that God wanted. The real mischief that had to be undone was not the bodily death of those men; there was a worse evil than that, there was the loss of faith in God, the fracture of a loving dependence on God. That is the essence of all sin. Sin is disobedience to God. It means that you snatch your life out of God's hand, that you will not live according to God's will, that you make yourself your God; you will be your own master, you will take your own way—you can do better for yourself than God. Now, mark, you never would choose that sinful course as long as you trusted God. Loss of faith, that is sin. It is no good talking of cures, no good talking of salvation, unless you undo the mischief done by sin. Loss of faith: that is the beginning, the essence, the end of sin. Ah! that doctrine of salvation through faith that men mock at and call a legal sophism, it has got the heart of all truth in it, only I think we are to blame that we have so much talked of faith as the means of salvation as if it were some external condition attached by God to salvation. Faith *is* salvation; Jesus Christ hangs there on the cross as Moses lifted up the brazen serpent. The moment a man believes on Him he is saved from sin. How? Through some magical virtue in the cross, in the Body hanging there, in the blood poured out, or in the man's mental act of faith? Never, never. That Christ hanging there is the living embodiment of faith in God: His life, His death, are the incarnate declaration that all sin is error, that all sin is an outrage, that men erred and went wrong when they disobeyed God. He condemns all sin by His life of holiness, by His death of antagonism against sin, hanging there on the cross, wrestling with sin, seeking to undo it, offering to God the world's love and obedience that sinful men have failed to give to God, dying in their stead, obeying in their stead, making Himself a perfect sacrifice and substitute for this world of ours. All that still would not be salvation, is not salvation, to you until the sight of it turns you, regenerates you, makes you see that all your sin was madness, folly; fills you with hatred of it. When once the love of God binds you over to follow that Christ in obedience to God, in trust to God, in love of God, that is faith in Christ, that is salvation.

That serpent became an object of idolatrous and superstitious worship. It was very natural, and it is very evil. Hezekiah with his reforming zeal took it, and with real reverence, though with seeming external irreverence, dashed it in pieces. Has not that also a parallel, hundreds of parallels in Church history? Hezekiah rightly interpreted the heart of God; he believed that the great heart of God up there in heaven was pained every time that a poor ignorant Israelite, man or woman, poured out on that brazen image the gratitude that should have gone direct to Him. And so it is that in the Church's story you find that whenever priests have set up any channel or means of actual grace divine, grace supernatural, and have attached to it undue reverence, and made it bulk too largely in the eyes and worship of common men and women, so as to come between them and God, then God has raised up infidels and unbelievers to break it and dash it to pieces. Was not that what was done by the Reformers? At the Reformation, when the Mass had been set between eager longing hearts of men and women seeking forgiveness and the great loving heart of God that gives it, it was taken and shattered. Ay, and when this Bible of ours—this Protestant Bible of ours, or our great evangelical doctrines, are taken and have given to them a place of importance in our salvation and in our belief that they ought not to have, once again be sure of it God will create a true, lawful, and blessed recoil, and you will have these sacred things even dashed down to a position of undue depreciation. It is God's ways of leading us to Himself. Ah! there is a grand thought in that—the unutterable glory about our God that shines for me through all the tale of that great battle about belief, and doctrines, and Church institutions that makes up the Church's story—through it all what I see is the heart of God our Father longing for the touch of our hands in His hands, the gaze of our eyes into His, giving us things that shall help us to Him, lesson books to teach us about Him, steps that shall lead us to His feet. But the moment we make these a barrier that keeps us far from Him, things sacred and good are dashed away. What does that mean? It means to you and me the revelation in all wonder, awe, and comfort of how tender, near, and true and clinging is the love of God's heart to you and me—of that God whom we sometimes think so awful and so terrible, but who in His inmost being through and through is love, wholly, absolutely love.

VIII.
THE GRADATIONS OF DOUBT.

Psalm lxxiii.

I AM going to ask you to study with me this morning the 73rd Psalm. Before I read the Psalm I had better tell you what it is about; then you will follow the line of thought in it with greater ease. The central faith of the Hebrew religion was that God governs this world according to the principles of morality, that He is on the side of goodness, and against wickedness. The facts of life clashed with that dogma of Hebrew faith. Good men in those old times found it as hard to believe in God and goodness as we do, and they got just as little, or just as much, supernatural help as we do. Therefore they could nowhere find an absolute certainty; they nowhere received from heaven a supernatural and complete explanation of the enigmas of life. God, because He loved them, deliberately left them to fight their battle for faith with the actual facts and the actual difficulties. He left them constantly trying to find a complete intellectual solution of the problem, and failing to do that, just as we fail; and so He shut them up to discovering a resting-place for faith in the heart when they could not get it in the head. A great many psalms have welled out of men's hearts, just like fountains away among the hills, and valleys, and slopes. This 73rd Psalm is brimful of human thoughts, and duties, and longings, pains, and battles, and victories, just like bits of your life when you were all alive to the real grandeur of your human existence, when your heart longed to think loftily of life, and to hold fast to God, and precisely because your heart was all alive you found it was not easy. I am going to ask you to follow this man's struggle against doubt, to watch the steps by which he descended into the valley of real questioning of God's goodness and of God's government of the world, and then to trace the steps by which he climbed back again to a hill-top of serene and tranquil certainty.

I have already indicated to you that I do not think that anywhere in the Old Testament, or in the New Testament, or in all Christian theology or philosophy, does there exist a complete demonstration of the fact that God is good, and that He is on the side of goodness. Whether that is true or not every intelligent believer will admit that this 73rd Psalm is no complete theodicy. It will not hold its own as a logical demonstration that the government of this world is moral or just. The man's certainty that there is a good God, and that God takes sides with good men, rests not upon sight, but upon faith; it is a solution of the heart, not of the head. Thank God! that is the universal law of religious experience. One thing I want to point out to you at the beginning, especially to those of you who are thinkers, and who study the various religions of the world. There is a very simple characteristic about the fashion in which the problem of life is dealt with in those Psalms, when we compare them, say, with the very finest of Greek devotion and Greek religion. In all Greek philosophy there is only one fixed quantity—that is, the world. The problem of Greek thought is this: Given the world, the clear, solid, certain fact, to find the God that made it. They took life as it stood, and from its elements and components they tried to determine what kind of a Maker this world has had. Now, at the very outset, all through Hebrew religious thought and philosophy, you find two fixed quantities. There is the world, but over against it there is God—God, holy, just, righteous; and therefore, while the Greek problem was always, Given the world, to construct God, the Hebrew problem is, Given the world as it exists, and given God as He exists, can those be reconciled? It is a very simple and striking contrast. I will tell you the picturesque aspect that it gives to the two literatures. Greek thought is all philosophical, speculative—great minds rising back to the First Cause, from this actual world; and this world being what it is, no wonder that at one time they reached iron Fate, at another time Materialism, at another time Pantheism, at another time Manichæism. Hebrew thought does not sway about in that fashion; it is simply concerned with this—the vindication of God's character; and there is the striking contrast. In Greek poetry, in all Pagan poetry, you will find warm-hearted, large-minded men contemplating life, with all its great wrongs, injustices, pains, sorrows, disappointments, and then breaking into pity and compassion for men. In Hebrew poetry, in Hebrew religion, you will everywhere find the same dark aspects of life fearlessly held up, acknowledged, and confronted; but what do you think is the supreme pain that breaks in upon the hearts of the Hebrew sages and seers as they contemplate the world's enigmas? It is anxiety for the character of God. It is not pity for poor men and women, ground under the wheels of this earth, but a terribly agonising question, "How can we defend God and God's goodness when the world is so evil and so dark?" Ah, you want to prove what the Bible is by its own light, to show that it has a right to be spoken of as a revelation and as inspired! Do not go to all the trivial Mediæval theories and doctrines about it; go to the book itself, and go to the world. It can hold its own, without claiming anything outside to buttress it up. Set the heart-life in it against the heart-life of any other religion, and you will see that it has the blue of God's heaven in it—unsullied, splendid, perfect. Now, I am going to take this one Psalm—to take one glimpse into that long, painful chemistry of revelation, as God came into human hearts with pain and perplexity, with struggle, with triumph, with glory, and made those hearts know Him, not through explanations, but by His indwelling in them, His life, His love, His holiness, echoing and throbbing into their heart life.

I am now tempted to break off here for a moment, and say to you what always strikes me when I look at that aspect of this revealed, inspired Bible—that it does seem just possible that the good Christian Church we belong to in our time is not in quite the right way of thinking about religious doubt. I am not talking about doubt of the head, the intellect, and the schools—intellectual fence, that sort of triviality; let it alone, it is not worth taking notice of. But the real doubt of any age, the doubt of any man's heart and head—what are we to think of that? Are we to stamp it as devilish? Are we to denounce it, and excommunicate it? Why, we might be fighting against God. If I read my Bible aright, real, genuine, patient struggle for faith means just the birth-throes of God's revelation of Himself in men's hearts. Now come to this point, and see what it reveals to you that is sacred, pathetic, instructive in the heart of a man dead hundreds of years ago. Look into his heart, and you may learn a great deal about your own heart. The problem that confronts him is the fact that has always been very evident in every age, that honesty is not by any means always the best policy, if by that you mean that it pays you best. I am putting it in homely language. It is a big question. Do the world's good things go predominantly to the good men? or do they go to the clever and unscrupulous men? In the professions is it your honest, truthful man, of modest merit, that succeeds best, or your humbug, impostor, flatterer, self-advertiser? In the State, in politics, is it your honest man, that speaks truths to the people, that is lauded and flattered? or is it your skilful adventurer? In the

City does strict honour make a man's fortune? or are profits bigger in proportion as a man can wink at things? Anywhere on the large scale are the virtuous classes the most prosperous? Are the powers of this world raised up to their lofty elevation by goodness, or rather in spite of badness? Is God on the side of goodness? or does He not care? or is He rather on the side of violence, and wrong, and wickedness? Now, this point is the real struggle in the poet's heart, to solve that difficulty of life. I am going to read it to you, giving you the headings of the various parts of it, the steps of emotion and of thought through which his heart has passed.

He begins, first of all, with the point at which he ends. This is the right result of that struggle of doubt and faith within him; he believes that God is on the side of goodness. But there is a curious little word, very difficult to reproduce in English, that expresses how the firm conviction that he has of goodness having God backing it was reached through painful conflict. "Surely"—yes, after all—"God is good to His people, good to such as are pure in heart." Then we come to the history of doubt, the progress of doubt, in the man's soul. That you have in the first fourteen verses. The first step of it was his recognition of the fact of prosperous wickedness. It is a little difficult to divide the Psalm exactly, and I do not give you the divisions that I am choosing as certainly the precise, original structure of the poem, but roughly they bring out the outstanding thoughts. The first division would be verses 2 to 5—the fact of prosperous wickedness: "But as for me, my feet were almost gone; my steps had well-nigh slipped. For I was envious at bad men—at successful bad men—when I saw the prosperity of the wicked. For they have no barriers, no entanglements; they are never tripped up on to the time of their death"—that, I think, is the real translation—"but their success remains firm. They are not in trouble like other men; neither are they plagued like other men."

That is the first step of doubt. Then comes the second, the effect upon themselves: "Therefore pride is like a golden chain round their neck; violence covers them as a garment. Their eyes stand out with fatness; they have more than heart could wish. They scoff, and in wickedness utter oppression, pour forth oppressive taunt; they speak loftily. They have set their mouth in the heaven, and their tongue stalketh through the earth."

Then there is a third step of doubt, the effect upon good men: "Therefore God's people are prevented that way, and the waters of a full cup are drained by them. They say, How can God know? and is there knowledge in the Most High? Behold, these are the wicked; and being always secure, they heap up wealth."

Then there is the effect on the poet himself: "Surely in vain have I cleansed my heart, and washed my hands in innocency. For all the day long have I been plagued, and chastened every morning." You see here the doubt reaching its last full result.

Then we come to the recoil, the restoration of faith. That also is set in three steps. The first is the perception of the fact of retribution. Verse 15: "Had I made up my mind, I will speak thus; behold, I should have dealt treacherously with the generation of Thy children. When I thought how I might know this—how to read this riddle—it was too hard for me, until I went into the sanctuary of God, and considered the last end of them. Surely Thou didst set them in slippery places; Thou hast hurled them down to destruction. How are they become a desolation in a moment! They are utterly consumed with terrors. As a nightmare when one awaketh, so, O Lord, when Thou awakest Thou dost despise [flout] the presentment of them."

Then there is the next step, the perception of his own stupidity: "My mind was in a ferment, and I was pricked in my heart. How brutish I was, and how ignorant! I was no better than a proud beast before Thee; and I am continually with Thee, held by Thy right hand."

Then there is the last step, the perception of the immeasurable joy, the intrinsic superiority, of goodness. "Whom have I in heaven but Thee? and there is none upon earth that I desire beside Thee. My flesh and my heart faileth; but God is the strength of my heart, and my portion for ever. For, lo, they that are far from Thee shall perish; thou hast destroyed all them that go straying away from Thee. But it is good for me to draw near to God: I have made the Lord my refuge, that I may tell all Thy works."

Now, for our own help and instruction, let us follow, step by step, the struggle of that good man's heart. Is it evident on the face of things that goodness has the best of it in this world? Now, I am going to say to you a thing that perhaps many of you will think little of me for saying, but I cannot help thinking that the poet exaggerated the actual facts; and I am quite persuaded that a great many people who think themselves very wise, and are very wise, at the present day, make far too much of the external material advantage gained by dishonesty. I am quite prepared to admit that goodness often keeps a man back from earthly joy. I am quite prepared to admit that the prizes of this world go far too much to men that possess no real right to them. There are endless social wrongs and individual wrongs. Things are not rightly adjusted, either in the Church or in the world, in professions or in business. All that is true. Nevertheless, I rather think that the amount of it is exaggerated. I do not think that is the predominant aspect of life. It is only when a man is morbid, when existence is pressing too hard on himself, when he is sharply injured and wronged, that he would take upon him to say that evil out and out, clearly and without question, has the best of it. I am talking, of course, of our society nowadays; but I rather think that in all states of society it could never have been the case that wickedness absolutely had the best of it. I will tell you why: Because this world cannot stand without a good deal of love and a good deal of faith, a good deal of honesty, a good deal of mutual trust. Why, if business were the utter mass of cheating and unscrupulosity that some men would have us believe, you would have an end of all credit, of all business. There must be some brotherliness; there must be a certain trustworthiness; there must be a considerable amount of honesty. It is the very salt of the world; it maintains it; the world would come to an end without it. But all the same, I am willing to admit that that is the superficial aspect of existence, and that it is a very staggering blow to men's faith, especially faith that is inherited from one's father, that is not a man's own; it is a thing to make a young man's heart bitter; it is a thing to make him hesitate and doubt whether he ought to hold to the pathway of honour. It is not, I think, the paramount, the predominant aspect of life, looked at calmly and dispassionately, quite apart from religious faith, but certainly it is a very prominent aspect—prominent because it is superficial. Well, then, that fact of successful wrong-doing is the cause of religious doubt, but not by any means a very dangerous cause.

We come to the second source of doubt and questioning—an infinitely more subtle and hazardous one. It is the perception that successful ill-doers do not seem to be miserable. You know how we are all taught that bad men have such terribly evil consciences, that harpies are always behind them, that their hearts are gnawed with dread and anxiety, that they cannot sleep at night, that remorse haunts them. Not a bit of it. You go into the world and pick out men who have gained their wealth, who have wrung it out of the heart's blood of their fellow-men—got it by downright dishonesty; their eyes stand out with fatness, they roll about in their carriages, they have splendid houses, and everybody bows down to them and makes much of them; their faces are wreathed with smiles of self-satisfaction; you sit at their tables, and they tell you how successful they have been; they expect you to envy them; they are not humble and miserable. Then the deadly question comes to you, Where, then, is God? Ah, one can quite understand God letting the external world run its own course! One might explain in some way that God allows, to try men, the prizes of wealth and the joys of life to go to men that do not deserve them. As a good man once said to me, "It is plain that God does not think much of money—why, look at the kind of people he gives it to!" That is so; but the one thing you would believe is this, that in that strange inner world of the human heart, the mind, the conscience God could not keep still. If He gives them the external gift, if He sends them the desire of their flesh, He will send leanness into their soul. Why do you not see their faces haggard? Why can you not trace the lines of care? Why does not shame and degradation sit upon the wealthy man's face who gained his wealth by cheating and lying, by dishonour and meanness? Oh, they seem so happy, so contented, so pleased, so proud, so arrogant! Why does their tongue reach up to heaven, in its pride, and haughtiness, and complacency? Well, you would think that that is a deadly enough doubt to be gnawing at a good lad's heart; but there is a still deadlier one. Here you have the deadliest cause of doubt, when a man, pressed hard by the great fact of prosperous ill-doing, staggered by that blow, does not see the inner, ethical, moral vengeance of God stamped on it. He looks round for confirmation to the good men in the Church; he looks at religious Christian society, he falls back on it, to let it support him, to let it help him; and what does he discover when his eyes pierce through and penetrate? In the heart within him he begins to recognise the hearts of others. Everywhere the Church is secretly doubting too; good men are longing for a share in the ill-gotten gain—ay, tampering with their consciences, themselves turning into the same direction, drinking of the waters of the same cup, and then some of them, more reckless or more honest, speaking straight out: "Yes, I was brought up, like you, to believe in virtue, in honesty, in God, and in goodness; but I have seen throughout that this world is not governed by a good God. If there is a good God, He does not know or does not care; He does not step in; it is the wicked that have the best of it in this world; I am going to take that course." Ah, the moral perversion, the tainted breath of the base, selfish, greedy, unscrupulous world! that detected in the heart of his own father, the good elder, the church member; that detected in his own mother, not valuing or choosing for the society of her home the honourable, the pure, the good, the true, but the people with money, and tainted reputations, and all the rest of it; that is the deadliest thing; that makes the real doubt, the real unbelief; that carries a lad, not to books of philosophy—he will never take much harm from them, even if he has head enough to understand them—but carries him clean away from religion, into shady company too, and takes the virtue and morality out of him, making him sell himself for money in life's sacredest relationships: it is that—the perversion of good. Oh, how much we Christian men and women have to answer for when we denounce sceptics and worldlings, the ungodly young men who stop going to church, and all that! Ay, poor souls, they will have to answer for it! but how much shall we have to answer for it too? The Church, is it not tainted by worldliness? Do we go and take the bravest, the most patient, the most loyal, the most prayerful, the most devout Sunday-school teacher, a working man, and put him in the chair of our Sunday-school assemblies in Exeter Hall? No, no; it is not pure goodness. I do not know that we can help it, but it would be worth while trying that system, instead of the Church, for want of faith, making so very much of the world, of social position, and of purse power.

But I have rather wandered from my point. Doubt has now run its course, completed its curriculum. The question is often raised, Does it matter what a man believes? No, not what he believes about the abstract theories or explanations either of philosophy or theology—it will not matter much what he thinks about these abstruse questions; but it matters infinitely and eternally what he thinks about God, and goodness, and life. Ah, there a man's heart-faiths make his life-conduct! It was so with the poet here, when those dark, demon doubts had filled his soul, when his mind was in a ferment, when his heart was pricked and bitter within him, when he heard good men—men that were good once—round him saying, "Does God know?" and when he felt himself in a God-forsaken world, where there was nothing but each man snatching the best he could get, where everything was given over to wickedness and evil. Ah, then, such a man does not stop at theoretical atheism and scepticism! he goes farther. "Surely in vain have I kept my hands clean; I have been a fool to deny myself forbidden joys and pleasures; I have been punished, I have been injured; those that were unscrupulous, and impure, and dishonest have had the best of it; I have done with being a fool; I am going to have my share too." Now doubt has reached its most dangerous point; it is going to hurry into forbidden action.

It was at this moment that the recoil came. I will tell you how. If a man has got any heart at all, he can go any length in his own head with his doubts and questions about whether there is a God or a heaven, or whether it is worth while trying to be holy, and pure, and honest; but if he has any heart at all, the moment that he says, "I am going to be pure no longer, but I am going to be foul," then there is something in him that draws him back. He sees himself, or rather he feels, that he is not doing harm to any one with those doubts that are in his own intellect, but the moment he says, "I am going out into the world, in the train, in the town, in the warehouse, and I am going to tell it, right and left, that I count it an old wife's fable that there is a God and heaven, that I count the man an idiot who denies himself any fleshly joy that he can get without coming within the grasp of the law"—I say, if he has any heart at all, he suddenly thinks to himself, "If I say that to my younger brother, if I say that to that innocent maiden, I shall be doing a cruel wrong to the generation of God's people." Oh, there is an eternal, immovable fact! Doubt may have all logic on its side, but doubt and the denial of God and of virtue are the world's damnation. It may be an advantage to a man to cheat and steal, but it cannot be an advantage to his neighbours. Take the worst man in the City, and ask him if he would wish that all goodness, all virtue, all religion should be so crushed out that every man should become a thief, a robber, a burglar. No; he does not want that. Even in the case of an infidel, if he be a man of fine conscience and fine heart—I have known such—not for his life would he tell his doubts to a child, not for his life would he say a word to stop that mother teaching her boy to pray. I have known such men who told me that they were thankful that the mother of their children kept on doing it. Yes, that Psalm is far away from our theoretical theologies or intellectual apologies and the rest of it. See how intensely human it is—that recognition that doubt held within the intellect is not very harmful, but let it go out into the world, and it will do unspeakable mischief; it is that that gives the doubter check. Ay, and there is reason in it, rationality. When a man recognises that fact he has got to go farther. If doubt manifestly would harm the world, if the denial of God, and goodness, and the earth's moral government would damage human society, then there must be something wrong in the reasoning that leads up to that denial. The facts cannot be as I have fancied, or else my inferences are wrong; for never, never can it be evil to know the truth. Therefore that denial of mine that there is a good God, or that if there be a God He governs this world by goodness, must be false. Now all things appear to the man in a new light. Why? Because he has got up to a great elevation. Suddenly it darts upon him, "Before, I was looking at this world out of my little self; I judged everything by its effect upon my own personality, my own life. I was suffering, and therefore all things must be wrong." What a poor little aspect that is! Now he has risen up to a point where he stands as God stands; he looks at the big world out of himself, and he sees that the doubt, the denial, would destroy all that is best in the world. And he looks farther; he has reached to God's sanctuary. Now his eyes travel over wider reaches of human story. Before he was like a man down in a valley where there is a winding river, and just where he stood the river seemed to flow in one direction, and he went away and proclaimed to men that the river ran north. Now he has travelled away up the mountain, and he is able to look over the whole extent, and he sees that there was a winding and twisting in the stream, but observes that its great ultimate course is to the southern seas. The man stands up above this world of ours, he looks over the great spread of its course and history, and what is the absolute conclusion? That everywhere in the end immorality has death in it; that violence, wickedness, selfishness ruin themselves; that oppressive dynasties have fallen, and corrupt peoples have been struck down; that sin everywhere has God's vengeance set in it, and ends in death. Everywhere in the end virtue does triumph and survive, goodness proves superior. That is a fact which the evolutionist tells us. This world seeks and reaches the moral, the good, the true, the noble in intellect, heart, and soul. It was made, the religious man says, by a good God, and it is making for goodness. Yes; but there comes another revelation. For the good man says to himself, "Now, how came it that I could not see that before?" and suddenly an overwhelming shame falls upon him. "How could I not see that before? Oh, because I was such a little soul, because I lived in such a despicable, little world! I failed to see the truth because I was as base as those bad men. What makes them forsake God and goodness? Because they count earthly gain the supreme thing. Why was I so bitter against their getting the earthly gain? Because I counted it the supreme thing. I, a man made in God's image, a man held by God's hand, a man whose will was being overshadowed, and led, and guided by God's Spirit, through all was so ignorant and so brutish that I thought God's best gift that He had to give to His children was money, or fleshly pleasure, or earthly adulation. I was no better than a brute beast. To the brute beast God can give nothing more than meat, and drink, and fleshly sensual delight; but that a man held in God's hand, loved by God, should have great joy about these things! Ah, my doubt grew not out of the world's enigmas alone! it grew out of my own low morals." Now he stands in a new position. He sees as God sees, and he says to himself, "Ah, let this world grow as ill as it may; even if it were the case that money, power, social ambition, earthly rewards did go predominantly to wickedness, what then? Here am I, a man loving honour, truth, justice, mercy, purity, God; shall I hesitate for one moment if I must lose all the world? Can I hesitate for one moment? No; goodness alone, with no earthly reward, is heaven, and far more precious than all worldly gain." Why? Because goodness has in it the very breath of God, the throb of His Spirit, the echo of His heart. The good man has God in him, loving him, continually with him, he continually with God; and this world lies beneath him, and death beneath his feet. Ah, the best this world can give trembles before death and the grave, and breaks and is gone! but in goodness the human heart clasps God, and doubt is at an end.

Oh, how much our world to-day wants that supreme daring faith in goodness just for itself, and that close fellowship with God, that defies all questionings, all doubts, that would stand if all the evidences about our Gospels and Epistles were swept away, still sure that God is up there, that God loves men, and that God draws them to Himself to make them holy, as their Father in heaven is holy!

IX.

THE STORY OF QUEEN ESTHER.

Esther iv. 13-17.

THE subject to which I invite your attention to-night is the Story of Queen Esther. The kernel of it has been read to you in the fourth chapter. I shall read the closing verses, so as to give you the key-note to the meaning of the narrative. After Esther had refused to go and plead for the Hebrews with the King of Persia, "Mordecai commanded to answer Esther, Think not with thyself that thou shalt escape in the king's house, more than all the Jews. For if thou altogether holdest thy peace at this time, then shall there enlargement and deliverance arise to the Jews from another place; but thou and thy father's house shall be destroyed: and who knoweth whether thou art come to the kingdom for such a time as this? Then Esther bade them return Mordecai this answer, Go, gather together all the Jews that are present in Shushan, and fast ye for me, and neither eat nor drink three days, night or day: I also and my maidens will fast likewise; and so will I go in unto the king, which is not according to the law: and if I perish, I perish. So Mordecai went his way, and did according to all that Esther had commanded him."

It is a very difficult task to calculate how much religion there is in the world—true religion, that God accepts. Elijah once tried to calculate, and concluded there was nobody true to God but himself; blind to the seven thousand that had not bowed the knee to Baal. It is quite possible to take superficial, indulgent, optimistic views of the progress made by mankind, but God knows there are as deadly and wicked and more blasphemous errors committed by good men, who talk of this world as if it were given over to the devil to reign and rule in it, as if things were growing worse and worse, as if the number of men and women whose hearts are God's were few. I think the blunder comes from looking for goodness often in the wrong place, from a mistaken idea of what true religion is. It won't do to reckon up our church members; they are not all genuine. It won't do to count our acts of worship, our prayer-meetings, our praises. These are often mere sound, breath, empty air. If you want to know how much of Christ there is in this world, you must go outside the churches, into the workshops, into the homes of the people. Ay, you must go to lands where Christ's name is not often heard, and you have got to listen with a sympathetic ear, and whenever you hear the accents of Christ's human voice ringing out in any way of genuine love and tenderness, whenever you see duty done patiently, and loyally, and uncomplainingly, whenever you see a heart or a soul follow the light, however dim and glimmering, understand that there you are touching Christ, and stand on a bit of the kingdom of heaven. The eleventh chapter of Hebrews is the golden roll of the Old Testament heroes, men of God, stamped by God Himself as genuine; and the deeds recited, too, as having been done by them, that gave them their degree and title as heroes, and nobles, and princes in heaven's kingdom, are not the preaching of sermons, or the writing of books of theology, or the fighting about petty little trivialities of doctrinal explanation, or the performance of rites and ceremonies and acts of worship, but brave deeds of battle, noble, dauntless generalship, heroism, and courage, and self-sacrifice, loyalty to the cause of truth and righteousness in this world. These are the deeds that were done, following the guidance of God, under the inspiration of Heaven, and the men who did them are recited in one long unbroken chain, and linked on in line direct with Jesus Christ, whose death and redemption are presented as the crown and consummation of that long series of priests, and kings, and prophets, and warriors, and heroes, true-hearted men and women who lived for God and fought for God in the olden time. It is sometimes said that Christ was not present in the Old Testament times. True, the human Jesus of Nazareth was not there, but oh, the spirit of Him was! He was the very heart-beat, and pulse, and inspiration of all that long, continuous struggle to bring heaven down into earth, for that is what the Old Testament story presents to us. In every brave deed, in every true word, in every pure and righteous life, it was not the heart of man that glowed, but the very spirit of Christ—Christ coming to full birth and maturity in this world's story.

Some people are puzzled to discover how the Book of Esther comes to be in the Old Testament. It is said to be a romance of history. It contains no religious teaching. The name of God is not once mentioned in it, from the first verse to the last. How comes it in the Bible?

Now, it is quite true that there is no direct dogmatic teaching of religious truth. It is absolutely true that the name of God is not to be found in its pages. But what of that? what of that, if the book is one of the most powerful presentations of God's providence working among men, if the book itself has for its very soul and idea the conception of God overruling events in a marvellous fashion to preserve His kingdom on earth? Is the great thing to get the name of God, spelt with its three letters, or to be shown God? Ah! it is the same kind of blunder that causes us to make so much of mere forms of words in the Church, instead of looking to see if the Spirit of God animates the man and woman and the preacher who inhabit the professed house of God on earth. There may be no teaching of religion, no prophesying of Jesus, no foreshadowing of the evangelical truths of redemption in the Book of Esther; but what it does paint for you is a majestic picture of a human heart struggling against its own weakness, rising to a grandeur that had in it the glory of Christ's own self-sacrifice. The name is not there, the phrase is not there; but the core, and kernel, and heart of Christ's love, and faith, and redemption of men are pulsing and beating in the book.

It is a puzzling book. There is a great deal in it that is revolting. The background on which Esther's deed of heroism was done is ugly and repulsive. She lived in a social state that was degraded and base, containing in it customs and habits that almost sicken us who, through Christ's mercy, have been lifted into comparative purity and sweetness.

You remember the story. A dissolute Persian monarch, in a drunken frolic, requires of his queen to do a deed that ran against all that was womanly within her, and she refused. Mercilessly he deposes her from the throne, and he sets to select another queen. The fair maidens of the land are collected, and in a very disgusting fashion presented to the tyrant, and from among them he chooses the beautiful young Jewess Esther, and makes her his queen. One cannot but pity her for having lived in such a time, for having had to play a part on such a stage of the world's story. One may even fairly ask the question, if it had not been nobler if she had not been presented by her guardian in such a revolting competition? But it is no good for us finding fault with the actual course of the world's story. If God was not too fine to lead men in all the bygone days—polygamy and such like practices were tolerated in the Old Testament time, because of the lowness of men's hearts, as Christ explains to us—it is a mistake in you and me being too fine to recognise God where God was numbering Himself among transgressors, that He might lift mankind to His own level. And then the narrative proceeds; presents to us a succession of cruel, unscrupulous intrigues, mainly between Esther's guardian, Mordecai, (a Jew whom one cannot admire and love, taking the picture of him drawn in this book) and the king's favourite courtier, Haman. In the course of the rivalry between the two, the very existence of God's people throughout the Persian empire is imperilled. Partly through Haman's scheming, but also through dauntless devotion to what they believed to be the cause of God, and which was the cause of God, in spite of the earthliness and imperfections attaching to its soldiers and defenders, partly by evil fixed to them, partly through nobility and goodness, a drama is presented to us, a struggle of heroism and bravery, and in the centre of it is that young queen doing a deed that we cannot but call Christlike.

Now, I want to say this to you: Men's lights in the world are very diverse. The possibilities of goodness and attainment for one man are far greater and far higher than for another. Some of you may be so entangled with evil customs and habits of commercial or of social life that you feel your very position there is impossible to make quite consistent with the full requirements of Jesus Christ. Thus things are. It is no good blinking them. And what are you to do? To despair, to give up any attempt to be good, and pure, and noble? Never! never! Look at all that Old Testament story—men far behind in their notions of common morality, yet on that low, degraded background discerning always a higher that may be done, a lower that may be avoided. No matter where you may stand, no matter how difficult the achievements may be, the one great question is, not what is the framework, but what is the painting you put in it. Are you living for self? or are you living for God? living to your own self-will, or striving to do your duty as far as you can do it?

From a very lowly lot Esther rose to be the first lady in the land, and I suppose all her sister Jewesses envied her, and thought that there was nothing that was not happy, and prosperous, and pleasant in her position. Yes, it was a position of great advantage, of great pomp, flattering to her pride—rich raiment, jewellery, the adulation of fawning courtiers, the admiration of the great monarch of the mightiest kingdom in the world, promoted to the throne as queen, wielding power over the destinies of man. Ah! it was a very enviable, happy lot, and yet not altogether so very enviable. I will tell you why—a thing that we apparently forget. When we all of us enter into our estates, when we come of age, nearly all good fortune in this world is heavily mortgaged. It is encumbered estates that we come heir to; and without disloyalty, without being renegades and dishonourable, we cannot cast off these encumbrances. The present has always got to pay the purchase price to the past. You must not kick away the ladder by which you rose to fortune. Ah! and sometimes into the bright sunshiny present the past comes with a very long bill to pay—comes with a very stern face and a demanding hand, and bids you, perhaps, risk all that is making your heart so warm, and so proud, and so gay.

That was the case with Esther. She was a Jewess. She owed her birth and her breeding to that despised, exiled people. She had won her proud position on the emperor's throne through the planning, and toiling, and sacrifice of her Jewish guardian. And now her people's destiny hangs on the balance. A deadly conspiracy against them has brought it about that on a given day, rapidly approaching, there is to be a universal merciless massacre of these defenceless Jews. And through the mouth of her old revered guardian the demand comes to her—the one human being that might have influence with the cruel king to cancel the decree and save the lives of men, women, and children—at the risk and peril of her own life in asking it, to go and intercede for them.

Hard! oh, how hard! Don't you judge harshly the poor queen when she shrank away from it and could not face the stern summons. Think of it, the young flesh, the soft heart—a woman's heart—within her, and think of the cruel death by torture that was wont to be inflicted upon any one that, unbidden, dared to force his way into the king's presence; coming, too, in the bright noonday of all her good fortune. It would have been easier to risk life when she was an unknown Jewish maiden; but oh, in this good luck, this fortune, this love, this adulation, this admiration, with her right fair beauty all upon her, to take it all and go and confront grim death! it seemed too much to ask. And so Esther began arguing within herself: Was she bound to hazard her life for these Jews? After all, what had they done for her? They were her race, her kindred, but what of that? Had she not come out from among them? Has not destiny taken her lot and separated it from theirs? Why cannot she live her own life apart from them? Why should she come down from the throne and take her stand among them, exposed to cruel massacre and death? What is the obligation? Where are the ties that bound her lot to theirs? Ay, where were the ties of love and the obligations to generosity? They are too fine and impalpable to be proved by argument. The moment you begin discussing them or questioning them—ties that bind brother to brother, sister to sister, child to parent—they vanish like life dissected for. You destroy them. They have to be felt, not proved, but are more real, more solemn, more important in determining a man's destinies than all the legal bonds and moral obligations that bind him in society.

But then, again, the queen would ask herself, What would be the good of her running such a risk? Is it reasonable that she, a single weak woman, unskilled in the ways of courts and of cunning courtiers; that she should be asked to plunge into a whirlpool of race-hatreds and furious feuds between unscrupulous nobles and potentates about the court; that she should confront the reckless rage of the royal tyrant—she, so defenceless, so impotent, so frail? Ah, yes! once again the argument was good to shirk the path of heroism; but once again, what business had she to argue? When duty comes to you it is not a thing to reason about. You have got to just go and do it.

Mother, when your little one was struck down with the deadliest and most infectious ailment, did you reason for one moment whether you could be expected to risk your life, whether you were not too delicate to make it worth while doing it, whether you would not be throwing away your existence? If any man came and suggested that to you,—"No!" Love, duty, they do not argue, they command.

The fact of the matter was, the queen was standing in a false position. She could not see the truth, she could not see the right, where she stood. I hope I have been able to show you how very plausible, how very weighty, the grounds were on which she made her refusal to risk her life. But have not you yourselves felt something about a home atmosphere in which such reasoning moved that is contemptible and despicable? Have not you recognised its infinite pettiness and littleness? Oh, what a narrow, contracted, selfish world that woman's heart is living in! It has been all a question about Esther—Esther's life, Esther's risks, Esther's obligations, as if that were the whole. Why not break down those prison walls of littleness? Look at those thousands of Jews—fathers, mothers, young maidens, brave lads, little children with their bright eyes, and with terrible death impending over them. How is Esther so forgetful of them, with their white faces and their anxious eyes, and of God's purposes in this world? Ah, no man can ever choose the path of right, of heroism, of goodness, of duty, till he sees and feels himself in God's big world, and with God above him up in heaven!

Mordecai recognised the root of the queen's cowardice, and swiftly and sternly he sent back a reply that shattered those barriers of her selfishness, and lifted her out of her little self-centred world, and set her on the pinnacle whence the whole line and way of duty shone out unmistakably. "Go back," said he—"go back and tell the queen to be ashamed of her despicable selfishness. Does she imagine that she lives separate and unconnected in this world of God's, so that she can save her own life by sacrificing, cowardly, the lives of her kinsmen? Go, tell the queen that she does not live in a will-less, random world, where she may pick and choose the best things for herself. Go, tell her that confronting her, sweeping round her, seizing her in its currents, the great will of God is moving on down through the centuries. If she will not save God's people, then God will find another deliverer, and she herself shall be dashed aside. Go, tell the queen she may refuse the task, but the deed shall be done. God's purpose in His chosen people shall not be baulked. Deliverance will come to the Jews, but she, poor blind queen, may have missed a noble vocation. Go, bid the queen look at the strange providence that picked her out among her people, that placed her on the throne, that set her by the side of the despot in whose hands the fate of her people is held, and then bid her ask whether she thinks God did that deed out of partial, indulgent favour of her petty self, or whether it is not clear as noontide that just for this hour of peril, and of danger, and of death, to be the redeemer and the saviour of the Jews, God gave her that dignity and set her on the throne."

Ah, what a new world we are in now! what a new light floods everything! The queen felt it. All that was noble, all that was good in her waked and gained the upper hand, and crushed down her baseness, and her meanness, and her selfishness. And yet heroism had a struggle with the weakness of the flesh. That is nothing strange. Remember Christ in Gethsemane: "Oh, watch with Me, with your human sympathy and fellowship, in My dire hour of need!" It was a cry like that that made Esther send back that message to Mordecai. She wanted to feel the binding force of the ties of common human brotherhood that connected her with her people to make her strong. She saw how it was. Away from them, and living alone, proudly, selfishly, her heart had got hard, and she could not go out among them; but it would mean a deal for her during those days if she knew that in every Jewish home men and women, young men and maidens, and little children, from morning till night, were fasting, and by the pain and abstinence of fasting kept thinking, from morning till night, of the deadly danger hanging over them, and Esther steeling herself to risk her life for love of them. Oh, wrapped round with that sense of human sympathy, nerved and braved by the thought of all these human lives hanging on her heroism, the weak woman conquered, and she could go and do the deed of valour!

But one thing more: the other element, the sense of her own weakness, her own impotence—for that she needed to fall back on God. Ah, if it were the case simply of a nation pleading with her to intercede on their behalf, she could not have done that all alone! But when she herself, through those two days, lived face to face with God, till this world was filled with His presence, till all the old stories of the generous rescues of bygone days were blazing resplendent before her eyes, guaranteeing that it was a call of God, that God would be behind her and with her and that His strength would be sufficient for her weakness—so backed with intimate love and sympathy with her fellow-men, and a strong faith in God, she could go and do her duty. Look at this striking contrast. Read that first refusal of hers—selfish, self-centred, cowardly, prudent. I think you feel all through it a restlessness, a dissatisfaction, a vacillation, a nervous excitement, a sense of uneasiness, a hidden doubt whether in saving her life she may not be losing it. Read that reply now, when she pledges herself to go and dare the king's deadly rage. How grand, and majestic, and calm it rings out! solemn, earnest, like the voice of a brave veteran going on a forlorn hope, but with the tranquillity, the serene certainty, of a brave heart doing what it knows to be duty. Ah, the man that goes through this world regardless of right or wrong, not asking what is duty, taking and choosing what shall be for his own advantage, trimming, and chopping, and setting his sails to catch every breeze of dishonourable prosperity, the restless heart that made response hanging upon himself, every step his own, if wrong then the upbraiding and the remorse all will be his. Oh, the sweetness, the grandeur, the calmness of the man who has asked simply, in any circumstances of danger and difficulty, "What is right? what is duty? what is the will of God? what alone can and ought to be done?" and then does it, ay, with death hanging over. He can sleep tranquilly. He is not responsible for the issue, no matter what it be. Here on earth he has done the right, done his duty, and the responsibility rests on God.

Esther, by that deed of heroism, delivered God's people from destruction. In her measure she did the same thing that Christ did perfectly later. Like Him, too, she laid her own life down on the altar. That it was not sacrificed does not diminish the value of the offering. A man does not need to perish in saving another from drowning, if he plunge into the wild, stormy sea, to deserve an admiration as great as if he had perished in the task.

She did a deed of Christ. That deed roused the admiration of her day and generation. That deed of hers was told with kindling eyes and ringing voice, and pride and triumph, from father to child, generation after generation. That deed of hers stood out as a pledge, a guarantee, of the reality of God's purpose for His kingdom on earth. By her deed, in her own day and generation, she saved God's people from imminent destruction; by that deed, preserved in history, she lifted up and made strong the hope and faith of generations after. And so, rightfully, her story finds its place in that long record of the hearts, noble, and brave, and true, who, for love of men and faith in God, at the bidding of Heaven, loved not their own lives to death, but laid them down for their brethren.

Oh, we men and women have got to learn this lesson from this Bible of ours—the real service of God, that is real religion, and that does build God's kingdom on earth, is done not altogether, by a long way, in our churches, in our religious exercises of worship; but done in purity, love, and truth, and goodness, out of generous kindliness to one another, at the bidding of God, through all the common chapters that make up our daily life.

X.
THE EXAMPLE OF THE PROPHETS.

"Take, my brethren, the prophets, who have spoken in the name of the Lord, for an example."—JAMES v. 10.

WE possess the books produced in olden times by a number of different nations. Each national literature has its own peculiarities. The literature of Israel has various features that are very characteristic of it. Among them all, one stands out and is unique. All along the nation had a conviction that they were destined to be the greatest nation in the world, and they believed that this destiny of theirs lay in the fact that through their government the world was to be made good, righteous, holy, and happy. They believed that God had a large plan, embracing the whole world in its operations; they believed that God was using all the different races as tools to work out that design of His; but they held that infinitely beyond all lesser instruments, He had made up His mind to employ Israel in accomplishing that great purpose of His high heart; through Israel He was to make the whole world into one Divine kingdom, ruled by Himself, and reverencing Himself as the one only God and Lord.

The mass of the people constantly forgot that sense of a lofty destiny; they constantly tired of that great ideal; they chose to prefer present gain and advantage; they disregarded that predicted end of their history in determining their contemporary policy in relation to other nations; they were dumb, and blind, and deaf to that feeling of God's movement in history and His purpose for the future. Nevertheless, in every age down through that nation's story there existed in their midst men who were possessed by a supreme conviction of this presence, and power, and purpose of God, men who sacrificed bread, profession, home, happiness, and life itself, that they might seek to carry out that intention and desire of God. In every age they declared what God wanted Israel to be and to do. In every age they recommended a policy founded on that destiny of Israel and that design of God. The darker the national history grew, the more decided was their certainty of the fulfilment of God's purpose. But this singular change took place in the form in which they conceived that fulfilment: In the earlier times Israel—the whole nation—was to be the minister of God's intention; but as age after age exhibited the depravity, the unholiness, and the jealousy of the nation, the thought of the coming kingdom of promise, and of gladness and goodness, concentrated itself not so much about the people, but about the King. More and more, it was not the chosen *people* of Israel, but it was the chosen *Son* of Israel, the chosen Heir of David, the coming Deliverer, the King, that was to bring it in. It is a strange spectacle to behold how God, by His external dealings with the people of Israel, and by the development of their conduct, led His servants the prophets to see that if ever this grand purpose of God for mankind was to be accomplished, it could not be done by the whole people, or any number of them, but must be done by one single individual, who should combine in his character all the goodness, and all the truth, and all the knowledge, and all the power of God that were necessary to make a kingdom of God on earth. So it came to pass that inside the progress of Israel's history, as a wall down the long march of that history, there was a line of men first of all foreseeing a grand future, mainly connected with Israel in the government of the nation, and gradually defining more brightly the covenant, and the establishment, and the maintenance of that kingdom as contained in the person, in the character, in the work, in the heart, in the sufferings, in the triumph of a great coming Messenger of God, a Man of God, a Son of God, yet so stamped with Divinity that He gets names which set Him on a level with God. It is the long procession of prophets, the line of foreseers, who, in succession to the patriarchs, touch, ages in advance, the coming of Christ, and make the world expect it, and preserve faith in mankind till Christ does come.

The history of these men within their own nation is striking. As a rule, they stood in a small minority, were despised and disbelieved, had to maintain the truth of their Divine conviction in the face of almost universal denial, were ill-treated and persecuted, were declared to be impostors or traitors to the national cause, were cast out, and an immense number of them were killed. But as time rolled on the development of events proved that those men had seen the calamities and vengeances of God which had been foretold as about to fall on Israel, because of Israel's sin. The people were cast out of their own native land; they were driven into captivity, and in captivity they remembered what the prophets had spoken; and then, with humble hearts and penitent spirits, they said to themselves "Those men were right; they spoke true; they anticipated what has come to pass; God was with them; they were His messengers; we were in the wrong; it was a true word from heaven that they uttered amongst us;" and so the old contempt and disbelief vanished away, and there came a reverence and a faith for those prophets that almost reached the verge of superstition; they gathered together their writings; they treasured them, and made the books of those prophets into their Bible. It is in that fashion that our own Old Testament of the prophets was formed. The prophets were first rejected, derided, put to death, and, then with repentance and humility, accepted as the true messengers of God, taken as authoritative interpreters of God's mind and will; their writings were treasured and preserved, and made into the national Bible.

It is these prophets that the Apostle James bids us take as an example. He means that every Christian man and every Christian woman is, in a measure, to be a prophet; He means especially that every Christian man and every Christian woman in the battle of life stands in some measure between God and others, and is to be a prophet. He means further that every father is to do for his children what those prophets did for Israel—he is to make them know God. He means that every mother is to be the very channel of making her children come into contact with God's character, and comprehend God's intentions for them. He means especially that every Sunday-school teacher is to be just what those old prophets were in Israel—to make others who are more ignorant than he is sensible of the presence, and purpose, and progression of God's designs through life in his own present age and time. He means that every preacher, and every teacher, and every man who speaks about religion is, in his conduct and character, and what he teaches and what he preaches, to be a prophet. And above all, he means that one and all of us of this age shall, even down to the humblest Christian, who hardly has any influence, act as a mediator or interpreter between other men and God, as did many of the prophets, with an unswerving belief of the truth, and with a patience and perseverance of spirit in every unenlightened time, and amidst the most adverse circumstances, founded upon the certainty of the fulfilment of God's promise that Christ should come, and shall come again.

Now I want to say a few things to you about the character and the office of those prophets in the world, that we may see some respects in which we may and certainly ought to imitate them. What was a prophet? I imagine that many of us are content with a very superficial notion of the part played in actual life by those men. I imagine, because of the class of books that has been written in great profusion in our present century, and is still written, that we are apt to think of a prophet simply and only as a man who predicted things that were going to happen—incidents and events that were to fall out in the unfolding of history. The prophets did a vast deal more than that, and the very essence, and life, and grandeur of their character and conduct appear only in a small fragment in that portion of their office. Their real movement and meaning are in quite another department.

If we wish to know what a prophet is, we may, first of all, take the names given to the prophets in the Bible. Then, again, we may remember who were the prophets. And then we may take their writings, the records of their deeds, the history that tells of their fortunes. What are the names given to a prophet in the Old Testament? The first and holiest is "a man of God"— "the man of God." All that that tells us is that in a peculiar sense the prophet belonged to God. The next name is "the servant of God." That tells us that he belonged to God in the sense of serving God, doing things for God. Then he is called "the ambassador, or the messenger, of God." That tells you that he served God by bringing messages from God. Then he is called an interpreter. That tells you that it was to men he took God's message, and that he had to make it understood by them. The next thing that we come to is a "seer," connected with the word "watchman," a spier or seer. It means one who saw what other men could not see, who saw into God's mind, who saw God, who saw what God was about. It tells us how he got to know his message, how he learnt it; it was by insight, seeing into the hidden, underlying purposes of God. Then the last name of all is what we translate "prophet," and it literally means a man who bubbles up and runs over, whose heart gushes out, in the sense of being poured into, that what is poured in comes out of him. It tells us that he pours out what he has learnt, to other men; and it adds this shade of meaning (the very form of the Hebrew word does so), that he is, as it were, spoken through; it does not end with himself, nor does it take its rise with himself, but it comes into him like a flood, and it overflows; he cannot help himself; he is possessed, he is pressed; he is compelled to utter what his God tells him.

The names of a prophet, therefore, tell us this; this is his function; he, beyond other men, has to do with God, belongs to God; he belongs to God in being God's servant; he is God's servant in being God's messenger; he is God's messenger in bringing things to men that God wants men to know; he learns what he has to tell men by seeing it himself, by knowing it, understanding it, feeling it, and then he utters it by a resistless compulsion and impulse, the fire burning in his heart, a pressure being put on him to tell what God has taught him. Already you have got the thought of a man with a grandeur, a greatness, a significance, and a meaning immensely above what you think of when you think of a man who can tell you where an axe which has been lost is to be found, or whether a sick person will die or live, or whether a town is going to be destroyed or not. What you have is a living, breathing, warming channel of communication between the great God in heaven and the human hearts of men on earth.

Then, who were the prophets? Moses was a prophet, the greatest of all the Old Testament prophets. He was a prophet because of his whole life-work, not because once or twice he predicted a thing which was going to happen. Because he was Moses, the moulder and the maker of Israel, and the giver to them of all their knowledge about God which is contained in God's law, therefore Moses was a prophet. Samuel was a prophet; Saul the king was a prophet for one night, when he lay on the ground in an ecstasy, and uttered strange sayings. There were all kinds of prophets; I cannot deal with them all. Isaiah was a prophet; Daniel was a prophet supremely. Christ was *the* Prophet, and the complete Prophet. How? Because He foretold the doom of Jerusalem? Because He foretold His own death? Undoubtedly because He did those things; but that was not why He was called the Prophet. Why was it? A very excellent book, the Shorter Catechism, puts it better than I can: "Jesus Christ is a Prophet in making known to us the mind and will of God for our salvation."

I put this deliberately and very strongly, almost unduly depreciating the idea of foretelling future events, just because I know from my own experience, and certainly from the experience of others, that one thinks that the latter is the whole meaning of the word. It is startling and intensely interesting when you can pick out a prediction which was uttered ages before, and which was afterwards fulfilled. By all means take that; but never forget that, just like

Christ's miracles, it was, as it were, only the accompaniment of the prophet's main work as a prophet, and that the real work of a prophet is making known unto us the whole character, and heart, and mind, and will of God, as these are revealed in working out the world's salvation.

If you turn to the writings of the prophets in the Old Testament you instantly discover that that is the true idea of a prophet. Take Isaiah, take Micah, take Jeremiah, take any prophet you please; every here and there you come upon a prediction—"Babylon shall be destroyed;" "Nineveh shall be destroyed." Yes, but it is one prediction, as an impassioned declaration of God's ways to men, showing how He must punish their wickedness, and must visit the impenitent. But the story of God's character and dealings for the world's redemption is, after all, the grand substance of Old Testament prophecy; it is a record of God's pity for mankind, and His determination to make them holy and happy, and of the fact that it is all to be done by the great coming Christ, the world's Sacrifice and the world's Saviour.

And when you are told to take the prophets as your example do not go away saying, "I cannot predict future events, and astonish people, and make them feel that I have some supernatural power." No, they could not be *that* example to you. A prophet was a man who knew the character of the true and living God; and because he knew and loved Him, and was living with Him, he made other men know Him, and feel Him, and understand Him too.

I have no time to enter into all the questions concerning the precise manner in which the prophet got to know God's mind and will—by dream, in ecstasy, in lofty rapt thought, in wonderful insight into the Spirit of God, and sometimes by a vision like that of Isaiah, where he "saw the Lord, high and lifted up," on His throne. Or, the prophet got to know God in a similar way to that which we read of in the case of the child Samuel, when the voice of God in the lonely Temple struck upon the child's ear so that there was nothing startling, and he thought it was his master's voice calling him; but he lived to see the terrible fulfilment of the first teaching which God gave to the child, in that which befell the master. I have no time to go into all that, nor to enter largely into the place and purpose of the prophets in working out that history which shows, when properly understood, nothing else but the growth of the Spirit of Jesus Christ through the ages, till that Spirit came in its completion in Jesus the Son of Mary; for *there* is the whole meaning of the prophets in

Israel; they were an incarnation of the very same heart, and mind, and will of the Divine dispensation and of God for the world's redemption which were in Jesus; it was the Spirit of Jesus. And do not put away the words as a mere figure unless you put away the words as a mere figure when you read that Jesus was the incarnate Son of God. It was the very Spirit of God. The same Spirit as was consummate in Jesus, the perfect Prophet because the perfect Revelation of God, in its measure was present in every prophet who made the people believe God as they had never done before, and recognise His presence in the history of their time. The prophets taught them to repent of their sin, to live for God, to take their share in the great conflicts for righteousness that God was fighting in their age. In a measure the Spirit of Jesus Christ, the Son of God, the Saviour of the world, was present in every age of it. There is scarcely any occurrence, any story, any Psalm, in the prophecies of the Old Testament, which has not an application to Jesus Christ, and a meaning showing that He is in it. It is made a specimen, as it were, of all that is practically to be found in Him. The history of Israel in prophecy, which was the rising and the beginning of the future history of Israel, was just the growing of Jesus through the ages, till at length He culminated in the Son of Mary.

I want to-day rather to tell you some of the qualifications of a prophet—some of the elements of character that a man must have if he is to play the part of a prophet to the people he lives among, bidding myself and you take the prophets as an example. One thing is remarkable—the office of a prophet was not hereditary. The great departments of God's government, and teaching, and dealings with Israel were the kingship, the priesthood, and the prophethood—the rule, the fellowship, and the teaching and guidance. Now, all these culminated in Jesus; He is Prophet, Priest, and King. In Israel no mere man or body of men was fit in unity to fill those offices; they were distributed. The burden was too great, the power was too grand, for any single man, except the perfect Son of Man, to combine them in their fulness, and so they were divided in Israel, to be reunited in the perfect embodiment of Israel, God, Prophet, Priest, and King to the people. God's meaning was that all Israel in its completeness should be king, and prophet, and priest, without any active, separated, divided government; that it should be a theocracy, as God's kingdom, ruling themselves, every one of them being a king to God, every one of them being a priest, every one of them being able to come direct to God for himself, and to bring his prayers to God without any intervention of man; in the same way every man, as a prophet, hearing God's voice direct to his heart, and being taught the truth that God revealed. God wanted them all to be prophets; God wanted them all to be priests; God wanted them all to be kings: but they were not fit for it, and so among them special men had to be cultivated to fill those offices. Now, there is this distinction between those divided offices or faculties of God's rule and guidance in Israel: the kingship was hereditary; the priesthood was hereditary: the prophethood was never hereditary. A priest's son was born a priest; a king's son was born a king: a prophet's son was not born a prophet. The prophets were selected, not born. Why? Because it was the supreme and grandest office, the most difficult, the most responsible, the most sacred. Any man was fit to be a priest, to conduct the ritual and external ordinances of worship, through which men's hearts were brought to God. And any man, comparatively, might be a king, so long as he devoted to his office that amount of thought and time which was necessary. It needed no special moral qualifications and no special insight. A man was the better who had these, but he could be a good enough king without them. But a prophet could not be born a prophet; a prophet had to be chosen, a prophet had to be made by God. And the reason was this: the prophethood was a creative office and function. God's dealings with Israel were not done when He had given the ancient economy of a religious priesthood and kingdom. God had to reshape, and remodel, and adopt His laws, and teaching, and meaning, and the outward ordinances of religion to every age. As the nation both externally and internally altered, new teaching had to come to it at the hands of the prophets.

Were the priests the channel by which God could do it? Their duty was fixed, and in the law, as well as in the form of government, men could not err; they could follow the Divine precepts exactly in administering them. But when an addition has to be made, and a remoulding to take place, it wants a man capable of entering with strange, grand insight into God's purposes, a man with eyes, with soul; it needs a man lifted up. And so the prophets' office was never hereditary; they were always selected; God chose them; why? Why did God choose one man, and not another? I think that He chose a man, first of all, who had a natural adaptation, who had rare powers of mind, who had rare genius and sympathetic feeling, and not a mere presentiment of the movements of the world and its destiny as it went on round about him. I think that, as a rule, God selected a man with a natural adaptation, and prepared him for all that he had to do and tell. It transformed a man's life; it took him clean out of the common world in which men lived. We presume that it was so from what is recorded, and from the facts which we know concerning the prophets' characters and lives. God caused something to happen to a man that made God appear to him what He was not to common men. An awful vision was presented to Isaiah of the great, grand God, and thenceforth all earthly considerations were nothing to Isaiah. He had seen *God*, and the future was God's making. In the face of empires, however mighty in name and in armies, it is the will of God that settles the future, and such a man disregards all earthly advantages; he knows that God means to do His deed; he says, "It shall be done; and if you set yourselves against it there is no other end than destruction, which is sure to fall upon you, for God will do the deed which He means to do." It was a revelation of *God* which made the man a prophet; it made him a man who felt God to be supreme; it made him to be certain of God's sovereignty, and absoluteness, and the goodness of God's authority; so that nothing could induce him to swerve from the path that God appointed for him. He was a man who stood like a rock amidst the earthly, selfish, planning, scheming men of his time, and declared the future truly, because he had seen God's meaning, and held men to it; and when they would not be so held he was content to die, declaring the truth of his message, and looking forward to the time when the future would manifest its truth. He was a fit prophet, a living teacher, who spoke of the future—a grand man, with a grand office and a grand destiny to play in the world.

The man, the father, the mother, the teacher, the preacher, who takes the prophets as examples, who will play his destined part in his own little home, in his own Sunday-school class, in his own congregation, in his own neighbourhood, in the great world round about him, must be a prophet; he must be a man who knows God; he must be a man who feels God to be all about him; he must be a man who is not merely orthodox in theology, and believes all that is written about God's dealings in the past; but he must be a man that will make you know that God is living, and moving, and loving in the events of his own time; he must be a man who recognises God in the providences of his own life; he must be a man who does not shape his conduct for earthly gain or for social advantage; he must be a man despising all these things, and paying heed to his own high destiny, yet whose character and conduct move on the lines which I have indicated; who says, "God is making me great, but He bids me live as He lives—but He bids me sacrifice friends and home; I *must* do it; I *must* tell this truth, though all good men should be against me, for I have learnt it of God, at my risk of having mistaken its meaning; yet I must speak it." Ay, even if such a man makes mistakes in learning this new lesson of God, and does not read it quite right, even if he goes wrong, nevertheless he has life in him, Divine life; he has honesty; he is a true man; he is a man who is not of the world; he is a man who is not a mere ecclesiastic; he is a man who is not a mere self-seeker. That man does God's work on earth. And I venture to say that in the Church's story you will find that there has been a succession of men who have done what was the work of the priest in the old time, and there has been a succession of men who have done the work of the prophet. You need both; you need the priest, to keep alive, as it were, the ordinary level of religion, to preserve some sort of uniformity; and in the Church's story you will find that God has raised up prophets, men who sometimes broke loose, who were not always true, who sometimes mistook God's meaning, who had but little of the character of the old prophets, and yet who taught truth, and adapted the old ecclesiastical doctrines to the new necessities, suiting their work to the age; and though disbelieved and openly denounced in their own day, they have become our teachers since. What of the Reformers? what of Wesley? what of Whitefield? what of many another name, much nearer our own time, but which does not diminish the effect of the general principle? Ay, and what of men not so good and great as these, but who had life in them; who broke up the stagnation of ecclesiastical life, and brought new faith to men; who by their dazzling earnestness, and spiritual insight, and their teaching brought up the ordinary level of God's presence? Thank God it is so. It is the lot of the human prophet and priest, and of similar teachers, in our day, to make men know that there is a God, and a Christ, and a soul to be saved, and that they are men, and not mere machines. Thank God for it; but pray God to make you and me true prophets; pray God to give us the passion of prophets, to give us sympathy with all the wants of the age, to give us to know that He is moving, to give us to know what new teachings come from Him; pray God to give us generosity, and self-sacrifice, and liberality, and largeness of heart, with our means, with our abilities, with our whole soul, with our prayers and spirits, and all that we have, to play our part as faithful prophets in the world's story, showing men God, and winning them to follow Him.

XI.
THE MAKING OF A PROPHET.[2]

"In the year that King Uzziah died I saw the Lord sitting upon a throne, high and lifted up, and His train overspreading the temple floor. Seraphs were poised above, each with six wings, with twain veiling his face, with twain veiling his feet, and with twain hovering. And those on one side sang in responsive chorus with those on the other side, saying, 'Holy, holy, holy is the Lord of hosts.' 'The fulness of the whole earth is His glory.' And the foundations of the threshold trembled at the sound of that singing, and the house was filled with incense smoke. Then cried I, 'Woe is me! for I am a dead man; because I am a man of unclean lips, and I dwell in the midst of a people of unclean lips; for mine eyes have seen the King, the Lord of hosts.' Then flew one of the seraphs unto me, having in his hand a burning ember, which with a tongs he had taken from off the incense altar; and he touched my mouth with it, and said, 'Lo, this hath touched thy lips; and thine iniquity is taken away, and thy sin purged.' Thereupon I heard the voice of the Lord, saying, 'Whom shall I send, and who will go for us?' Then I cried, 'See me; send me.'"—ISAIAH vi. 1-8 (*annotated*).

ISAIAH was a prophet. A prophet, we say, was a man who foretold future events. It is not an apt description. He did that, and much more besides. He interpreted past, present, and future alike in the light of eternal truth. But his supreme concern was with the present, and he cared for the past and the future only as they threw light on the problems of instant, pressing duty. The prophet was no dealer in futurities, no dreamer babbling to an age unborn. He was a potent actor in history, living and working amid the actual sins, and sorrows, and struggles of his day and generation.

Read the memoirs of Isaiah, and you will see how intense and intimate was the part he played in the life and movement of his age. One day you will find him at the Temple, scathing with scornful reprobation the hypocrisy and hollowness of the established ritual of religion. Another time he has taken his stand over against the fashionable promenade of Jerusalem, and as he watches the passing procession of pomp and opulence, built up on the misery and

---

[2] Preached at Nottingham, before the Congregational Union of England and Wales, on Monday evening, October 8th, 1888.

degradation of defenceless poverty, his heart grows hot with honest indignation, and he breaks into impassioned invective against the stream of selfish luxury, as it rolls by with a smiling face and a cruel heart. Again, he forces his way into a meeting of the Privy Council, fearlessly confronts the King and his advisers, denounces the iniquity of a faithless foreign policy, and sternly demands its abandonment. In every department of national life, in every section of social and religious existence, his voice was heard and his personality felt. Yet nobody ever mistook him for a mere politician, philanthropist, or reformer. He was ever, and was ever felt to be, a prophet. For he did not speak like other men, he did not act like other men, he did not reason like other men. He spoke not for himself, but for God. He claimed for his speech, not the persuasiveness of human probability, but the imperativeness of Divine certainty. He relied solely on the coercive power of truth. He did not touch the tools of political partisanship or scheming statecraft. He cared nothing for the suggestions of expediency; he defied the most certain conclusions of earthly wisdom, and followed absolutely the bidding of an unseen guidance. He was a man taken possession of by an irresistible perception of the will of God, and an all-absorbing passion to have that will done on earth. He held in the commonwealth the place that is held by that inexorable voice which, deaf to all balancings of earthly gain or loss, unflinchingly proclaims the antithesis of right and wrong, and imperatively demands that right shall be obeyed. The prophet was the conscience of the nation. Preachers and teachers of religion, that is what England asks of us. It is a high calling.

The office of a prophet was not an easy one. The man had to hazard or sacrifice most of those things that men count dear—property, popularity, home. Every day he had to take his life in his hand, as he risked the rage of a royal tyrant, or faced the fury of insensate mobs. Still harder was it to stand alone in his faith and opinion, rejected by the multitude, by the wealth, by the wisdom of his day, mocked or pitied as a madman; hardest of all to see his efforts foiled, his country humiliated, his people depraved, to feel his heart sink within him, to struggle with dark misgivings, to doubt the reality of the Divine prompting, and despairingly to ask whether this world were indeed governed by a righteous Will, or were not rather the sport of blind caprice or the slave of iron fate! Ah! it was not easy to be a prophet. Before a man could become a prophet he needed to possess a knowledge of God of such absolute certainty as nothing could shake. Once at least in his life he must have come into actual contact with God.

The experience that made Isaiah a prophet took the form of a vision. It happened in a period of distressing perplexity and gloom. Wrestling passionately with the darkness, craving wistfully for light, the yearning to see God in the man's soul became so intense and sensitive that the great Heart in heaven answered the longing of the heart on earth, and aspiration leapt into realisation, and faith flashed into vision. On a throne, high and lifted up, crowning and dominating all things, fixed on immovable foundations, untouched by the changes of time, unshaken by the shocks of history, Isaiah beheld, seated in sovereign supremacy, a Form of ineffable splendour, the power and presence of the Eternal in awful actuality, beyond all doubt or question the Lord of the universe and the Arbiter of destiny. Henceforth he could never doubt the being and the might of God. That is a great experience, but it leaves the heart unsatisfied. We want to know the nature, the character of this God, who holds our fortunes in His awful hands. Is He good, and just, and gentle, or hard, and cold, and cruel? The answer came to Isaiah in the seraphs' song of adoration, with its ascription of perfect triune holiness. It told him that in God is light, and no darkness at all. Through and through, utterly and absolutely, in every chord and fibre of His being, there is no baseness, no harshness, no injustice; there is nothing but stainless purity and splendour, nothing but radiant justice, goodness, and truth. "Holy, holy, holy is the Lord of hosts." Still, one wistful doubt, one anxious question, lingers in the human heart. For what were our poor world the better of this holy God if He be content to sit aloof in the light and glory of heaven, leaving the web of human story to be woven by the blundering fingers of sinning, erring men on earth? That fear, too, was laid for ever in Isaiah's soul by the comforting response of the seraphs' chorus. God does not sit apart in frigid isolation, but with His own hands He guides and controls our lost world's course. Into its strange, sad, perplexing progress He is pouring the goodness, truth, and love of His holy heart; and so when the record is finished and fulfilled, every page and syllable shall shine with that hidden holiness come to manifested light and splendour. "The fulness of the whole earth is His glory!" That sight of God—the living, holy, loving God—made Isaiah a prophet. Preachers and teachers of to-day, if we are to be prophets, we need just such a sight of God.

The vision of God made Isaiah a prophet; but the immediate effect was something very different. The first effect of contact with God was to produce in his soul an intolerable sense of sin. "Woe is me! for I am undone; because I am a man of unclean lips, and I dwell in the midst of a people of unclean lips: for mine eyes have seen the King, the Lord of hosts." Was, then, Isaiah an exceptionally wicked man? Hardly, when God chose him as His ambassador. But if not, is, then, the proper effect on a good man of an access of nearness to God an overwhelming consciousness of personal defilement? What else should it be? Had Isaiah been a Pharisee, he would have seized the opportunity of his sudden vicinity to the Almighty to direct the Divine attention to his virtues, and excellence, and superiority over other men. Had he been one of those philosophers in whom the heart has been overlaid by the intellect, he would have calmly proceeded to make observations on the Divine for a new theory of the Absolute and Unconditioned, in sublime insensibility to the deepest problem of existence, the awful antithesis of human sin and of Divine holiness. Because Isaiah was a good man, his new proximity to God woke within him a crushing horror of defilement and undoneness. And it was so precisely because he had never been so near to God before, and had never felt himself of so much importance. Away down here, sinning among his fellow-men, the blots and blemishes of his soul seemed of little moment. But up there, in the stainless light of heaven, with God's holy eyes resting on him, every spot of sin within him grew hot and horrible, every defiling stain an insult and a suffering inflicted on the sensitive holiness of God. What he does has an effect on God; what he is, is of consequence to God. Never had Isaiah felt himself so near to God; never had he felt himself of such importance to his Maker; and therefore never had he felt his sin so black and so unpardonable. Believe me, these two things are linked together, and no man can divorce them—the dignity of humanity and the damnableness of sin. You cannot tamper with the one without touching the other. Men may, of laxity or of pitifulness, seek to extenuate the guilt of sin and its infinite possibilities of woes; but be sure of this, they will be compelled ere long to attenuate the moral grandeur of our human nature, and to surrender its majestic birthright of immortality. Two things go hand in hand through the Bible, from the first chapter to the last, and mark it out from all other books: the one is its unique and awful sense of the guiltiness of sin; the other is the quite unapproachable splendour of its conception of the dignity of man, made in the image of God, and destined for His service here, and the fellowship of His love for evermore.

The ethical process by which, in the imagery of the vision, Isaiah's sense of sinfulness came home to him, is finely natural and simple. It was at his lips that the consciousness of his impurity caught him. "Woe is me! for I am undone; because I am a man of unclean lips." That, judged by our formulas and standards, might seem a somewhat superficial conviction of sin. We should have expected him to speak of his unclean heart, or the total corruption of his whole nature. But conviction of sin, actual conviction of sin, is very regardless of our theories, and is as diverse in its manifestations as are the characters and records of men. Sin finds out one man in one place, and another in a quite different spot, and perhaps the experience is most real when it is least theological. Isaiah felt his defilement in his lips, for suddenly he found himself at heaven's gate, gazing on the glory of God, and listening to the seraphs' ceaseless song of adoring praise. Isaiah loved God, and instinctively he prepared to join his voice to the seraphs' chant, but ere the harmony could pass his lips he caught his breath and was dumb. A horrible sense of uncleanness had seized him. His breath was tainted by his sin. He dared not mingle his polluted praise with the worship of that pure, sinless host of heaven. Oh, the shame and agony of that disability! for it meant that he has no part or place in that fair scene. He is an alien and an intruder. Its beauty and its sweetness are not for him. He belongs to a very different scene and a very different company. He is no inhabitant of heaven, no servant of God; but a denizen of earth, and a companion of sinners. Down there, amid its squalor, and shame, and uncleanness, is his dwelling-place, remote from heaven, and holiness, and God. "Woe is me! because I am a man of unclean lips, and I dwell in the midst of a people of unclean lips." With that, the horror of his situation reached its climax. He stands there, on the threshold of heaven in full sight of God and of His holiness, dumb and praiseless, while all heaven rings and reverberates with the worship of its adoring hosts. The awful tremor of that celestial praise passed into Isaiah's frame, and it seemed like the pangs of instant dissolution. He, a creature of God's, stands there in his Maker's presence, alone mute, alone refusing to chant his Creator's glory, a blot and blank in the holy harmony of heaven, a horrible and foul blemish amid the unsullied purity of that celestial scene. It seemed to Isaiah as if all the light, and glory, and holiness of heaven were gathering itself into one fierce lightning fire of vengeance, to overwhelm and crush him out of existence. "Woe is me! for I am undone; because I am a man of unclean lips, and I dwell in the midst of a people of unclean lips: for mine eyes have seen the King, the Lord of hosts."

Isaiah in the presence of God felt within him the pang of that death which must be the end of unpardoned sin in contact with the Divine holiness. He felt himself already as good as dead, yet never in all his life had he so longed to live as now, in sight of God, and heaven, and holiness. He did not ask to escape. He was too overwhelmed to pray or hope. But to God's heart that cry of despair was an infinitely persuasive prayer for mercy. Ah! Heaven needs no lengthy explanation, nor requires the recital of prescribed forms or theories. The moment a sinful soul turns loathingly from sin, and longingly to God and goodness, that instant the Heart above responds, and meets it with pity, pardon, hope. Ere the piteous echo of Isaiah's cry had died away, one of the seraphs flew with a burning ember from the incense altar, and laid it on Isaiah's mouth, and said, "Lo, this hath touched thy lips; and thine iniquity is taken away, and thy sin purged." The action is of course symbolic, but the thing symbolised is a great spiritual fact. In it we have mirrored the very heart of the process of redemption. The cleansing efficacy of the burning ember resided not in the ember, but in the Divine fire contained in it. In the imagery of sacrifice the fire is always conceived as God's method of accepting and taking to Himself the offering. The sacred flame that comes down from God, licks up the sacrifice, and in vapour carries it up to heaven; a sweet-smelling savour represents, therefore, the pitying holiness of God, that stoops forgivingly to sinful men, and graciously accepts and sanctifies them and their sacrifices. Contact with that has sin-cleansing power, and nothing has besides. Pagan sages and Christian saints alike unite in proclaiming the overmastering strength of sin. Mightier than nature's most potent forces, stronger than all influences of persuasion, not to be reversed or uprooted by any resources of earthly origin, is the grasp of inveterate sin within the sinner's soul. Is there, then, no possibility of recovery, no way of cleansing, no ray of hope? One there is, and one alone. If Divine Purity would but stoop in pity to the sinful one, would but enter, in claiming love, into his polluted soul, would but come into actual contact and conflict with the sin and uncleanness in a decisive struggle of triumph or defeat, then which must prove the stronger, which must conquer—human sinfulness or Divine holiness? Ay, if only God so loves our sin-stained race as that His stainless purity enters really into our humanity, and wrestles with our impurity in a contact that must be suffering to the Divine holiness, and is sin-cleansing to us, that were salvation surely, that were redemption. But is it a reality? Brethren, Jesus Christ has lived, and died, and lives again, and we know that His Holy Spirit dwells in us and in our world. That, and that alone, is salvation—not any theories, nor any rites, but God's Holy Spirit given unto us.

It was at Isaiah's lips that the sense of sin had stung him, and it was there that he received the cleansing. The seraph laid the hot ember on his lips, and it left about his mouth the fragrance of the celestial incense. He felt that he breathed the atmosphere and purity of heaven. He too might now join in heaven's praise and service; no more an alien, but a member of the celestial choir and a servant of the King. That act of Divine mercy had transformed him. He was a new creature, and instantly the change appeared. The voice of God sounds through the temple, saying, "Whom shall I send, and who will go for us?" And the first of all heaven's hosts to offer is Isaiah. A moment before he had shrunk back, crushed and despairing, from God's presence, feeling as if the Divine gaze were death to him. Now he springs forward, invokes God's attention on himself, and before all heaven's tried and trusty messengers proposes himself as God's ambassador. Was it presumption? was it self-assertion? I think if ever Isaiah was not thinking of himself at all, if ever he had utterly forgotten self, and pride, and all things, and was conscious only of God, and goodness, and gratitude, it was then, when his heart was running over with wonder, love, and praise for God's unspeakable mercy to him. It was not presumption; it was a true and beautiful instinct, that made him yearn with resistless longing to do something for that God who had shown such grace to him. Oh, the tender love and irrepressible devotion of a forgiven heart! Nothing can restrain it, nothing hold it back. Salvation, real salvation, springs resistlessly onward into service.

XII.
FOR AND AGAINST CHRIST.

"He that is not with Me is against Me: and he that gathereth not with Me scattereth."—LUKE xi. 23.

"He that is not against us is on our part."—MARK ix. 40.

IT has never been an easy task to settle with any degree of exactitude who among men should be reckoned the Saviour's friends, and who His foes. But perhaps no time has surrounded the problem with such difficulties as those that arise from the circumstances of our own age. On every side we see truth and error intertwined in such a perplexing tangle that we scarce know on which side to rank men and parties. The Church of Christ is divided into so many divergent sections, within which good and evil are so strangely combined, that you can hardly tell if they are for Christ or against. You find men of unexceptionable profession and ample creed, but with a jarring life and scant morality. On the other hand, you see men whose creed is erroneous or imperfect, but whose life and character are instinct with the spirit of Christ. And amid such anomalies you feel it almost impossible to determine, with even an approach to certainty, whom you shall count followers, and whom foes, of the Lord Jesus Christ.

True, we are not called to sit in judgment on the inner state of heart, the hidden attitude of men's spirits, which is cognisable only by "larger, other eyes than ours;" yet we must for practical guidance form a conditional opinion regarding the position and action of our fellow-men; for so alone can we determine our treatment of them; so alone can we decide whether it is our duty to oppose or co-operate with them, to acknowledge them as brethren or deny to them the name of Christ.

Besides, for your own comfort, you must have some standard or test to determine who are Christ's and who are not, for otherwise how shall you be able to adjudicate on your own case? You are confronted, it may be, by large and influential bodies of Christians who declare you to be no member of Christ's Church at all, because you do not follow after them. You feel all the weight that attends such a verdict; you are sensible of the solemn, tragic awfulness of the question; you are humble, diffident, uncertain yourself of many things, and so, perchance, your heart knows little rest or peace. You would give much to ascertain some sure test by which you could settle, once and for ever, whether you are on Christ's side or against Him.

For our guidance in such matters we can do no better thing than to try and understand how the Saviour, when He was on earth, estimated the attitudes of men to Himself. Let us try, then, to determine the principles that guided Him.

He had come with a very definite aim in view, viz., to establish a kingdom of heaven on earth; that is to say, to secure the domination of men's hearts by God's will, so that they should always act in accordance with the Divine decrees. Or, in other words, He had come to perform this work of delivering men from sin, of making them pure, and holy, and Godlike. For this end, He sought to bring them under His immediate influence, to gather and attach them to His Person, to inspire them with faith and love for Himself. All who aided in this, all who contributed to draw men to Him, all who strove to make Christ and His word accepted and esteemed, all who were at one with Him in His aim, manifestly, were counted by Him as friends; while, on the contrary, those who exerted themselves to thwart Him, who endeavoured to alienate men from His Person and doctrine, all such were His enemies, were against Him.

"But," you may be inclined to say, "while it is true there were some men who did devote themselves to active support of Christ, and others who did commit themselves to declared hostility, was there not, between these two opposing classes, a large number who took sides neither for nor against Him, but preserved a sort of neutrality? What, then, does Christ say of these?" The two sayings of our Lord which I have taken for my text have both been applied to solve this problem. At first sight they have the appearance of clashing with one another. "He that is not with Me is against Me" seems to be a declaration that all who were not positive friends were really enemies, and thus to imply that the Master classed this whole body of neutrals as foes; and so some use it. But again, the second saying, "He that is not against us is on our part," has the appearance of asserting that all who are not declared foes are in reality the Saviour's friends, and so, according to this principle, all neutrals should be counted as allies. The appearance of discrepancy only lasts when you look at these sayings singly and apart from their occasions. They speak not of neutrals at all. Taken in conjunction, they are seen to enunciate, in fact, quite a different principle, viz., that in regard to Christ, indifferentism, neutrality, is impossible, and that every man must be either for or against the Saviour. "He that is not a friend is a foe," while "he that is not a foe is a friend;" consequently there is no such thing as a position of neither friendship nor enmity.

Let us, then, run cursorily over the incidents that gave rise to these two sayings, in order that we may see what is the essential character of the two attitudes of being for or against Christ, and so exhibit how neutrality is impossible.

One day a man possessed of a dumb devil was brought to Jesus. By His word of power Jesus cast out the evil spirit, and immediately the man regained the power of speech. The crowd looking on were filled with wonder and admiration. They were pleased at the good deed which had been done. They partook in the dumb man's joy and gratitude, and they regarded the Saviour with increased reverence and esteem. The influence of the miracle was to attach men to Himself, and draw them towards the kingdom of God. But among the spectators there were some who had no pleasure in the act of healing at all. They were not glad to see their fellow-man in new possession of speech and soundness of mind. On the contrary, they wished it had not been done, for they grudged the credit it brought to the Saviour. His popularity was gall to them. It pained them to see men revere or trust Him. They did not wish that men should be drawn to Him. Accordingly, they attempted to turn the people's admiration into distrust by flinging out a dark suggestion that it was by the aid, not of God, but of the evil one, that the Lord had been able to work the cure. The effect designed is manifest. Such a suspicion would have the effect of turning men away from Christ, of preventing them from submitting to His guidance. Their purpose was not to draw men to Him, but rather to alienate from Him any who were attracted. Thus they were in direct antagonism to Christ's purpose and striving. They did not like Himself, nor His teaching, nor His aims, so they set themselves to oppose Him in every way. It was of such men our Lord said, "He that is not with Me is against Me; and he that gathereth not with Me scattereth."

Turning to the second story, we find that Christ's disciples had come upon a man casting out devils in the name of their Master. It is evident this man had not been much in direct communication with Christ, if at all, for apparently he was not known previously to the disciples, and their grievance is that one who did not with them follow Christ should thus employ the Master's name. It cannot but have been, therefore, that this man knew very little of Christ's Person or teaching. His knowledge of Him must have been very much more imperfect than that of the disciples, and he did not deem it his duty to become an immediate follower of the Lord. Nevertheless, he had made the discovery that Christ's name had power to cast out devils, and for this beneficent purpose he was in the habit of using it. The disciples, perhaps jealous that another, not of their number, should possess the same power, and believing that he could not be one of the Lord's privileged servants, forbade him to make any further use of the Saviour's name. On reporting this to the Master He countermanded their decision and gave His grounds for so doing. They were these: Though he did not attach himself to the personal company of Christ, though he might be very ignorant, etc. etc., nevertheless, by performing miracles of healing through Christ's name, he was bringing new honour and reverence to that name; and again, while he was thus in deed spreading Christ's fame and arousing belief in Him, he was not likely to imitate the Pharisees in slandering the Saviour—for in our Lord's words, "There is no man which shall do a miracle in My name that shall be able easily to speak evil of Me." That is to say, "By using My name to perform a miraculous cure, he puts himself out of a position to say anything that would detract from My credit." Such an one was certainly not a scatterer, but a gatherer. And "he that is thus not against us is on our part."

Reverting now to the first narrative see how the active antagonism of the Pharisees was the inevitable outcome of the fact that inwardly they were not with Him in heart and aim.

Because they did not like Him, and did not desire Him to gain influence with the people they would not unite in the general approbation of the crowd. Such conduct was marked and demanded an explanation. Apparently a good and wonderful miracle had been wrought. It will not do for them to merely refrain from approving. They must justify their reticence. Neutrality is impossible. If they will not adore they must malign. So they are forced to impugn the character of Christ's act. To justify their want of sympathy they must disavow its claim to their approbation. There is no alternative between frank acceptance of the miracle or open repudiation and disparagement of its character.

Still you must take sides for or against Christ, and you cannot be neutral. For His claims reach you not as external facts to be passively gazed at, but as imperative, active demands that lay hold of you, and insist that you shall take action upon them. You must yield or you must resist. You must comply or you must oppose. Christ lays His hand on you and if you will not obey you must shake that hand rudely off. In countless forms that strange, drawing power lays hold of you, and you must follow or reject. It may be a call to you to yield your reverence, your support, your participation to some benevolent or religious movement. If you will not, while others do accede to this claim, you must seek to justify your refusal. So you are forced into disparaging it, depreciating it, slandering it. You cannot own it to be of God and yet remain a rebel against its demands. So you must, with evil, malignant tongue, sneer at it as folly, or revile it as delusion—thus imitating the Pharisees who set down Christ's work to be the doing of the devil.

Remember, too, what a black-hearted, hateful sin that was they were guilty of. Try and picture that gentle, beneficent, holy Jesus. Realise the cruel blow such a thought was to the man just healed. Surely caution, reserve, would have made men hesitate to speak so. But they cruelly, malignantly, eagerly cry, "By Beelzebub He casteth out devils." It was in the face of such light, such considerate helpful words of Christ, that they did it. Think of the gracious words He spoke, and of the beauty of all that life, which in our days bring from the hearts of unbelievers encomiums that sound like adoration. In spite of all that, they were not made reverent, careful, slow to condemn. Nay, they were exasperated by it all.

But you may say, "They were zealous, mistaken men, wrongly trained; they thought Christ a heretic; they were the victims of an erroneous creed. So many had deceived them, so many false Christs had appeared! Besides, did not Moses say that they were not to believe a miracle simply, but to judge it by the teaching of the worker?" It is true, there were many such. But you do not find them among the number who ascribed Christ's works of healing to the devil. There were, indeed, honest but timid souls who were staggered by the pretensions and claims of Christ, but how did they act? Remember how one such came to Christ and went away with mingled feelings of attraction and perplexity; but when the body of Christ lay lone and forsaken Nicodemus came and did honour to the sacred dead. But these men were not such as he; their error was not of the intellect, but of the heart. They did not yield to the beauty of Christ's character, life, and teaching. They were not one with Him in His longing to establish God's kingdom on the earth. There was an inner antagonism of spirit, of nature. They were proud, haughty, self-righteous, and they were hypocrites, evildoers, cruel. They hated Christ because His pure life shamed and pained them, and they dreaded the loss of their own prestige and power. The secret and the essence and seat of their antagonism was not intellectual error, but deep, dark, moral perversion and evil of heart and conscience. Thus, because they were not with Christ, even in so far as to have sympathy with the undeniable good in Him, therefore they were in act and word against Him.

Finally, from the second narrative see what it is to be with Christ and how those who inwardly are not against are by His own verdict on His side. And, first of all, note the error into which the disciples fell. Very like the conduct of the Pharisees is theirs. They find a man doing good in Christ's name. He is not all he should be, not one of them, and not a constant pupil of Christ's. But instead of seeking to draw him to more perfect light, they intolerantly forbid him to do the good he was doing. So mistaken an action must have come from a wrongness of heart. They, too, fell before that evil, monopolising tendency that grudges to another God's gifts which we possess. It was a cruel thing to the man, a harmful thing, and might have turned him from Christ. Let us take the lesson to ourselves. Let us beware of refusing to allow good in those who differ from us; let us beware of rashly judging those who are not just the same as we. Harm—grave harm—is often done by treating imperfect, immature followers of our Master as if they had neither part nor lot with Him. But mark how this man was with Christ; only, remember, he is not an example of what we should be, rather he is a specimen of one just over the borderland: but over. It was not intellectual orthodoxy; not a perfect knowledge of God's mysteries that he possessed. He was very ignorant about God, about Christ. He did but know a little of the power of Christ and His majestic character and stupendous work. Yet so far as his knowledge went of Christ He had received it gladly. He rejoiced in the power of the Saviour's name to cast out devils, to cure the troubled ones. He did the good he knew. He acted up to his light. In his measure he gave glory and reverence and obedience to the Saviour. He was working for good and mercy and truth and God in the world. Thus he was not against Christ in these his aims, and so was for the Lord. It is only of those who are not against Christ in *this* sense that He says they are on His side.

Friends, there is warning and comfort in that. Warning there is, for, mark, that vain dream is dispelled which would read Christ's words as meaning that if only you do not oppose Him actively you are to be counted on His side. No! if that is your position, you are not for Him; you must be against Him: for passivity, neutrality is impossible.

Comfort there is, on the other hand, to you who feel yourselves very feeble, very imperfect; to you who find it hard to understand; to you who fear you are mistaken about many things. Ah! men may condemn you; the disciples may dissuade you from taking His name and counting yourself His, but do not fear. If you do, as far as you see how, strive to do the good He has taught you; if you do, it may be afar off, follow in His footsteps; if you have learned to find in Him in any degree a power that helps you to cast out the evil spirits in your soul and in the hearts of men: be sure that though you may not follow with other disciples, though you may be very deficient, very immature, a very unworthy servant—be sure that, nevertheless, you are not against, but for Him, and that in the end of the days He will not forbid you to claim His name, but will acknowledge you for His own.

XIII.
THE PROPHECY OF NATURE.

"When I consider Thy heavens, the work of Thy fingers, the moon and the stars, which Thou hast ordained; what is man, that Thou art mindful of him? and the son of man, that Thou visitest him? For Thou hast made him a little lower than the angels, and hast crowned him with glory and honour. Thou madest him to have dominion over the works of Thy hands; Thou hast put all things under his feet."—PSALM viii. 3-6.

"But now we see not yet all things put under Him."—HEB. ii. 8.

THE Eighth Psalm is a very striking one. It lifts the mind of the reader to a lofty height where he seems to have soared above sin and sorrow. It exults in man's greatness and Nature's grandeur. It is not Hebrew and theocratic, but human and universal. What it says is said of man as man; of man as he ought to be, was meant to be, may be. The subject is Humanity.

The New Testament writer of the Epistle to the Hebrews takes what is said in this psalm to be true of Christ, and he thinks that he has a right to find in the words a prophecy of Christ's coming. If you read the psalm without thinking of what is said in the Epistle you would not immediately apply it to Christ. How, then, is there a real connection between this old Hebrew utterance and the coming of our Lord?

It is a fact that the patriarchs expected the coming of some great and wonderful blessing in the future, and it is a fact that in the coming of Christ a gift came to men in the lines of anticipated blessing; but far greater than they ever dreamed of.

Reflecting on those predictions and anticipations of future blessing, might there not be in the very structure of the world, of the material universe itself, in the course of events as they have fallen out in history, something to lead men to expect the advent of their Christ? God makes His plans looking, as a wise man looks, to the end. We should expect, then, in all the foundation-laying, that that was provided for and expected which should be the crown of all.

Is there not in creation an aspect of things which makes men think that there is something great and grand in store for their race? The writer of this psalm conceived his poem as he stood in the open fields and looked up into the solemn sky, and watched the unhasting and untiring motion of the shining stars—worlds upon worlds burning and throbbing in the abyss of space. Away from the hum and tumult of men, no one can look at those hosts of silent stars without a subdued and awed sense of the mystery of being, of the infinite possibilities that the universe discloses. The star-studded heaven at night makes a man irresistibly think of God. It makes a man think, too, of himself. The silence, the shining, the mystery and the solemnity of the starry heavens make a man's beating, living life, as it were, become heard. A man is intensely conscious of himself. That is exactly what passed through the heart of this writer. It was not he who chose to have these thoughts, no more than it is our wish to have these thoughts. God was playing upon the strings of this man's heart—more directly, more rigorously in him, but just as He plays upon the strings of your own when you have had great solemn thoughts of God on a dark night, beneath the burning stars. The man's thoughts went up, and then they went down into himself, when he looked up into heaven, when he saw the moon and the stars, when he realised all their wondrous being, the regularity, the order, the vastness, the distance; then he thought of God, and God became great and grand and majestic, and then he burst out, "O Lord, our Lord, how excellent is Thy name in all the earth!" That is what he said. Then he looked into himself, his own conscious life, met its failure, and his first thought was of his own terrible pettiness. In the face of these countless worlds revolving in the far heaven, "what is man?" And then there came another thought to him: "And yet how great is man!" That mighty moon, millions of times vaster than man, does not know its own shining, its lustre, its own motions, its majesty. It is blind, and deaf, and dumb, and insensate, and man sees it and wonders at it, measures and weighs it, and understands its nature; and so man in all his meanness, in all his smallness, in all his weakness, in all the fragility of his life, is greater far than sun and moon and stars, and all revolving worlds. How little is man—and yet how great, O God! Here down below on earth man watches the stars, and up in heaven God watches them too. Man thinks; God thinks; man creates, God creates; man loves, God loves; so little, so great, and yet so like; Father and child, the One so grand, the other so insignificant.

Then he turned to the earth on which he stood, and with a grandeur of soul he recognised man's position on earth sharing the likeness of God, gifted with God's power of thought and of plan, of will and of love; man stands lord of all lower things that have been made, king and ruler with power to control, with mastery to move them, he is lord and master over all their ways, uncontrolled by aught, undismayed by aught, king, god of earth: "Thou hast made him ruler over all the works of Thy hands."

Is it not a grand poem, that? If I could read to you the best poems written in other lands by men of other days, by men of other faiths, if I could compare the thoughts of this psalm with other thoughts of God's plan and of man's position, you would understand what I mean when I say the psalm is grand, the psalm is a revelation of man and of God.

If I had the capacity or the time to try and show you how these thoughts about God and about Nature and about man, give man all the dignity, all the elevation of character, all the powers and abilities to shape and fashion the world he is in, one could not but wonder at the grandeur of that psalm. The faith about God, and the faith about man's destiny written down in that psalm—that faith is the Magna Charta of humanity that has emancipated men from the slavery to sun, moon and star, and all the powers of Nature.

The psalm is a true conception of man's relation—upwards to God, and downwards to Nature. It has been perfectly described by a German commentator as a poetical echo of creation! A psalm, a poem, such as this flings a spell about you. You forget actualities. It is so good, it seems so true, it is so human, it is so living, you yield your soul to it, you are filled with its glow and joyfulness, you are warmed with its strength and triumph. You hail it;—and then you begin to think, you look round, and what do you see? Mankind lord over lower things, yourself lord over your own body, master of your appetites? Your neighbours kings? The best of men enslaved! Bound down by the greed of gain! So that the nobler powers of mind and body, and soul, are degraded and cramped in them—men and women slaves of superstition, slaves of prodigies and foolish fancies wrought into their very nature.

"We see not yet all things put under him." If exultation was the mood made by the picture of the psalm, depression is the mood made by the picture of mankind; and are we to end with that? No. The writer to the Hebrews has given us the key by which we can unlock the secret, and have confidence in the triumph of man's better nature, and hope for a better future.

Let us look a little deeper into things, let us do men justice. Has man ever acquiesced in his sinful, sorrowful slavery? Never. It is always under protest that he regards it. It is always with a sense of fallen greatness. It is always with discontent. It is always with an unconquerable conviction that man was made for something better. Proof, do you want? Why is it when you read a story of heroic generosity, like that of the captain who gave away his own life for that of a wretched boy the other day, that you feel life to be worth living? What is the meaning of that sense of grandeur, of greatness, of triumph, that comes over you? How is it? What is it? When you see a brave deed of self-denial; at another time, when we hear of a cruel, mean deed done—how do we feel towards each? Are we all bad? If that were our natural lot we should acquiesce in the evil deed, we should have no shock, no surprise; instead of that there is a sense of surprise and revolt. There is an error somewhere—a disaster, a calamity. It is a sin—sin—a thing that robs us of our heavenly nature. Do we recognise it as a part of human nature? No. Sin is unnatural, sin is horrible. That is the meaning of the death scene in Macbeth. A knock at the door reveals to the murderer the distance his crime has set between him and the simple ordinary life of man. Sin is something unnatural, it is a calamity, an intrusion, it ought not to be there. Fellowship with God! Impossible to us! Why? Because we were never meant to have it? No. If there be a God at all, if He made this world, if He made men to think, and feel and understand, then God meant the world to be like a written book that should speak of Him. Why does not all Nature so speak to man? Because we have sinned, because we have lost the lineage, because we are not like Christ, the sinless Son: to Him the lilies had the touch of God on them, the birds in every song proclaimed His praise.

So, then, while we see that all things are not put under man, we see plainly that God meant it otherwise, and that God made man to be lord of creation. What God does not wish is hardly likely to stand. If man has missed being what he was meant for, there is good possibility that he may regain it. If God be love, there is certainty. I enter a master-painter's studio, and I see upon his easel a spoiled picture. I can see the majesty of the design, the beauty of the ideal, but from some defect in the pigment or flaw in the canvas, it has gone wrong; it is blurred and dim and spoiled. But not so to himself; that man will not allow the disaster to prevent him creating in visible form the vision of beauty that once charmed his heart. The man would not be a man of will and determination if he allowed the disaster to hinder him in his purpose. God is unchangeable. God is God.

Man is not what God made him for; man is not what God made him to be; and God is God. His purpose may lapse for a little, His designs may be delayed on the way, but if the beginning points to the grand end, that end will be reached. God meant it. God means it. God shall do it.

We stand farther on along the track of God's providential dealings with men. We see more than the writer to the Hebrews saw. He, too, remembered that psalm when he described man as he ought to be. Why did he still let it live and exist as a thing that is true? He could wait. What was he waiting for? And what were the singers thinking of as they chanted that psalm? They thought of a good time coming, they thought not the less of the disaster, they thought of God redeeming men, of God causing a Man to be born who should be a Deliverer, they thought of Him reaching out hands of help to all who came to Him, and the writer to the Hebrews writes truly when he says that that is prophesied of Christ. It is a prediction of His coming. God cannot be foiled. Man is not yet what God created him to be, the crown of all the earth-creation, but in the divine heart and mind there has been that vision—man wanting but little of exaltation to be next to God—man the lord of all—and the writer to the Hebrews was able to say, "God has achieved it; in Christ, crowned King and Lord of all creation, the psalm is fulfilled."

What depth of meaning and of wonder, of future joy and triumph, there is in that feeling he has of Christ as the Flower and Fruit of God's design in all creation! What depth of meaning there may be I do not dare to fathom, of good to all mankind; but this I will think,—that in the end of time when all things have been summed up and restored in Jesus Christ, when God shall have gathered together in one the broken threads, when the whole creation that with man groaneth until now, shall be delivered from its bondage—God will be seen not to have failed. What future revelation of grandeur, and of Divine goodness, and of redemption beyond our utmost thoughts, there may be, I do not think we were meant to know. I do not think we should dare to dogmatise; but we were meant to have our eyes drawn away to that glorious, radiant, splendrous future, and we are bidden there to see all God's loving pity and wise provision for us. Ah! God is working; He is creating, loving; He is providing, planning; He is redeeming creation, gathering together into one grand whole a restored humanity and a ransomed creation; and all mysteriously and strangely wrought into a great unity with Christ, and through Christ, with God.

XIV.
CHRISTIAN GIVING.

**Preached in Willesden Presbyterian Church,
September 24th, 1882.**

"O death, where is thy sting? O grave, where is thy victory? The sting of death is sin; and the strength of sin is the law. But thanks be to God, which giveth us the victory through our Lord Jesus Christ. Therefore, my beloved brethren, be ye steadfast, unmovable, always abounding in the work of the Lord, forasmuch as ye know that your labour is not in vain in the Lord."—1 COR. xv. 55-8.

"Now concerning the collection for the saints, as I have given order to the churches of Galatia, even so do ye. Upon the first day of the week let every one of you lay by him in store, as God hath prospered him, that there be no gatherings when I come. And when I come, whomsoever ye shall approve by your letters, them will I send to bring your liberality unto Jerusalem."—1 COR. xvi. 1-3.

I HAVE read this passage for one single purpose; it is to draw your attention to the singular way in which St. Paul passes from the doctrine of the Resurrection to the practical duty of Christian giving. It almost startles us, who have not quite St. Paul's way of thinking about collections, to hear him pass from that triumphant apostrophe of death, "O death, where is thy sting?" to "Now concerning the collection"

This seeming incongruity in the Epistle, and in the Church's work, is not confined to the Bible or to the Church; it runs all through life. Man has a poor, fleshly body, needing food, and drink, and sleep, and nursing; and he has an immortal soul. Say what you will, we cannot deny that the body is there; and I do not think we shall ever come to deny that the soul is there too, and will live, so long as goodness, tenderness, and devotion, and truth, and being last. Life has got into it; and the material framework which carries that soul-man's life corresponds to himself. In our homes, in our national life, in our business life there is the strangest intermingling of tragedy and comedy, of what is reverent and sacred, and what is most secular, and common, and mean. You cannot divorce the two. You may dislike the commonplace, and the mean, and the material; but if you hope to preserve the region of the spiritual and the sympathy of the good, that you can only do by preserving the body; they are gone when you forget the body.

What is it that is the brightest, heavenliest thing in the whole earth? It is love. No amount of mere common propriety, in the humblest action, will make up for the absence of that which comes out in a sudden tear or looks out in a sweet smile. We all know it, however earthly and material we are. But what I have to say is this: Look at that sacred thing, that love, which is almost too refined to put its hands on the soiling things of earth; what do you find it doing? Nursing at the sick bed, doing tasks that are repulsive, planning, with all kinds of material medicaments, and helps, and reliefs, to ease bodily pain. Now, it is easily possible for a coarse heart and poor bodily eyes to be in the midst of all that is sacred, and secular too, and to call it all common, and poor, and mean. It needs a quick, warm heart, and it needs almost, I may say, some imagination, some touch of a fine fancy, something of that Divine power which comes of tender affection and love, to do such acts for God.

In the life of Christ's spiritual family, which we call "the Church" (and by calling it "the Church" so often put it clean away out of all control of common sense and of affection), the very same law holds. The Church is worth nothing if it is not lit up and warmed with heavenly devotion to Jesus Christ. It may look solemn at the Communion-table; but it is not worth having if it does not reach men's hearts with fingers which squeeze out their hardness, and make them penitent for their sins; it is not worth having if it has not God, and Christ, and the life of the soul all throbbing through it. And yet it has a body, and material buildings, and expenses to maintain its earthly fabric and framework; and the spiritual life and the spiritual love that will have nought to do with these "cares of all the Churches," which Paul, the greatest preacher and Apostle, carried, or with collections and planning for the maintenance of preachers, thereby destroy themselves. If we try to put away that, and say, "It is not spiritual," or "It is a low thing," we are simply committing suicide of the religious life. It cannot live without that. Christ Himself had to plan how His preachers were to be maintained; and He spoke a great word when He said that they were to go and live on those who could not preach; not taking it as charity—never!—but taking it as a helpful service, which, combined with their searching of the Divine Word, should make it triumph in the world. "He that receiveth" into his house—maintaining him, that he may preach—"a preacher" (that is the meaning of "a prophet"), "in the name of a preacher"—not because he brings honour to the house, and because he is a great man, but because he is a man who is converting souls, a man that takes God at His word, and prays, and preaches unto men—will have the same "reward" in heaven, Christ providing for the spiritual wants and for the bodily wants of the preacher, and for his maintenance. And so, if once we lived in good earnest into that real, loving, great, broad thought of the actual life of Christ, we should not feel any surprise when we read how St. Paul passes from the great triumph of the doctrine of the Resurrection to the enforcement of Christian liberality.

Now I am going to spend the time at my disposal this morning in a very practical way. I hardly think that it needed that introduction to justify this use of the time at a Sunday morning's service; still, possibly, what has been said may be of use, not so much as a justification, but just as a preparation. I think that these things are for you. The subject is not a mere question of Church business; it is not a mere question, either, of interest to the men whose minds have a little of the statesman in them, and who consider the problems of Church government and Church management, as well as of national government and management; but I will say that it is a subject which ought to have a thorough interest to every one of you. I have been led to take it as my subject this morning because I was sent, a fortnight ago, by our Synod, as a deputy to one of our largest Presbyteries in the North, in order that I might interest congregations there in our Church's financial system of maintaining the preaching of the Gospel throughout this country; and I had the feeling, when I was doing it, and I had the assurance from those whom I visited, that it did them good. I have thought, therefore, that it might do my people good. Moreover, I had this feeling about the very strong and plain things that I said to them, that I should hardly be an honest man if I did not care openly to say the same things to my own people. Nay, I was led in some things to speak of my congregation, and what they had done not only for their minister, but for all the schemes of the Church, as an example; and therefore I feel my honour somewhat pledged that our congregation should not only do well, as it has done, but should do better. I say these things that I may have your sympathy in what I am going on to explain and to say to you.

The special subject, in our Church's government and economy, of which I want to make you understand a little is what is called the "Sustentation

Fund." I wish to be short and to be simple. Let me begin in this fashion: We believe that wherever there are Christian congregations who have the love of their Master in them, and some spiritual life, all these are blessed spots and centres, wherever they stand. We know how sorrows are soothed away by that Christian brotherhood and friendship, by those common prayers and praises, and by those words of truth which are read out of the Bible and often spoken by preachers. We believe that, or we do not believe in Christ at all. That is how Christ comes to men and women, and boys and girls, and little children, on earth. Oh, He does nothing for them like that! Well, now, it is a very practical question, that comes to all Christian men and women who are gathered together into any section of Christ's Church, how they can make their ministers, and their managers, and their elders, and their deacons, and their office-bearers (by whatever name you call them), and all their members, most useful and effective for good. It is the first question that their Master puts to them. He says, "Do your best." It is the duty of every Church in England just now to do everything in its power, by business methods as well as by spiritual methods, to make every congregation have a happy, harmonious, earnest, liberal, joyful, successful Christian life.

Now I will say this: It seems to me that the good which will be done by any denomination in England just now depends, of course first of all on its possession of the living Spirit and heart of Jesus Christ in its members; but that is not my subject to-day; I am talking of the material side, the body surrounding the soul; I say, the good which will be done by any Church in England will depend upon three things: first of all, that it shall have devised a government which will exercise power—superior control—over individual members, office-bearers, ministers, congregations; which will preserve a harmonious, law-abiding, just, and generous spirit and conduct between them all; not leaving it to two individuals in the Church, or some individual member, to fight the thing out, if a disagreement arises, without asking, before an impartial tribunal, which party is right, and each of them being willing to take the right. I say that a government which, without the evils of undue centralization, without crushing individual freedom, and liberty, and enterprise, will combine all congregations into one strong, united body, powerful to do Foreign Mission work and Home Mission work, cemented together so that the strong carry the weak when they are overtaken by sickness or disaster—and the strong get the blessing when doing work like that—a government the likest to that is a government which will make the most useful and the most spiritual and successful Church in our England. I say that I have watched the progress of things in these times of profound interest, and it seems to me that men are looking at one another in the Churches for what is good and desirable. That I believe to be our attitude in watching other Churches, and to be the attitude of other Churches in watching us. I look forward to a powerful, happy future in consequence.

The second thing which seems to me to be a great spring of a Church's usefulness in this modern England is the earnestness and success with which it devises methods of instructing its young people; not merely winning their affections for Christ, but giving them a reason for the faith that is in them; not merely teaching them that there is a Saviour to protect them at the Judgment, but giving them the life and thoughts of Christ, and that knowledge which shall cause them to grow into the perfect manhood of Christ. I say, the Church that most successfully and thoroughly, from the children in the Sunday-school and in the Bible-classes to those under higher systems of instruction, carries forward a knowledge of the Bible, and of God's ways with man, and of human nature in its religious aspects, to its young people, will be the greatest blessing in England; and once again I see that all the Churches are awake to it.

And the third thing is this (not by any means that there are not other things, which are perhaps just as important, but these three stand out prominent on account of the state of men's minds in England just now): the Church that can devise a method which will fill its pulpits with men who are not merely earnest converted men, loyal to Jesus Christ, but men abreast of the intelligence and thought of the times, men who have a calm reliance in their own faith by having looked all difficulties in the face, men who have something of the self-control and the large thoughts that come with culture; men who will be, not despised, but respected by the people that come to listen to them, and with whom they come in contact in the sorrows and trials of life—the Church that can best fill its pulpits with such preachers, and put such pastors into its congregations, will do the best work in England. And, mark you, it is not merely a question of denominational success; God forbid that I should care for that; but that Church is best fulfilling its Master's command, best doing its Master's work, most contributing to the realisation of that time when Christ shall be King of men.

I now come to the particular part of our Church's method of government and order which I have chosen for explanation to you to-day. We aim at having all our ministers men who, with great differences of original natural ability, have at least had all the thorough discipline and culture that training can give them. Our ministers have all passed through a high school course, a University course, and a course of study at a theological hall. Now, all that means a period of education of something like at least twelve years. We aim at having men who have ability, men who will be able to bear themselves, in all the relations of life, with dignity. We aim at having men worthy to speak in Christ's name. It is a worthy aim. Well, now, how are you to have such men? By praying for them; by planning thoroughly disciplined study for them; by seeking them out in families, and persuading and inducing them to give themselves to the work of preaching Christ's Gospel, and keeping alive spiritual love and truth in people's hearts. It is a worthy object. But I will be very plain: the Church's hands are largely tied by a very mean, material fact; it is the question of the salary which is attached to that office. If it be a wretched pittance, then it is a simple matter of fact that you will not get men who are capable of taking a position in the Christian world with dignity and efficiency to devote themselves to the work of preachers. Why should they? You say, "Why should a mercenary motive act?" Very good; why should it? But it does. But why should it not? Sometimes it is said, "You must not make the ministry a bribe by the largeness of its emoluments." Does it cease to be a bribe when its emoluments are a pittance? You only lower the level of temptation to an inferior grade of men, as well as where nothing is paid at all. God meant that men should be tempted, and you cannot get rid of it; they must battle with it and withstand it. But how does the thing work? I do not think that many men of much ability will be tempted, at least till the Millennium comes, by the emoluments of preaching, however good they come to be. I, for my part, should regret if it ever became a temptation to the highest ability—a money temptation, I mean. But what I have to say is this: I am talking of a thoroughly adequate maintenance—not of *payment*. The kind of service that is done by a man who saves a human being from sin and hell is a service which cannot be *paid*. That man can only be maintained to do that work; there is no money equivalent to such a service.

Partly the same thing is true of a medical man's service; he saves a life. Why, if you paid him the commercial value of his service you must give him your fortune; he saves your *life*. There are some things which cannot be paid for. You cannot pay for the love of wife and children. The sweetest things cannot be paid for; you can only show your appreciation of them by a worthy maintenance; it would be a pity to talk of paying for them.

Now, suppose that the maintenance awarded to ministers, to preachers, be so small that they cannot live and bring up their children as men of such culture and such ability are made by God to require that they should be able to do; what is the effect of it? You often break that man's heart; you embitter it; he would be more than human if you did not. To go about begging for wife and child! That is the result; and it is not the result of mere disaster, but of stinginess and meanness in Christian England. I will tell you how it works. Where shall we get young men with brains, with talent, with ability, that they may give themselves to a life which is not thought to be worth a decent maintenance by Christian people? Look at it. Here is a young man, a member of some country Church; God has moved his heart, and made him wish to do all the good he can in the world. He has a feeling that he could do more if he were a minister. He would like to be one. He knows himself to possess powers to rise in the world and take a position of eminence, a position of dignity, and to do good in that fashion. Here is this youth with a warm heart, who wishes to be a minister. But I will suppose that the minister of his congregation has had some wretched pittance to live on, has been worn out with the cares of just making ends meet, has often been behindhand, has been talked of as such, and more than talked of, even by kind-hearted Christian men and women, with something of pity, and something of concern; and this youth says to himself, "That is the life of a preacher." He would be more than human if he thought it right and wise to choose it. And what of his father and mother—will they encourage him to do so? They would not be parents if they did. They will tell him, "Do not you suppose that there is anything so excellent, or dignified, or worthy, in a minister's work." Ah, you may say that it is a mercenary thing! True; but where does the mercenariness begin? who brings it in? After all, men will go by reason, and they will estimate what are the worth and dignity of the career of a preacher of the Gospel by what Christian men and women set them down at in pounds, shillings, and pence. That is reason.

I have said these things strongly; I have said them very strongly here, because, though I dislike to speak of things concerning ourselves, I am bound to say frankly that you to your minister have always acted with rare liberality and generosity, beyond what sometimes I have thought was proportionate. You will perfectly understand, then, that in what I speak it is not to reproach you; far from it; it is to interest you, and make you feel the importance of this question.

Since I came to be myself a teacher of theological students, and to take a pride in my students, and to seek that they should be able ministers, I have come to feel how my hands are hampered and crippled, and that the best men are kept out by such poor, mean drawbacks as these. You will understand me.

I now come to explain more fully the working of the particular method adopted by our Church to maintain an honourable, able, dignified Christian ministry: We call it the "Sustentation Fund." The immediate aim is this, to gather together the strength and liberality of rich congregations, and distribute them in districts where they are poorer. In that way the poorer congregations are able to give a more handsome maintenance to their ministers. In that way, instead of the Church having men of parts, and culture, and dignity in the wealthier charges only, it has men of at least fair eminence, and dignity, and ability in all its branches; and that is an immense advantage. If it is a bane to society to have too great extremes of wealth and poverty, it is the same with the Church. If any Church is bound to avoid it, it is *our* Church; for one of the central principles of our Church is that its ministers and office-bearers should all sit as equals in a deliberative assembly, and that none should be able to make their will press upon others. If you have one set of ministers begging for doles from other and richer ministers, what have you? You have destroyed the Church as a brotherhood, as a family. Now I have given you in that a reason why we endeavour to distribute the generous strength of the richer among the poorer congregations by the Sustentation Fund. Another method would be by an Augmentation Fund, by which wealthier congregations would dole out money to poorer congregations. That is not our system; our system is this: Every congregation is asked to give, "as God has prospered them," to a fund which we prefer to call by our old Scotch term, a "Sustentation" Fund; they have to give all that it is in their hearts to give to that fund, and they send it up to a central committee, charged with the duty of distributing it. The whole amount is divided by the number of the ministers, and an equal share is sent to each. Note how that works. It does not preclude the wealthier congregations from adding a supplement, as it is called—adding as much as they like to the income of their own minister. It would be unreasonable that a man should not give more to the minister to whose ministrations he has attached himself, and who has drawn out his sympathies; and therefore no such liberality is asked to this fund, which goes among all the ministers.

Again, the weaker congregations are urged to contribute a sum which is equal to their common share; but if they come short the deficiency is made up by the surplus from the other Churches. For instance, suppose the distributed sum is £200, and one congregation sends £230. Of that sum £200 comes back, £30 remains, and goes probably to some congregation in Northumberland who have only sent up £170.

Now, I have no time to go into details, or to talk about objections, technical objections, and so on; but just let me show you very briefly some of the advantages of this way of working. I have spoken about the sentiment of the thing. Ministers, like men, have feelings. The poorer ministers prefer to get their larger stipend in that fashion, rather than getting the money as a dole. That point has to be considered; and when you remember how great a part feeling plays in all our life you will not disregard such a thing, even if it is only sentiment. But look at the thing practically. It may be said, "What is the use of sending up the whole amount? What good is there in a congregation sending up £230, and getting £200 back? What good is there in a congregation sending up £170, and getting £200 instead? Cannot you just as well send the £30?" If you did that it would become a Dole Fund; it would not be a Sustentation Fund. Then is it a mere difference of arrangement or sentiment? Not a bit of it. I will show you how the thing works practically. It is one of those secondary sorts of advantage which generally go, more than anything else, to prove a principal good. I suppose that, if you have ever thought of it, you are not surprised to find that Church business is constantly done in a most slovenly way. I suppose you are aware that even down in the City there are many offices where things are done in a slovenly, hap-hazard fashion. If that is so in business, and parish matters too, it is worse in Church matters; for even Church people seem to think that Church business need not be done with the same method and regularity as that with which secular matters should be done. Now, that is especially the case in country congregations, and the bearing of it upon finances is that moneys are not collected as they should be; they are not asked for, and are lying out when they ought to come in. A man who can give a shilling a month cannot get up twelve shillings at the end of the twelve months. All of you who are business men know what an immense advantage it is to business to have the whole of the book-keeping, and everything, done in an efficient manner. I saw, in this visitation of mine, congregations that had not connected themselves with this Sustentation Fund whose business affairs were in a shameful condition. It meant that the minister did not get his salary; it did not come in at the time; not that the money would not be given the moment it was applied for, but the treasurer was careless about it, and never thought of it. You can see the foolishness of such a position, and what a bad thing it is for the Church. What do they care about giving, when the thing is done in that careless fashion? Now, the Sustentation Fund means that the whole money collected for the minister's maintenance goes up to London; and the country people down in Northumberland try not to disgrace themselves in the eyes of the central officers in London, and the central officers in London have no hesitation in giving them a reminder. The advantage is the same as it is to a business house every year to have all its books and business pass through the hands of an accountant. It makes a man careful; things do not fall behind. This mode of working brings regularity and punctuality, not merely into the Sustentation Fund, but into the whole of the funds of all our charges. Well, but you may say, "What is the use of aid-giving congregations sending up their £200?" They do it, who do not need it, to get the others, who do need it, to do it too.

I have shown you what a very practical thing the Sustentation Fund is. I am now going to mention an advantage which requires a little more of Church statesmanship to appreciate it. It is not the minister, but the congregation, who gets the greatest benefit; I will tell you how. Ministers do not like to go to congregations where they are kept in arrears, and where they do not get that proper maintenance which they should, just through carelessness, or where they have to ask the treasurer for money. To revert to the commercial illustration, you would not go as partner into a firm where all the books were carelessly kept, and everything was in a slovenly, negligent condition. And the congregation that has its whole business arrangements and financial affairs completely regular and punctual stands in a much better position when it has to seek a minister than one that has not; it will get a better man. That is a very real consideration.

Once more, the system of the Sustentation Fund acts in such a fashion that does not allow congregations to impose on it. The Committee of the Sustentation Fund say this: "We fix with the poorer congregation how much of the money it shall send up, and we undertake that it shall share with the richer congregations so long as it does its duty." If they find that it is imposing on them, then they act very sharply; but if there is some local disaster, the loss of a wealthy member, or some sweeping misfortune, the Sustentation Fund will do what a family does for a sick child; it will nurse the sick child till it is strong again, and will not let it die out.

Once again, look how this system improves the position of the congregation (to use a commercial phrase) in the ministerial market. See what the Sustentation Fund amounts to. You know how the credit of a weak State is improved when a powerful State backs it up; it can borrow at a lower rate interest. Any man, or any firm, whose business is punctually done, and whose books are properly kept, can get money from a banker much more readily than one who has the reputation of being slovenly. And the system of the Sustentation Fund improves the character of a congregation; it gives the shield of the whole Church to an individual congregation; it says that disaster shall not depress it; it carries such a congregation through a time of difficulty. A minister has more heart to go to a weak charge, to a congregation exposed to such disasters, when that congregation has its credit backed by the general credit of the whole Church. That is a businesslike and statesmanlike consideration, and it is a very real one.

There are a great many other things which I could tell you. Let me mention one fact to show what our Sustentation Fund has already done. It has always been weak hitherto, and there has been a great deal of opposition to it, and there have been a great many difficulties in introducing it. It has not been able to do what it would do if it were strong; but I will tell you what it has done already. In Northumberland, where our Churches get the best members and Church officers—young men brought up properly—young women brought up with prayers morning and evening—Churches with full light in them, but very poor—in these Northumberland Churches the annual ministerial stipend has in many cases been nearly doubled. Of course you may say that many ministers are not worth even £200 a year. That is true; but if they are not worth £200 a year they are not worth anything; it is better to have them out. It is not a question of degree or amount, but the question is, Is the man doing a minister's work in an honest way? If he is, it is not fair that he should have to struggle on upon such a pittance as many of the ministers have been receiving. Well, now, I will tell you what the Sustentation Fund has done. With the exception of two or three charges that have to be nursed by the Home Mission Fund, and put, as it were, on the child platform, this Sustentation Fund has given to every one of our ministers an annual income of £200; and what has it proved? That our giving it has brought before the congregations the duty of supporting their ministers as has never been done before. It has taught them to be more liberal in maintaining their ministers; it has induced them in that way to be more generous and liberal themselves.

Now I have left myself no time for some more spiritual thoughts with which I wanted to end. I do not think that it much matters, if you remember how the spiritual lives on the practical material working of Church organisation; but I just want to say this (I wish I could feel it for myself, and I do wish that our members could feel it), that there is a great risk of well-to-do congregations unconsciously growing very selfish, and being shut up in themselves. That position brings a curse with it if it brings a blight in the heart, and if we come to Christ just to get our souls saved, and then selfishly congratulate ourselves upon that. Christ wants a great, loving heart, panting to do good to every one, and to save him from sin. He says, "Do not be satisfied with just coming to say your own prayers, and sing your praises, and get your sorrows comforted, and have your joys brightened, by belonging to a congregation; but think of all the great Church everywhere, and whether you might not do something for it." I think that God gathers us into congregations just for the same reason that He gathers us into families. Our love is too weak to be left spread out—it would die altogether; it would be chill and cold as the world—and so he shuts it in, and bids a man love wife and child with family affection; and so he nurses that love, and makes it profound. What is it that causes the love of father and mother to be so strong and tender? Is it not that there are such endless demands upon them for giving their money, and time, and prayers? It is God's greatest gift. But sometimes I see men and women misuse it, and make gigantic walls, and turn them into prison walls, and they do not care for any human being outside their little circle. It becomes a blight and a curse to them. Our Church is strong now in England under the Presbyterian system, while others are isolated. There is a real danger that our hearts will be dried up and narrowed; and I put it to you that here is one means of counteracting it, by giving with a warm heart, thinking of the manses away in the North, and the ministers' homes, that will be made happier and better by the liberality of those whom God has prospered. The Church that shows most liberality and loyalty to others is the Church that will have most love and loyalty to the Master.

XV.
OUR LORD'S TREATMENT OF ERRING FRIENDS.

Sunday Readings.

I.
Read Ps. cxxxviii., and John xiii. 1-17.
THE SELF-ASSERTING.—John xiii. 4, 5.

ON the evening before He died, Jesus washed the disciples' feet. This touching action of our Lord is constantly taken and turned into a picture of spiritual truths, and it is a very fair use to make of the story. No wonder if there is ever an overflowing surplus of meaning in all the things that Jesus said and did. But we must not forget that their symbolic use is a matter of secondary moment, and we must take care, first and chiefly, to recognise in our Lord's words and deeds that simple, direct meaning which He intended them to have. In the present case He has Himself told us why He did this strange and beautiful act of self-abasement to His faulty followers, and what effect the memory of His great humility ought to have on our hearts and characters, if we would be like Him, divinely wise and good in our treatment of erring friends.

In the country where Jesus lived the roads were hot and dusty, and the people wore sandals that left the upper part of the foot exposed. In the course of even a short journey the skin became covered with an irritating kind of sand. Therefore, on the arrival of a visitor, it was the first duty of hospitality to offer water to wash and cool the weary feet. When a feast was made the guests, as they entered, would lay aside their sandals, and take their places on the couches that surrounded the table. Then the humblest servant of the house was wont to come with basin, towel, and pitcher of water, to kneel behind each couch, to pour the water over the projecting feet, to wash them clean and free from stain, and to wipe them gently dry. It was a comfortable and kindly custom, and we know, from the anecdote of Simon the Pharisee, that our Lord missed it when it was omitted, and gratefully welcomed it when it was observed.

This night Jesus and His disciples are gathered for supper in the upper room of a strange house in Jerusalem. The room has been lent for the occasion, and so there is no servant in attendance on them. In such circumstances it had been customary among the little company for one of their number, ere the meal began, to do this needful service for the rest. In a corner of the room stood the pitcher and basin, with the towel folded by their side. They had all taken their places round the table, and the time to commence supper had come (so read verse 2). But this night—the last of their Master's life on earth—none rose to wash their feet, none stirred to perform that friendly office. One and all, they kept their places in painful and embarrassed silence. Their refusal of the lowly but accustomed task was due to an unwonted access of pride and self-assertion in their hearts. That very day, in the way, there had been a fierce contention among the disciples as to which of them was greatest. The dispute reached the Master's ear, and he firmly rebuked their rivalry and quelled the quarrel. The storm of passion was silenced on their lips, but the sullen surge of anger had not quite died out of their hearts. Not yet would it be easy for any one of them to forget his dignity, and do a humbling service to the rest. And so it came to pass on that solemn evening, when their Master's heart was so soft and tender, their hearts were hard with pride and anger, and though they felt the painfulness of the pause and the wrongfulness of their obstinacy, not one of them had the manliness to rise and end it, and by humbling himself make peace and harmony in their hearts.

The consciousness of discord entered the holy heart of Jesus and pierced it. His soul was filled that night with love unspeakable, and He longed to pour out to His friends the joy and the pain of His mighty purpose. But that could not be while their breasts were possessed by petty rivalries, and mean thoughts, and angry feelings. He must first shame away their pride, and melt their hardness, and make them gentle, lowly, and loving. How can He do this most quickly and completely? "He riseth from supper, and laid aside His garments; and took a towel, and girded Himself. After that He poureth water into a basin, and began to wash the disciples' feet, and to wipe them with the towel wherewith He was girded." Who is not able to picture the scene—the faces of John, and James, and Peter; the intense silence, in which each movement of Jesus was painfully audible; the furtive watching of Him, as He rose, to see what He would do; the sudden pang of self-reproach as they perceived what it meant; the bitter humiliation and the burning shame! The way John recites each detail tells how that scene had scorched itself on his soul and become an indelible memory. Truly his Master had "given him an example." To his dying day John could see that sight, and many a time in the hour of temptation it crossed his path and made him a better man. May that same vision of our Lord's great humility rise before our eyes, when life is full of pride and rivalry, and our hearts are hot and angry; and may its sweet influence come on our spirits like cool, pure water, to wash these evil passions out, and to make us good and gentle, like Jesus!

II.
Read Job xvi., and Matt. xxvi. 31-46.
THE UNSYMPATHETIC.—John xiii. 1-3.

The preface to the narrative of the feet-washing is long and involved. The ideas move in a lofty sphere, seemingly very remote from the simple scene they prelude. At first sight the reader is tempted to count the introduction cumbrous, and to question the relevancy. A more profound appreciation of its contents and connection changes questioning into admiration, and transforms perplexity into wondering delight. We perceive how the thoughts of the prelude light up the whole scene with a golden glow of human tenderness and Divine grandeur, so that, like a picture set in its true light, we now discern in it a depth of meaning and a wealth of beauty previously unsuspected. The perplexing preface proves to be the vestibule that leads into the innermost shrine of the temple.

The Gospel of St. John was not written till half a century later than the events it records; yet it is written as though it were but yesterday the Apostle had witnessed the scenes he describes. Those recollections had not been casual visitants, but constant inmates of his mind and heart. There was hardly ever a day he had not thought about them. At night when he lay awake and could not sleep he had thought about them. He conned them over in memory, he pored over them in his mind, he cherished them in his heart lovingly. And the promise his Lord had given came true to him, for the Holy Spirit took of these things of Christ, and showed them unto him, so that they grew to his eyes better and better, and more beautiful, and more full of meaning, till their inmost heart of Divine goodness was revealed to him. Ah! when we first get to know Christ it is but His face, His eyes, His outer form we see. That is a great sight! But to see and know all the heart of God that was in Him—that takes a very long time; it takes half a century; it takes eternity to get at that! John lived in that high quest almost all his life, gazing at the Master, worshipping and adoring, laying his heart on the Master's heart; and the result was that he got to know Jesus far better than he did when he lived with Him. Hence it is that the fourth Gospel is so different from the other three. They just tell us what Jesus said and what Jesus did. But John's Gospel mixes up the acts and words of Jesus with John's own thoughts and explanations, so that it is sometimes hardly possible to tell whether we are reading what Jesus said or what John thought about it. He is ever passing behind the loveliness of the human life, to trace its explanation in the inner heavenly nature. He paints for us the tree with its beauteous branches, leaves, and blossoms, and then he bids us behold the great root in God's earth out of which it grew; that wonderful root, which is Divine, and which is the source of all the sweetness that is brightening the upper air. The Jesus of John's Gospel has more of God in the look of face and eyes, and in the ring of His voice, than the Jesus of Matthew, Mark, and Luke. It is the Jesus that lived and grew on in John's loving memory, year by year becoming greater, holier, Diviner in the illumination of the Holy Spirit, that was brooding over that home of Christ in the heart of John. It is, indeed, Jesus coloured by John's thoughts and John's feelings; but then they are true thoughts and true feelings. And so it is that sometimes, in the evangel of the Beloved Disciple, we almost lose sight of the outer form and familiar features of our Lord, but only that we may see more clearly the glory of His inner nature and the beauty of His heart Divine.

It is to this loving industry of John's mind that we owe the preface of our story, so laden with great thoughts. It bids us, before we scan the picture of our Lord's humility, gaze into His heart, and see how that night it was filled with contending emotions of exaltation and agony, of tenderest devotion and unrequited love, and then, in the light of His inner grandeur, grief, and forlornness, measure the marvel of this wondrous act of self-abasement. He who washed the feet of those sinful men was the Son of God and the world's Saviour. He made Himself their servant! He washed their feet! But more than that, He was a dying man that night, and He knew it. His hour was come. Already the presaging pangs of the bloody sweat, of the scourging and the spitting, of the anguish and forsakeness of the cross, had broken like stormy waves of a troubled sea on Christ's sensitive spirit. The pain, and the parting, and the solemn awe of death had fallen upon His soul. He was going to bid good-bye to the faces He had loved, to the things that were so beautiful in His eyes, to the lilies and the birds, to those He had clung to on earth, to mother, and brother, and friend, to all that was sweet and dear to His human heart. His thoughts were preoccupied that night. He was preparing Himself for death. His heart was already getting detached from earth. Oh, if ever there was an hour when He might have been forgiven, if He had had no thought but of Himself, it was that night! If ever He might have held Himself exempt from thinking of others, and expected them to think of Him, it was that night. If ever there was an hour when He might have counted selfishness unforgivable, and bitterly resented want of sympathy, it was that night, when His grief was so great and His love so warm and tender. And yet, says John, it was on that night that amongst us all, engrossed in our petty, selfish rivalry, He was the one that could forget Himself, could lay pride aside, and humble His heart, and do the lowly act that made peace amongst us, and melted all our pride away, and made us good, and loving, and fit to hear the wondrous thoughts of grace and love that were glowing in His heart for us and for all mankind.

The lesson is one for good men and women. They are too apt to think, because they have set out on some great enterprise of goodness, that therefore they are exempt from the little courtesies and forbearance of lowlier service. They mean to do good, but they must do it with a high hand and in a masterful fashion. They cannot stoop to conciliate the lukewarm and to win the unsympathetic. And so too often their cherished purpose ends in failure, and we see that saddest sight in Christ's Church—beautiful lives marred and noble service spoiled, because the sacrifice is not complete enough, because pride lingers in the heart, and self-assertion and selfishness. We cannot be faithful in that which is greatest unless we are willing to be faithful also that in which is least.

III.
Read 2 Sam. xxiv., and John xxi. 15-23.
THE WILFUL.—John xiii. 6-10.

The character of Peter stands clear cut in the Gospels. He had a warm heart, an eager mind, an impulsive will, a quick initiative, and a native aptitude for preeminence. He took the lead almost unconsciously and without premeditation, but none the less he was conscious of a keen pleasure in being first. Prominence with him was not a choice of calculation, but rather an innate instinct and necessity of nature. Alike by what was best and by what was worst in him, it was natural for Peter to stand out from the rest, and whether right or wrong, to be their spokesman, champion, and chief.

As Jesus went round, washing the disciples' feet, there was perfect stillness in the room. None ventured to speak in explanation or remonstrance till He came to Peter. But as He prepared to kneel down behind him, Peter stopped Him with a protest: "Lord, dost thou wash my feet?" It looks on the face of it altogether good, and pure, and manly. But then Christ was no narrow-hearted pedant, eager to find fault, and imagining offence where none existed. Yet Peter's protest, instead of being approved, is gently but firmly refused. "What I do thou dost not understand now, but thou shalt understand presently." Beneath the fair surface of the remonstrance there must have been some unlovely thing that had to be rebuked away. What was the jarring chord? Had Peter's motive been contrition, and contrition only, would he have waited till it came to his turn? Would he not have leapt to his feet at once, and insisted on taking the Master's place, and washing the feet of them all? Did he sit still, ashamed for himself and them, but angrily ashamed, resolving first that he would not basely allow his Lord to demean Himself, then thinking hard things of the others, who suffered it without protest? And so, when it came to his turn, was his heart full of censorious thoughts, and a proud resolve that he would come out of the humiliation better than the rest? If, without breach of charity, we may take this to have been his mood, then we can understand Christ's kindly deprecation of his words and act. He fancied his impulse all good and noble. He did not know the treachery of his own heart. He did not fathom the necessity for the humbling experience of having to be washed by his Master. With the cleansing of his feet in simple obedience, his heart would be cleansed also of pride and of anger. Then he would understand what his Master was doing, and how He had to do it to put right so much that was wrong in the heart of His wayward follower.

It is not easy to obey without understanding. What was noble in Peter, and what was base, combined to hold him back from yielding. Peter's love recoiled from the humbling of his Master. Peter's pride shrank from the humbling of himself. "Thou shalt never wash my feet." Truly a noble, proud refusal! There was in it a strange mixture of good and evil. Peter wanted to come back to right, but he wished to come in his own way. Christ's way was painful, and the disciple would fain choose another that did not lead through the Valley of Humiliation. But then, if you have gone wrong through pride you cannot get right again and yet keep your pride. If you would be good you must abase yourself. Peter's refusal meant that his spirit still was not quite subdued, his heart not quite humble and contrite. In that mood he could not enter into the sacred communion of his Master's dying love. With that spirit cherished and maintained he could not belong to His fellowship. "If I wash thee not, thou hast no part with Me."

Christ knew Peter's heart. The man loved his Master with a passionate personal attachment. These words fell on his spirit with a sudden chill. To have no part with Christ—that was more than he could bear. "Lord, not my feet only, but also my hands and my head." It is as though he would say, "A great part in Thee!" And we might readily count the request blameless, and the mood that uttered it commendable only. But Jesus declines it, and in refusing suggests that it has in it something of unreality and excess. So then, without his knowing it, there must have lurked in the thought Peter's love of pre-eminence. First of all, he had wished to differ from the others in not being washed at all. Now that he must be washed, he would be the most washed of all. Ah, the subtle danger of wanting to be first, even in goodness! We cannot safely try to be good for the sake of being foremost. We must be good just for goodness' sake, with no thought of self at all. And surely silent submission had become Peter better than any speech. When a man knows he has gone wrong again and again, and Christ has undertaken to set him right, his wisdom is to offer no resistance, nor make any suggestion, as if he knew better than Jesus what had best be done.

Self-will in choosing the way in which we are to be saved and sanctified is a blunder from which few are quite free. We cannot leave our souls simply in

God's care and teaching. We catch at Christ's hands, and distrust the simplicity of His grace, and dictate to the Holy Spirit the experience and discipline we deem best. Surely it is not becoming and it is not wise. When a man has been taken into God's hands, and has been forgiven his sins, and is being taught by God, he should just keep very still and very humble, and let God make of him what He will.

IV.
Read 1 Sam. xxiv., and Luke xxii. 47-62.
THE FAITHLESS.—John xiii. 11.

Jesus enjoined us to love our enemies. We count it a hard saying. An enemy is not lovable. The sight of him wakes instinctively not affection, but antagonism. It is not easy to wish him well, to do him good. We find it difficult to endure his presence without show of repugnance. Still harder is it to pity him, to help him, to do him a service. But there is something worse than an enemy, something more repulsive, more unforgivable. That is a traitor—the faithless friend, who pretends affection with malice in his breast, who receives our love while he is plotting our ruin, and under cover of a caress stabs us to the heart. Open hostility may be met, resented, and forgotten, but cold-blooded treachery our human nature stamps as the all but unpardonable sin. Its presence is revolting, and its touch loathsome. An honest heart sickens at the sight of it.

Among the guests gathered around the table, that night before our Lord's death, was Judas, who betrayed Him. He had sold his Master for thirty pieces of silver, and was watching his opportunity to complete the covenant of blood. He sat there while Jesus washed their feet. Jesus knew all his falseness, all his heartlessness, all his treachery. He knew it, and He washed the traitor's feet.

The perfection of our Lord's holiness is apt to mislead us into the idea that because it was faultless, it was therefore easy. We conceive His goodness as spontaneous, His sinlessness as without effort. But in truth He was a man tempted in all points like as we are. He was obedient unto death, but His obedience He learned by the things which He suffered. He was perfect in purity, meekness, self-denial, but only by humbling Himself and crucifying the flesh. His self-control was absolute, but it cost Him as much as it does us— perchance more. His sinless, holy heart shrank from sin's foulness, and suffered in its loathsome contact as our stained souls cannot. The base presence and false fellowship of a Judas must have been a perpetual pain to His pure spirit. But He endured his meanness with a heavenly self-restraint that curbed each sign of repugnance, and to the last He maintained for the traitor a Divine compassion that would have saved him from himself, and that in Jesus's nature compelled the very instincts of loathing to transform themselves into quite marvellous ministries of super-human loving. It was no empty show of humility and kindness, it was pity and love incarnate, when Jesus knelt at Judas's back, and washed the feet of His betrayer.

That seems to me one of the most wondrous, most tragic scenes in this world's story. Could we but have seen it—Jesus kneeling behind Judas, laving his feet with water, touching them with His hands, wiping them gently dry, and the traitor keeping still through it all! What a theme for the genius of a painter—the face of Jesus and the face of Judas—the emotions of grandeur looking out of the one, of good and evil contending in the other! If anything could have broken the traitor's heart, and made him throw himself in penitent abasement on the Saviour's pity, it was when he felt on his feet his Master's warm breath and gentle touch, and divined all the forgiving love that was in His lowly heart.

This was our Lord's treatment of a faithless friend. On the night of His betrayal He washed the feet of His bitterest enemy, of the man who had sold Him to death. He rises from that act, and speaks to you and me, and says, "I have given you an example, that ye should do as I have done to you." If you have a friend that has deceived you, do not hate him; if you have an enemy, forgive him; if you can do him a humble kindness, do it; if you can soften and save him by lowly forbearance, be pitiful and long-suffering to the uttermost. It is the law of Christ. If you call it too hard for flesh and blood, remember how your Master, that night He was betrayed, washed the feet of the man that betrayed Him.

V.

Read Isa. xl., and 1 Cor. xiii.
THE SECRET OF MAGNANIMITY.—John xiii. 12-17.

There is a contagious quality in greatness. Young hearts, generous souls, dwelling in the vicinity of a hero, are apt to catch his thoughts, and words, and ways. Christ's greatness is His goodness, and that is absolute. Men look at Jesus, behold His perfection, grow to love Him, and hardly knowing how, become like Him. We see His tranquillity, whose minds are so perturbed by life's worries and men's wrongs. We wonder at His infinite peace, whose hearts are so hot and restless with the world's rivalries and ambitions. Our spirits, tired, and hurt, and fevered, gaze wistfully at the great serenity of His gentle life, and ere we know it a strange longing steals into our breast to learn His secret and find rest unto our souls. Plainly the panacea does not consist in any change outside us, for, do what we will, still in every lot there will be crooks and crosses that cannot be haughtily brushed aside, that can only be robbed of their sting by being humbly borne and patiently endured. Moreover, the world was not least, but most unkind to Him, yet could not mar His peace, nor poison the sweetness of His soul. Within Himself lay the talisman of His charmed life, the hidden spring of His unchanging goodness. It was the spell of a lowly, loving, and loyal heart. This is the key to the enigma of His perfect patience. He loved us, and He gave Himself for us. And so, whether His friends were gentle and obedient or wayward and rebellious, whether they were kind and sympathetic or cold, and hard, and selfish, whether they were good or evil, He remained unchanged and unchangeable. "Having loved His own which were in the world, He loved them unto the end."

The machinery of life is not simple, but complex and intricate. In its working there cannot but be much friction. If the strains and jars of social existence are to be borne without irritation and ill-will, there must be between us and our neighbours a plentiful supply of the oil of human kindness. The pressure and constraint that from a stranger would be irksome or unendurable become tolerable or even gladsome when borne for one we love. Did we, as God meant us to do, love our neighbour as ourself, life's burdens would seem light, for love makes all things easy. But then the difficulty just is to love our neighbour as ourself. Here, as elsewhere, it is the first step that costs. For too often our neighbour is not lovable, but hateful, and our own self is so much nearer to us than any neighbour can be. Its imperious demands silence his claims on our kindness, and drown the calls of duty. Its exuberant growth overshadows his, and robs him of the sunshine. Its intense acquisitiveness absorbs all our care and interest, all our sympathy and affection, so that we have no time or heart to spare for his exactions—no, not even for his necessities. Clearly in this inordinate love of self is the root of the wrong and unrest of our life. Because we love our own self too much, we love others too little to be able to be generous and good like Christ. Wrapped up unduly in selfish anxiety for our own happiness and dignity, we become too sensitive to the injuries of foes, the slights of friends, the cuts and wounds of fortune. The reason why we lack the lowliness of Jesus, and miss the blessedness of His heavenly peace, is our refusal to take up the cross and follow Him in the pathway of self-sacrifice. It was His detachment from self that made Him invulnerable to wounds, imperturbable amid wrongs, good and kind to the evil and to the froward. Because He cared much for others and little for Himself, He was lifted above the strife and restless emulation of our self-seeking lives. The charm that changed for Him the storm of life into a great calm was the simple but potent spell of self-renunciation.

The thought is one that captivates fresh hearts and noble souls with the fascination of a revelation. It seems to unlock all doors, to break all bars, and to lift from life its mysterious burden of perplexity and pain. The pathway of renunciation opens before their eyes with an indefinable charm, unfolding boundless vistas of lofty achievement, haunted by sweet whispers of a joy and content, dreamt of many a time, but never before attained. It is a fond delusion, that experience soon dispels. At the outset the way glows with the rosy light of a new dawn, and our footsteps are light with the bounding life of a fresh springtide; but ere many miles are traversed the road becomes hard and rough, and we, with heavy hearts, drag hot and dusty feet along a weary way. For the way of the Cross has indeed blessedness at the end of it, but easy it cannot be till it is ended. To curb our pride, to crush our self-seeking, to conquer passion, to quell ambition, to crucify the flesh—these things are not easy. They have the stern stress and strain of battle in them. To be patient under injuries, to suffer slights and wrongs, to take the lowest place without a murmur, are conquests that demand a strong heart and a great mind. Where shall we learn a serenity that can be disturbed by no trouble, where find a peace that disappointment cannot break, where reach a goodness that no wrong can ruffle? What is the secret of magnanimity?

The answer comes to us from John's picture of his Lord's humility. In the forefront we behold Jesus kneeling on the ground and washing His disciples' feet, and we wonder at such lowliness. But now John's finger points, and our eyes rest on the heart of this lowly Saviour, and reverently we read His thoughts. "Jesus, knowing that the Father had given all things into His hands, and that He was come from God and went to God," washed the disciples' feet. There is at once the marvel of His condescension and its explanation. He was so great He could afford to abase himself. His followers stood on their dignity, and jealously guarded their rank. He was sure of His position. Nothing could affect His Divine dignity. He came from God; He was going to God. What mattered it what happened to Him, what place He held, what humiliation He endured, in the brief snatch of earthly life between? And we, if we would be great-minded like Him, must have the same high faith, the same heavenly consciousness. We must know that this world, with its wrongs and disappointments, is not all; that this life, with its pride and pomps, is but a passing show. We must remember ever the grander world beyond, the infinite life within, and even now, amid the glare and din of time, live in and for eternity. Then we should no longer fret for a thousand trifles that vex us, we should not trouble for all the wrongs that pain and grieve us. What dignity, what grandeur, what Divine nobility there would be in every thought, in every word, in every deed of all our life on earth, were the consciousness ever glowing in our hearts that we too came from God and are going back to God!

XVI.
A Hymn of Heart's Ease.

Sunday Readings for the Month.

"Lord, my heart is not haughty,
Nor mine eyes lofty:
Neither do I exercise myself in great matters,
Or in things too high for me.
Surely I have behaved
And quieted myself;
As a child that is weaned of its mother,
My soul is even as a weaned child.
Let Israel hope in the Lord
From henceforth and for ever."—Ps. cxxxi.

1.
FIRST SUNDAY.
Read Job xxvi., and 1 Cor. xiii.

THE SOURCE OF UNREST.
"Things too high for me."

WE are apt to think and speak as if difficulty of faith were an experience peculiar to our age. It is indeed true that at particular periods speculative uncertainty has been more widely diffused than at others, and our own age may be one of them. But the real causes of perplexity in things religious are permanent and unchanging, having their roots deep-seated in the essential nature of man's relation to the world and to God. There has never been a time when men have not had to fight hard battles for their faith against the dark mysteries and terrors of existence, that pressed in upon their souls and threatened to enslave them. What is this brief Psalm, echoing like a sea-shell in its tiny circle the heart-beat of a vanished world, but the pathetic record of a soul's dread struggle with doubt and darkness, telling in its simple rhythm and quiet cadences the story how through the breakers of unbelief it fought its way to the firm shores of faith, and peace, and hope? It reads like a tale of yesterday. It is just what we are seeking, suffering, achieving. Yet more than two thousand years have come and gone since the brain that thought and the hand that wrote have mouldered into dust.

The poem must have been penned at a time when the poet's own misfortunes, or the general disorders of the age, were such as seemed to clash irreconcilably with his preconceived notions of God's goodness, character, and purposes. The shock of this collision between fact and theory shook to its foundations the structure of his inherited creed, and opened great fissures of questioning in the fabric of his personal faith. He was tempted to abandon the believing habits of a religious training and the confiding instincts of a naturally devout heart, and either to doubt the being and power of the Almighty, or to deny His wisdom and beneficence. For a long time he was tossed hither and thither on the alternate ebb and flow of questioning denial and believing affirmation, finding nowhere any firm foothold amid the unstable tumult of conflicting evidence and inconclusive reasoning. At last out of the confusion there dawned on his mind a growing persuasion of something clear and certain. He perceived that not only was the balance of evidence indecisive, but also that the issue never could but be indeterminate. For he saw that the method itself was impotent, and could never reach or unravel the themes of his agonised questioning. A settled conviction forced itself upon his mind that there are in life problems no human ingenuity can solve, questions that baffle man's intellect to comprehend, "great matters, and things too high" for him. It was a discovery startling, strange, and painful. But at least it was something solid and certain; it was firm land, on which one's feet might be planted. Moreover, it was not an ending, but a beginning, a starting-point that led somewhere. Perchance it might prove to be the first step in a rocky pathway, that should guide his footsteps to heights of clearer light and wider vision, where the heart, if not the intellect, might reach a solution of its questioning and enter into rest. The quest he had commenced had turned out a quest of the unattainable, but it had brought him to a real and profitable discovery. He had recognised and accepted once and for ever the fact of the fixed and final limitation of human knowledge.

It is an experience all men have to make, an experience that grows with age and deepens with wisdom, as we more and more encounter the mysteries of existence, and fathom the shallowness of our fancied knowledge. What do we know of God, the world, ourselves? How much, and how little! How much about them, how little of them! Who of us, for instance, has any actual conception of God in His absolute being? You remember how in dreamy childhood you would vainly strive to arrest and fasten in some definite image the vague vision of dazzling glory you had learned to call God, which floated before your soul, awing you with its majesty and immeasurable beauty, but evading every effort to grasp it. With gathering years and widening horizon you watched the world's changeful aspects and ceaseless movements, till nature seemed the transparent vesture of its mighty Maker, but it was all in vain that you tried to pierce the thin veil and behold the invisible Worker within. You took counsel with science, and it told you much concerning the properties of matter and the sequences of force, but the ultimate cause, that which is beneath, that which worketh all in all, it could not reveal. You turned to philosophy, and you traced the soaring thoughts of the sages, that rushed upward like blazing rockets, as if they would pierce and illuminate the remotest heaven; but you saw how, ere they reached that far goal, their fire went out, their light was quenched, and they fell back through the darkness, baffled and spent. You betook yourself to revelation, counting that at last you were entering the inner shrine, and you did indeed learn much that was new and precious; but soon came the discovery that here also we do but see through a glass darkly, and that our best knowledge of God is no more than a knowledge in part. "Lo, these are but the outskirts of His ways; and how small a portion we know of them! But the thunder of His power, who can understand?" We are, as it were, surrounded on every hand by mighty mountain peaks, whose rocky sides foil every effort to explore the pinnacles that lie hidden in distant cloud and mist. The achievements of the human intellect are many and marvellous, but above and beyond its realm remain, and doubtless ever shall remain, "great matters, and things too high" for us.

SECOND SUNDAY.
Read Ps. xxxvii., and Matt. xi.

The Secret of Rest.
"Lord, my heart is not haughty, nor mine eyes lofty."

There is in the human intellect an insatiable eagerness and an indomitable energy of acquisitiveness. It carries in its consciousness an ineradicable instinct of domination, that spurs it to boundless enterprise and prompts it to spurn defeat. This lordly quality of the human mind is the natural outcome of its sovereignty over the physical creation, and the appropriate expression of its kinship with the Creator. It is part of man's Divine birthright, and the insignia of his nobility. But it brings with it the peril of all special prerogative, the inevitable temptation that accompanies the possession of power. It tends to breed a haughtiness that is restive of restraint, a self-sufficiency that forgets its own boundaries, and an arrogance that refuses to wield the sceptre of aught but an unlimited empire. So it comes to pass, when reason in its restless research is brought to a stop by the invisible but very actual confines of human knowledge, it resents the suggestion of limitation, and declines to accept the arrest of its onward march. The temptation that besets it is twofold. On the one hand, pride, irritated by the check, but too clear-sighted to ignore it, is tempted to refuse to admit any truths it cannot fathom or substantiate, and to deny the real existence of any realm of being beyond its natural ken. This is the characteristic error of Rationalism and Positivism. On the other hand, there is in the opposite direction a tendency, born equally of intellectual pride and self-will, to refuse the restriction, to ignore reason's incapacity, and so to venture to state and explain that which is inexplicable. Alike in the spheres of science and of religion men strive recklessly to remove from God's face the veil which His own hand has not drawn, and irreverently intrude into mysteries hopelessly beyond human thought to conceive or human speech to express. This is the transgression of rash speculation and of arrogant dogmatism, and it is in itself as sinful, and in its consequences as harmful, as are the blank negations of scepticism.

Each of these errors the author of our poem was fortunate enough to escape. Recognising the limitation of all earthly knowledge, he does not rage against the restrictions and beat himself against the environing bars. He does not take it on himself, by a foolish fiat of his finite littleness, to decree the non-existence of everything too subtle for his dim eyes to perceive, or too fine for his dull ear to hear. Where he fails to understand the wisdom or goodness of God's ways he does not intrude and try to alter them, neither does he wildly struggle to comprehend their meaning, nor madly refuse to submit to them. He adapts himself to the Divine dealing, and is content to obey without insisting on knowing the reason why. He curbs in the cravings of his mind, nor will suffer the swift stream of his thought to rush on like an impetuous torrent, dashing itself against obstructing rocks, and fretting its waters into froth and foam. He possesses his soul in patience, and does not "exercise" himself "in great matters, or in things too high" for him.

This attitude of acquiescence is the position imposed on us by necessity, and prescribed by wisdom. But, as a matter of fact, its practical possession depends on the presence of a certain inner mood or disposition. We have seen that the denials of scepticism and the excesses of dogmatism are alike the offspring of pride, and spring from an over-estimation of the potency of reason. Therefore, as we might expect, the poet's simple acceptance of limitation and contentment with partial knowledge are due to the fact that he has formed a modest estimate of himself. "Lord, my heart is not haughty, nor mine eyes lofty." His submission to restraint has its root in humility. He does not exaggerate his capacity. He takes the measure of his mind accurately. He does not expect to be able to accomplish more than his abilities are equal to. It seems to him quite natural that men should not be able to comprehend all God's ways. It is to be expected that there should be many things in God's operations beyond their knowledge, and in his thoughts passing their understanding. It is, therefore, no matter for surprise that men should encounter in God's universe "great matters," and "things too high" for them. Nay, the wonder and disappointment would be if there were no mysteries, no infinitudes, transcending our narrow souls. Would it gladden you if indeed God were no greater than our thoughts of Him? What if the sun were no brighter and no vaster than the shrunken, dim, and tarnished image of his radiance framed in a child's toy mirror? Alas for us if God and the universe were not immeasurably grander than mankind's most majestic conceptions of them! Measuring ourselves thus, in truth and lowliness, over against God, who will not say, with the poet of our Psalm, "Lord, my heart is not haughty, nor mine eyes lofty: neither do I exercise myself in great matters, or in things too high for me"?

THIRD SUNDAY.
Read Ps. lxxiii., and Heb. xii.

CALM AFTER STORM.
"Surely I have behaved and quieted myself."

Peace bulks largely in all our dreams of ideal happiness. Without repose of heart we cannot conceive of perfect contentment. But we must not forget that the peace of inexperience is a fragile possession, and that the only lasting rest is the repose that is based upon conquest. We speak with languid longing and ease-seeking envy of the peace of Jesus, because we forget that His peace was a peace constituted out of conflict, maintained in the face of struggle, and made perfect through suffering. Therefore it was a peace strong and majestic, and the story of His life is the world's greatest epic. A life that commenced with effortless attainment, proceeded in easy serenity, and ended in tranquillity were a life without a history, pleasant but monotonous, devoid of dramatic interest, and destitute of significance. The young cadet, in his boyish bloom and unworn beauty, furnishes the painter with a fairer model, but the grizzled hero of a hundred fights, with his battered form and furrowed face, makes the greater picture. It means so much more. And it means more precisely because the tried valour of the veteran is so much more than the promise of the untested tyro. Innocence unsullied and untried has a loveliness all its own, but it lacks the pathos of suggestion, the depth of significance, and the strength of permanence that make the glory of virtue that has borne the brunt of battle, and has known the bitterness of defeat, the agony of retrieval, and the exultation of recovered victory. We talk proudly of the faith that has never felt a doubt, that has been pierced by no perplexity, and shows no mark of the sweat and stress of conflict. We look askance on difficulty of faith, have no mercy on lack of assurance, and reckon them happy who are convinced without trouble and believe without effort. That is not quite the Bible estimate. The Psalms echo with the prayers of hard-pressed faith, and throb with the cries of agonised doubt. The New Testament speaks of faith as a fight, counts them happy who endure, and pronounces blessed the man who encounters and overcomes temptation. If "strait is the gate and narrow is the way that leadeth unto life," how should faith be easy, since faith is that gate, that way? The truth is that we invert the Divine standard of values, and put last what God puts first. We count enviable the land-locked harbours of unthreatened belief, that are protected from assault by their very shallowness and narrowness. We are blind to the providential discipline which ordains that men should wrestle with difficulty, and in overcoming it attain a tried and tempered faith possible only to those who have passed through the furnace of temptation. For sinful men there can be no real strength that is not transmuted weakness, no permanent peace that is not a triumph over rebellion, no perfect faith that is not a victory over doubt. The saints that have most reflected the spirit of Christ formed their fair character, like their Master, in lives of which it may be said, "Without were fightings, within were fears." The way of the cross has ever been a way of conflict, and it is they who come out of great tribulation that enter into the rest that remaineth. The deep lakes that sleep in the hollows of high mountains, and mirror in their placid depths the quiet stars, have their homes in the craters of volcanoes, that have spent their fury, quenched their fires, and are changed into pools of perpetual peace.

There breathes through our Psalm an atmosphere of infinite repose—a subdued rest, like the hush of a cradle song. Nevertheless, if we listen closely enough to its music, we catch under its lullaby the low echo of a bygone anguish, the lingering sob of a vanished tempest. Nature's most exquisite embodiment of calm is the sweet fresh air that is left by a great storm; and the perfection of the Psalm's restfulness is that it consists of unrest conquered and transmuted. For the poet's peace is the result of a great struggle, the reward of a supreme act of self-subjection. "Surely I have behaved and quieted myself;" or, preserving the imagery of the words, "Surely I have calmed and hushed my soul." His submissiveness had not been native, but acquired. His lowliness of heart was not a natural endowment, but a laborious accomplishment. His acquiescence in God's mysterious ways was a thing not inborn and habitual, but was rather the calm that follows a storm, when the tempest has moaned itself into stillness, and the great waves have rocked themselves into unruffled rest. For his soul had once been rebellious, like a storm-lashed sea dashing itself against the iron cliffs that bounded its waves, and impetuous like a tempest rushing through the empty air, seeking to attain the unattainable, and spending its force vainly in vacancy. He had longed to flash thought, lightning like, athwart the thick darkness that surrounded Jehovah's throne, and to lay bare its hidden secrets. It was all in vain. Hemmed in on every hand, beaten back in his attempts to pierce the high heaven, baffled in every effort to read the enigma of God's ways, he had been tempted to revolt, and either to renounce his trust in the Almighty's goodness or to refuse to submit to His control. It cost him a hard and weary struggle to regain his reliance, to restore his allegiance, to calm and hush his soul.

There was nothing wonderful in this conflict, nor anything exceptional in the experience. It is the common lot of men. True, there are some natures for whom the tenure of faith is less arduous than it is for others. But in almost every life there come crises when this same battle has to be fought. For it is not always easy to be content to trust without seeing, and to follow God's leading in the dark, when the way seems all wrong and mistaken. There are things in life that rudely shake our faith from its dreamless slumber, and sweep the soul away over the dreary billows of doubt and darkness. There are times when, to our timorous hearts, it seems too terrible to be compelled just to trust and not to understand. Such conflicts come to us all more or less. Painful and protracted the struggle sometimes is, but not necessarily evil, not even harmful. For if we do but fight it out honestly and bravely the fruits will be, as they were with our poet, wholesome, good, and peaceable.

FOURTH SUNDAY.
Read Ps. xlvi., and Phil. ii.

VICTORY BY SURRENDER.

"As a child that is weaned of his mother: my soul is even as a weaned child."

It is good to cheer men on in a noble strife by speaking of the certainty of victory, and by the story of heroic deeds to nerve their arms for battle and stir their hearts to war. But that is not enough. They want more than that. They want to learn how to wage a winning war, how to secure the highest triumph, how out of conflict to organise peace. In the good fight of faith what is the secret of success? Has our Psalm any light on that point? By what method did the poet still the turmoil of his doubt and reach his great peace? The process is finely pictured in a homely but exquisite image: "Like a weaned child on its mother, like a weaned child is my soul within me." What does that mean? Torn by an insatiable longing to know the meaning of God's mysterious ways, he had struggled fiercely to wring an answer from the Almighty. His heart was long the abode of unrest, and storm, and tempest. At length peace falls on the fray; there is no more clangour of contention: all is quietness and rest. How is this? Has he succeeded in solving the enigmas that pained him? Have his cravings for an answer from God been gratified? If not, how has he attained this perfect repose? His peace is the peace of a weaned child. Not, therefore, by obtaining that which he craved has he found rest; for the rest of a weaned child is not that of gratification, but of resignation. It is the repose, not of satisfied desire, but of abnegation and submission. After a period of prolonged and painful struggle to have its longings answered, the little one gives over striving any more, and is at peace. That process was a picture to our poet of what passed in his own heart. Like a weaned child, its tears over, its cries hushed, reposing on the very bosom that a little ago excited its most tumultuous desires, his soul, that once passionately strove to wring from God an answer to its eager questionings, now wearied, resigned, and submissive, just lays itself to rest in simple faith on that goodness of God whose purposes it cannot comprehend, and whose ways often seem to it harsh, and ravelled, and obscure. It is a picture of infinite repose and of touching beauty—the little one nestling close in the mother's arms, its head reclining trustfully on her shoulder, the tears dried from its now quiet face, and the restful eyes, with just a lingering shadow of bygone sorrow in them still, peering out with a look of utter peace, contentment, and security. It is the peace of accepted pain, the victory of self-surrender.

The transition from doubt to belief, from strife to serenity, is remarkable. We want to know what produced this startling change of mood, what influences fostered it, what motives urged it, what reasons justified it. Perhaps a glimpse, a suggestion of the process is hinted in the simile chosen from child life. The infant takes its rest on the breast of its mother—of its mother, whose refusal of its longings caused it all the pain and conflict, whose denial of its instinctive desires seemed so unnatural and so cruel. How is it, then, that instead of being alienated, the child turns to her for solace in the sorrow she caused, and reposes on the very breast that so resolutely declined to supply its wants? It is because over against this single act of seeming unkindness stand unnumbered deeds of goodness and acts of fondness, and so this one cause of doubt and of aversion is swallowed up in a whole atmosphere of unceasing tenderness and love. Besides, rating the apparent unmotherliness at the very highest, still there is no other to whom the child can turn that will better help it and care for it than its mother. So, since it cannot get all it would like, the little one is content to take what it may have—the warmth, and shelter, and security of its mother's breast.

This process of conflict between doubt and trust, rebellion and resignation, which half-unconsciously takes place in the child, is a miniature of the strife that had surged to and fro in the poet's soul. Pained and perplexed by the mystery of God's ways, foiled in his efforts to fathom them, denied all explanation by the Almighty, he was beset by the temptation to abandon faith and cast off his allegiance to his heavenly Friend. But he saw that that would not solve any enigma or lighten the darkness. Rather it would confront him with still greater difficulties, and leave the world only more empty, dark, and dreary. Then, benumbed and tired out, he gave over thinking and arguing, and was content for a little just to live in the circle of light and sunshine that ever is within the great darkness. Gradually it dawned upon him that in the world of men's experience there was much, very much, of goodness that could only be the doing of the God that moves in the mystery and in the darkness. The warmth of the thought crept into his heart, softer feelings woke, love and lowliness asserted themselves, and at length he became content to just trust God, spite of all perplexities, partly because there was so much undeniable proof of His tenderness, and partly because there was more of rest and comfort in this course than in any other.

FIFTH SUNDAY.
Read Gen. xxxii., and Rev. vii.

THE RECOMPENSE OF FAITH.
"Let Israel hope in the Lord from henceforth and for ever."

Who has not wondered why there is so much mystery in the universe, such perplexity in our life, and in revelation itself why so many doubts are permitted to assail our souls and make it hard for us to be Christians? Is this wisely or kindly ordered? Perchance it is necessary, but is it not evil? Can warfare ever be aught but loss and not gain? The question is natural, but the answer is not uncertain. The fight of faith is a good fight. Success means no bare victory, but one crowned with splendid spoil. We shall be the better for having had to fight. The gain of the conflict shall out-weigh all the loss, and in the final triumph the victors shall manifestly appear more than conquerors. This is no paradox, but the common law of life. The same principle rules in the homely image of the child. Weaning is not needless pain, is not wasted suffering. It is a blessing in disguise. The distressing process is in truth promotion. It is the vestibule of pain that leads to a maturer and larger life. In like fashion the struggles of doubt are inevitable, if faith is not to remain feeble and infantile. Only in the furnace of affliction does it acquire its finest qualities. Were there no clouds and darkness around God's throne, how should men learn humility and practise reverence? Human nature is too coarse a thing to be entrusted with perfect knowledge. A religion of knowledge only were a hard and soulless thing, devoid of grace, and life, and love; for sight and reason leave nothing for the imagination, and rob affection of its sweet prerogative to dream and to adore. Without the discipline of toil and the developing strain of antagonism, how should faith grow strong, and broad, and deep? Most of us start in the life religious with an inherited, fostered, unreasoning belief, which therefore is weak, puny, and unstable. It is the storms of doubt and difficulty that rouse it to self-consciousness, stir it to activity, urge it by exertion to growth and expansion, and compel it to strike deep roots in the soil of reality. For in such conflict the soul is driven in upon God. It is forced to make actual proof of its possessions, to realise and employ properties that hitherto were known to it only through the title-deeds or as mere assets available in case of necessity. With wonder faith discovers the rare value of its inheritance, and enters for the first time into actual enjoyment of its spiritual treasures. It is no longer faith about God, but is now faith in God. In its agony and helplessness the soul is compelled to press close up to God, to take tighter hold of His hand, to fling itself on Him for help and comfort, just as a sick child clings to its mother. And ever after such a struggle there are a fresh beauty and sacredness in its relation to God. There is that pathetic tenderness of affection friends have who by some misunderstanding were well-nigh sundered, but having overcome it, are nearer and dearer to each other than ever before. There are a quiet community of knowledge, and a restful confidentiality of affection, that were not there before, that come of having had to fight that you might not be severed from each other. The recoil of joy from the dread of loss, and the memory of the agony that thought was to you, make God dearer to you now than ever. Out of the very strife and doubt there is born a new assurance of your love, in the consciousness you have acquired of the pain it would be to you to be deprived of your Divine Friend.

The experience is of general application. It is the secret of serenity amid the world's mystery and life's pain and perplexity. Therefore, when at any time the clouds gather around you, and their blackness seems to darken on the very face of God, do not turn away in terror or anger, but cling the faster to Him, even if it be by the extreme hem of His garment. What wonder if your feeble eye fails to read clear and true each majestic feature of that Divine face which is so infinitely high above you? What matter if sometimes its radiance is obscured by the chill fogs and creeping vapours of earth's mingled atmosphere? The darkness is not on God's face, but beneath it. One day you shall rise higher, and you shall see Him as He is. Meantime, in your gloomiest hour, when overwhelming doubts, like hissing waves, wind and coil around your heart, and seek to pluck it from its hold, then do but let all other things go, and with your last energy cling to this central, sovereign certainty, that whatever else is true, this at least is sure, that God is good, and that He whose doings you cannot comprehend is your Father. And so, weary of dashing yourself vainly against the bulwarks of darkness that girdle His throne, be content to lay yourself down humbly as a tired child on the breast of your heavenly Father. Thus, with your questionings unanswered, with the darkness not rolled away, with a thousand problems all unsolved, be quieted, be hushed, be at peace. Lay down your head, your weary, aching head, on the great heart of God, and be at rest.

Doing this, you shall reach not merely passive resignation, but joy, and peace, and trust. For of humble submission hope is born. "Let Israel hope in the Lord from henceforth and for ever." Perchance all you can do now is just, in weariness, more out of helpless despair than active expectancy, to fall back on a faint, broken-hearted trust in God's goodness. It is an act of faith, poor enough, in truth, but it holds in it the promise and potency of a better confidence. For it is into the arms of God that it carries you. Resting there in the lap of His infinite love, you shall feel the warmth of His great heart penetrating softly into yours. The weary, throbbing pain will slowly pass away. Deep rest and quiet peace will steal into your spirit. And at length, out of a helpless, compelled, and well-nigh hopeless surrender, there shall be born within you fearless trust and winged reliance, and you shall hope in the Lord from henceforth and for ever.

XVII.
The First Chapter of Genesis.

THERE is in many people's minds a painful uneasiness about the relation of the Bible to modern science and philosophy. The appearance of each new theory is deprecated by believers with pious timidity, and hailed by sceptics with unholy hope. On neither side is this a dignified or a wholesome attitude. Its irksome and intrusive pressure promotes neither a robust piety nor a sober-minded science. It is worth while inquiring whether there is any sufficient foundation for either alarm or expectancy in the actual relations of the Bible to scientific thought. We shall work out our answer to the question on the historical battle-field of the 1st chapter of Genesis. Results reached there will be found to possess a more or less general validity.

There are two records of creation—one is contained in the Bible, which claims to be God's Word; the other is stamped in the structure of the world, which is God's work. Both being from the same Author, we should expect them to agree in their general tenour; but in fact, so far from being in harmony, they have an appearance of mutual contradiction that demands explanation.

In studying the problem certain considerations must be borne in mind. There is a loose way of talking about antagonism between the natural and the revealed accounts of creation. That is not quite accurate. Conflict between these there cannot be, for they never actually come into contact. It is not they, but our theories, that meet and collide. The discord is not in the original sources, but in our renderings of them. That is a very different matter, and of quite incommensurate importance.

The Bible story is very old. It is written in an ancient and practically dead language. The meaning of many of the words cannot be fixed with precision. The significance of several fundamental phrases is at best little more than conjecture. Since it was penned men's minds have grown and changed. The very moulds of human thought have altered. Current impressions, conceptions, ideas are different. It is hard to determine, with even probability, what is said, still harder to realise what was thought. Certainty is impossible. No rendering should be counted infallible, not even our own. Every interpretation ought to be advanced with modest diffidence, held tentatively, revised with alacrity, and adjusted to new facts without timidity and without shame. This has not been the characteristic attitude of commentators. The exegesis of the 1st chapter of Genesis presents a long array of theories, propounded with authority, defended dogmatically, and ignominiously discredited and deserted. Had a more lowly spirit presided over their inception, maintenance, and abandonment, the list would perhaps not have been shorter, but the retrospect would have been less humiliating. As it is, we can hardly complain of the sting of satire that lurks in Kepler's recital of Theology's successive retreats: "In theology we balance authorities; in philosophy we weigh reasons. A holy man was Lactantius, who denied that the earth was round. A holy man was Augustine, who granted the rotundity, but denied the antipodes. A holy thing to me is the Inquisition, which allows the smallness of the earth, but denies its motion. But more holy to me is truth. And hence I prove by philosophy that the earth is round, inhabited on every side, of small size, and in motion among the stars. And this I do with no disrespect to the doctors."

The physical record is also very old. Its story is carved in a script that is often hardly legible, and set forth in symbols that are not easy to decipher. The testimony of the rocks embodies results of creation, but does not present the actual operations. Effects suggest processes, but do not disclose their precise measure, manner, and origination. You may dissect a great painting into its ultimate lines and elements, and from the canvas peel off the successive layers of colour, and duly record their number and order; but when you have done you have not even touched the essential secret of its creation. In determining the first origin of things the limitation of science is absolute, and even in tracing the subsequent development there is room for error, ignorance, and diversity of explanation. Of certainties in scientific theory there are few. For the most part, all that can be attained is probability, especially in speculative matters, such as estimates of time, explanations of formation, and theories of causation. As in exegesis, so in geology, all hypotheses ought to be counted merely tentative, maintained with modesty, and held open at every point to revision and reconstruction. The necessity of caution and reserve needs no enforcing for any one who knows the variety and inconsistency of the phases through which speculative geology has passed in our own generation. In this destiny of transitoriness it does but share the lot of all scientific theory.

Professor Huxley was once cruel enough to call attention to the fact that "extinguished theologians lie about the cradle of every science, as the strangled snakes beside that of Hercules." The statement is a graphic, if somewhat ferocious, reminder of a melancholy fact, and the fate of these trespassing divines should warn their successors—as the Professor means it should—not to stray out of their proper pastures. But has it fared very differently with the mighty men of science who have essayed to solve the high problems of existence and to make all mysteries plain? Take up a history of philosophy, turn over its pages, study its dreary epitomes of defunct theories, and as you survey the long array of skeletons tell me, are you not reminded of the prophet who found himself "set down in the midst of the valley which was full of dry bones: and, behold, there were very many in the open valley; and, lo, they were very dry"?

If it is human to err, theology and geology have alike made full proof of their humanity. That in itself is not their fault, but their misfortune. The pity of it is that to the actual fact of fallibility they have so often added the folly of pretended infallibility. The resultant duty is an attitude of mutual modesty, of reserve in suspecting contradiction, of patience in demanding an adjustment, of perseverance in separate and honest research, of serenity of mind in view of difficulties, coupled with a quiet expectation of final fitting. The two accounts are alike trustworthy. They are not necessarily identical in detail. It is enough that they should correspond in their essential purport. It may be that the one is the complement of the other, as soul is to body—unlike, yet vitally allied. Perchance their harmony is not that of duplicates, but of counterparts. They were made not to overlap like concentric circles, but to interlock like toothed wheels. In the end, when partial knowledge has given way to perfect, they will be seen to correspond, and nothing will be broken but the premature structures of adjustment with which men have thought to make them run smoother than they were meant to do.

To attempt anew a task that has proved so disastrous, and is manifestly so difficult, must be admitted to be bold, if not even foolhardy. But its very desperateness is its justification. To fall in a forlorn hope is not ignoble. To miss one's way in threading the labyrinth of the 1st chapter of Genesis is pardonable, a thing almost to be expected. If in seeking to escape Scylla the traveller should fall into Charybdis, no one will be surprised—not even himself. It is in the most undogmatic spirit that we wish to put forward our reading of the chapter. It is presented simply as a possible rendering. What can be said for it will be said as forcibly as may be. It is open to objection from opposite sides. That may be not altogether against it, since truth is rarely extreme. Difficulties undoubtedly attach to it, and defects as well. At best it can but contribute to the ultimate solution. Perchance its share in the task may be no more than to show by trial that another way of explanation is impossible. Well, that too is a service. Every fresh by-way proved impracticable, and closed to passage, brings us a step nearer the pathway of achievement. For the loyal lover of truth it is enough even so to have been made tributary to the truth.

The business of a theologian is, in the first instance at least, with the Scriptural narrative. To estimate its worth, and determine its relation to science, we must ascertain its design. Criticism of a church-organ, under the impression that it was meant to do the work of a steam-engine, would certainly fail to do justice to the instrument, and the disquisition would not have much value in itself. Before we exact geology of Genesis we must inquire whether there is any in it. If there be none, and if there was never meant to be any, the demand is as absurd as it would be to require thorns of a vine and thistles of the fig-tree. Should it turn out, for instance, that the order of the narrative is intentionally not chronological, then every attempt to reconcile it with the geological order is of necessity a Procrustean cruelty, and the venerable form of Genesis is fitted to the geological couch at the cost of its head or its feet. Either the natural sense of the chapter is sacrificed or the pruned narrative goes on crutches. If we would deal fairly and rationally with the Bible account of creation, our first duty is to determine with exactness what it purposes to tell, and what it does not profess to relate. We must settle with precision, at the outset of our investigation, what is its subject, method, and intention. The answer is to be found, not in *a priori* theories of what the contents ought to be, but in an accurate and honest analysis of the chapter.

The narrative of creation is marked by an exquisite symmetry of thought and style. It is partly produced by the regular use of certain rubrical phrases, which recur with the rhythmical effect of a refrain. There is the terminal of the days—"and there was evening, and there was morning, day one," etc.; the embodiment of the Divine creative will in the eightfold "God said;" the expression of instant fulfilment in the swift responsive "and it was so;" and the declaration of perfection in the "God saw that it was good." But the symmetry of the chapter lies deeper than the wording. It pervades the entire construction of the narrative. As the story proceeds there is expansion, variety, progression. Yet each successive paragraph is built up on one and the same type and model. This uniformity is rooted in the essential structure of the thought, and is due to the determination with which one grand truth is carried like a key-note through all the sequences of the theme, and rings out clear and dominant in every step and stage of the development. Our first duty is to follow, and find out with certainty, this ruling purpose, and then to interpret the subordinate elements by its light and guidance.

The narrative distributes the operation of creation over six days, and divides it into eight distinct acts or deeds. This double divergent arrangement of the material is made to harmonise by the assignment of a couple of acts to the third day, and another couple to the sixth—in each case with a fine and designed effect. We shall take a bird's-eye view of the contents of these divisions.

The chapter opens with a picture of primeval chaos, out of which God commands the universe of beauty, life, and order. Nothing is said of its origin. The story starts with it existent. It is painted as an abyss, dreary and boundless, wrapped in impenetrable darkness, an inextricable confusion of fluid matter, destitute of character, structure, or value, without form and void. It is the raw material of the universe, passive and powerless in itself, but holding in it the promise and potency of all existence. For over it nestles, like a brood fowl, the informing, warming, life-giving Spirit of God, sending through its coldness and emptiness the heat and parental yearnings of the Divine heart, that craves for creatures on which to pour out its love and goodness. This action of the Spirit is, however, no more than preparative, and waits its completion in the accession of a personal fiat of God's will, in which the Divine Word gives effect and reality to the Divine Wish. This is a feature of supreme importance, for in it consists the uniqueness of the Bible narrative. In the Pagan accounts of creation we find the same general imagery of dull, dead matter, stirred and warmed into life and development by the action of an immaterial effluence of "thought," "love," or "longing." But in them the operation is cosmic, impersonal, often hardly conscious; in the Bible it is ethical and intensely personal. In them the language is metaphysical, materialistic, or pantheistic; here it is moral, human, personal, to the point of anthropomorphism. They show us creative forces and processes; the Bible presents to us, in all His infinite, manifold, and glorious personality, the thinking, living, loving "God the Father Almighty, Maker of heaven and earth."

The result of the first day and the first Divine decree is the production of light. The old difficulty about the existence of light before the sun was made, as it was invented by science, has been by science dispelled. The theory of light as a mode of motion, which for the present holds the field, knows no obstacle to the presence of light in the absence of the sun. But this harmony is not due to any prescience of modern science in the writer of Genesis. His idea of light is not undulatory, and not scientific, but just the simple popular notion found everywhere in the Bible. Light is a fine substance, distinct from all others, and it appears first in the list of creation, as being the first and noblest of the elements that go to make up our habitable world. The emergence of the light is presented as instantaneously following the Divine decree. That is manifestly the literary effect designed in the curtness of the sequence, "Let there be light, and there was light." The light is pronounced good, is permanently established in possession of its special properties and powers, and is set in its service of the world and man by having assigned to it its place in the "alternate mercy of day and night." There is a very fine touch in the position of the declaration of goodness. It stands here earlier than in the succeeding sections. Darkness is in the Bible the standing emblem of evil. It would have been discordant with that imagery to make God pronounce it good, though as the foil of light it serves beneficent ends. The jarring note is tacitly and simply avoided by introducing the assertion of the goodness of light before the mention of its background and negation, darkness. The picture of the first day of creation is subscribed with the formula of completeness—"There was evening, and there was morning, one day," or "day first"—and has for its net result the production of the element or sphere of light.

The second day and the second Divine decree are devoted to the formation of the firmament. All through the Old Testament the sky is pictured as a solid dome or vaulted roof, above which roll the primeval waters of chaos. The notion is of course popular, a figment of the primitive imagination, and quite at variance with the modern conception of space filled by an interastral ether;

though it is well to remember that this same ether is no more ascertained fact than was the old-world firmament, and is in its turn simply an invention of the scientific imagination. It is of more moment to note that the real motive and outcome of the day's work is not the firmament. That is not an end, but a means, precisely as a sea-wall is not an object in itself, but merely the instrument of the reclamation of valuable land. What the erection of the firmament does towards the making of our world is the production of the intervening aërial space and the lower expanse of terrestrial waters. Since this last portion of the work is not complete prior to the separation of the dry land, the declaration of goodness or perfection is, with exquisite fineness of suggestion, tacitly omitted. The net result of the day is, therefore, the formation of the realms of air and water as elements or spheres of existence.

The third day includes two works—the production of the solid ground, and of vegetation. The dead, inert soil, and its manifold outgrowth of plant life, are strikingly distinct, and yet most intimately related. Together they make up the habitable earth. They are therefore presented as separate works, but conjoined in the framework of one day. Two sections of the vegetable kingdom are singled out for special mention—the cereals and the fruit-trees. It is not a complete or a botanical classification, and manifestly science is not contemplated. Those divisions of the plant-world that sustain animal and human life, and minister to its enjoyment, are drawn out into pictorial relief and prominence. The intention is practical, popular, and religious. The net result of the day is the production of the habitable dry land.

The fourth day and the fifth decree call into being the celestial bodies—the sun, moon, and stars. They are called luminaries; that is to say, not masses or accumulations of light, but managers and distributers of light, and the value of this function of theirs, for the religious and secular calendar, for agriculture, navigation, and the daily life of men, is formally and elaborately detailed. Were this account of the heavenly bodies intended as a scientific or exhaustive statement of their Divine destination and place in the universe, it would be miserably inadequate and erroneous. But if the whole aim of the narrative be not science, but religion, then it is absolutely appropriate, exact, and powerful. In the teeth of an all but universal worship of sun, moon, and stars, it declares them the manufacture of God, and the ministers and servants of man. For this practical religious purpose the geocentric description of them is not an accident, but essential. It is not a blunder, but a merit. It is true piety, not cosmical astronomy, that is being established. In the words of Calvin, "Moses, speaking to us by the Holy Spirit, did not treat of the heavenly luminaries as an astronomer, but as it became a theologian, having regard to us rather than to the stars." The net result of the fourth day is the production of the heavenly orbs of light.

The fifth day and the sixth work issue in the production of birds and fishes, or, more accurately, all creatures that fly or swim. It is evidently a classification by the eye—the ordinary popular division—and it makes no attempt at scientific pretension or profundity. As having conscious life, these new creatures of God's love are blessed by Him, and have their place and purpose in the order of being defined and established. The net result of the day is the formation of fowls and fishes.

The sixth day, like the third, includes two works—the land animals and man. The representation admirably expresses their intimate relationship, and yet essential distinction. The animals are graphically divided into the domestic quadrupeds, the small creatures that creep and crawl, and the wild beasts of the field. The classification is as little scientific in intention or substance as is the general arrangement into birds, fishes, and beasts, which of course traverses radically alike the historical order of palæontology and the physiological grouping of zoology. The narrative simply adopts the natural grouping of observation and popular speech, because that suffices, and best suits its purpose. With a wonderful simplicity, yet with consummate effect, man is portrayed as the climax and crown of creation. Made in the image and likeness of God, he is clothed with sovereign might and dominion over all the elements and contents of Nature. The personal, conscious counterpart and child of God, he stands at the other end of the chain of creation, and with answering intelligence and love looks back adoringly to his great Father in the heavens. Mention is made of lesser matters, such as sex and food; but manifestly the supreme interest of the delineation is ethical and religious. Science is no more contemplated as an ingredient in the conception than prose is in poetry. With the making of man the circle of creation is complete, and the finished perfection of the whole, as well as the parts, is expressed in the superlative declaration that "God saw everything that He had made, and, behold, it was very good." The net result of the sixth day is the formation of the land animals and man.

The six days of creative activity are followed by a seventh of Divine repose. On the seventh day God rested; or, as it is more fully worded in Exodus (xxxi. 17), God "rested and was refreshed." It is a daring anthropomorphism, and at the same time a master-stroke of inspired genius. What a philosophical dissertation hardly could accomplish it achieves by one simple image. For our thought of God the idea performs the same service as the institution of the Sabbath does for our souls and bodies. The weekly day of rest is the salvation of our personality from enslavement in material toil. During six days the toiler is tied, bent and bowed, to his post in the vast machinery of the world's work. On the seventh all is stopped, and he is free to lift himself erect to the full stature of his manhood, to expand the loftier elements of his being, to reassert his freedom, and realise his superiority over what is mechanical, secular, and earthly. What in the progressive portraiture of creation is the effect of this sudden declaration that the Creator rested? Why, an intensely powerful reminder of the free, conscious, and personal nature of His action. And this impression of such unique value is secured precisely by the anthropomorphism, as no philosophical disquisition could have done it. The blot and blemish of all metaphysical delineation is that personalities get obliterated and swallowed up in general principles and impersonal abstractions. In all other cosmogonies of any intellectual pretension the process of creation is presented as passive, or Necessitarian, or Pantheistic, and invariably the free personality of the Creator becomes entangled in His work, or entirely vanishes. By this stroke of inspired imagination the Bible story rescues from all such risks and degradations our thought of the Creator, and at its close leaves us face to face with our Divine Maker as free, personal, living, loving, and conscious as we are ourselves.

We have now got what is, I trust, a fairly accurate and complete summary of the contents of the narrative. It is not necessary for our purpose to discuss its relations to the Pagan cosmogonies. From the sameness everywhere of the human eye, mind, and fancy, certain conceptions are common property. There is probably a special kinship between the Biblical and the Babylonian and Phœnician accounts. But with all respect for enthusiastic decipherers, we make bold to believe, with more sober-minded critics, that the 1st chapter of Genesis owes very little to Babylonian mythology, and very much indeed to Hebrew thought and the revealing Spirit of God. The chapter strikingly lacks the characteristic marks of myth, and is on the face of it a masterpiece of exquisite artistic workmanship and profound religious inspiration. Proof of this has appeared in plenty during our brief study of its structure and contents. Let us proceed to use the results of our analysis to determine some more general characteristics of its structure and design.

The process of creation is portrayed in six great steps or stages. Is this order put forward as corresponding with the physical course of events? and, further, does it tally with the order stamped in the record of the rocks? Replying to the second question first, it must be admitted that, *primâ facie*, the Bible sequence does not appear to be in unison with the geological. Of attempted reconciliations there is an almost endless variety, but, unfortunately, among the harmonies themselves there is no harmony. At the present moment there is none that has gained general acceptance: a few possess each the allegiance of a handful of partisans; the greater number command the confidence only of their respective authors, and some not even that. It is needless to discuss these reconciliations, because if geology is trustworthy in its main results, and if our interpretation of the meaning of Genesis is at all correct, correspondence in order and detail is impossible. If the order of Genesis was meant as science, then geology and Genesis are at issue; but, on the other hand, if the sequence in Genesis was never meant to be physical the wrong lies with ourselves, who have searched for geology where we should have looked for religion, and have, with the best intentions, persisted in trying to turn the Bible bread of life into the arid stone of science. Now, we venture to suggest that in drafting this chapter the ruling formative thought was not chronology. It must be remembered that the narrative was under no obligation to follow the order of actual occurrence, unless that best suited its purpose. Zoology does not group the animals in the order of their emergence into existence, but classifies and discusses them in a very different sequence, adopted to exhibit their structural and functional affinities. If the design of Genesis was not to inform us about historical geology, but to reveal and enforce religious truth, it might well be that a literary or a logical, and not a chronological, arrangement might best serve its end. As a matter of fact, the order chosen is not primarily historical. Another quite different and very beautiful idea has fashioned, and is enshrined in, the arrangement. Looking at our analysis of their contents, we perceive that the six days fall into two parallel sets of three, whose members finely correspond. The first set presents us with three vast empty tenements or habitations, and the second set furnishes these with occupants. The first day gives us the sphere of light; the fourth day tenants it with sun, moon, and stars. The second day presents the realm of air and water; the fifth day supplies the inhabitants—birds and fishes. The third day produces the habitable dry land; and the sixth day stocks it with the animals and man. The idea of this arrangement is, on the face of it, literary and logical. It is chosen for its comprehensive, all-inclusive completeness. To declare of every part and atom of Nature that it is the making of God, the author passes in procession the great elements or spheres which the human mind everywhere conceives as making up our world, and pronounces them one by one God's creation. Then he makes an inventory of their entire furniture and contents, and asserts that all these likewise are the work of God. For his purpose—which is to declare the universal Creatorship of God and the uniform creaturehood of all Nature—the order and classification are unsurpassed and unsurpassable. With a masterly survey, that marks everything and omits nothing, he sweeps the whole category of created existence, collects the scattered leaves into six congruous groups, encloses each in a compact and uniform binding, and then on the back of the numbered and ordered volumes stamps the great title and declaration that they are one and all, in every jot, and tittle, and shred, and fragment, the works of their Almighty Author, and of none beside.

With the figment of a supposed physical order vanishes also the difficulty of the days. Their use is not literal, but ideal and pictorial. That the author was not thinking of actual days of twenty-four hours, with a matter-of-fact dawning of morning and darkening of evening, is evident from the fact that he does not bring the sun (the lord of the day) into action till three have already elapsed, and later on he exhibits the sun as itself the product of one of them. Neither is it possible that the days stand for geological epochs, for by no wrenching and racking can they be made to correspond. Moreover, it is quite certain that the author would have revolted against the expansion of his timeless acts of creative omnipotence into long ages of slow evolution, since the key-note of the literary significance and sublimity of his delineation is its exhibition of the created result following in instantaneous sequence on the creative fiat. The actual meaning underlying the use of the days is suggested in the rubrical character of the refrain, as it appears rounding off and ending each fresh stage of the narration—"And there was evening, and there was morning—day one, day two, day three," and so on. The great sections of Nature are to be made pass in a panorama of pictures, and to be presented, each for itself, as the distinct act of God. It is desirable to enclose each of these pictures in a frame, clear-cut and complete. The natural unit and division of human toil is a day. In the words of the poet—

> "Each morning sees some task begin;
> Each evening sees it close."

In Old Testament parlance, any great achievement or outstanding event is spoken of as "a day." A decisive battle is known as "the day of Midian." God's intervention in human history is "the day of the Lord." When the author of Genesis i. would present the several elements of Nature as one and all the outcome of God's creative energy, the successive links of the chain are depicted as days. Where we should say "End of Part I.," he says, "And there was evening, and there was morning—day one." Moreover, it is needless to point out how finely, from this presentation of the timeless flats of creation in a framework of days, emerges the majestic truth that not in the dead order of nature, nor in the mere movement of the stars, but in the nature and will of God, Who made man in His image, must be sought the ultimate origin, sanction, and archetype of that salutary law which divides man's life on earth into fixed periods of toil, rounded and crowned by a Sabbath of repose.

If this understanding of the structural arrangement of the chapter be correct, we have reached an important and significant conclusion regarding the author's method and design. He does not suppose himself to be giving the matter-of-fact sequence of creation's stages. His interest does not lie in that direction. His sole concern is to declare that Nature, in bulk and in detail, is the manufacture of God. His plan does not include, but *ipso facto* excludes, conformity with the material order and process. He writes as a theologian, and not as a scientist or historian. Starting from this fixed point, let us note the outstanding features and engrossing interests of his delineation. We shall find them in the phrases that, like a refrain, run through the narrative and form its key-notes, and finally in the resultant impression left by its general tenour and purport.

The recurrent key-notes of the narrative are three—God's naming His works, His declaration of their goodness, and the swift formula of achievement—"and it was so." The naming is not a childish triviality, nor a mere graphic touch or poetical ornament. It does not mean that God attached to His works the vocables by which in Hebrew they are known. Its significance appears in the definition of function into which in the later episodes it is expanded. Name in Hebrew speech is equivalent to Nature. When the story pictures God as naming His works, it vividly brings into relief the fixed law and order that pervade the universe. And by the picturesque—if you will, anthropomorphic—fashion of the statement, it attains an effect beyond science or metaphysics, inasmuch as it irresistibly portrays this order of Nature as originating in the personal act of God, and directly inspired by and informed with His own effluent love of what is good, and true, and orderly. Thus the great truth of the fixity of Nature is presented, not as a fact of science or a quality of matter, but as rooted in and reflecting a majestic attribute of the character of God. The interest is not scientific, but religious. In like fashion, the unfailing declaration of goodness, though it might seem a small detail, is replete with practical and religious significance. The Pagan doctrines of creation are all more or less contaminated by dualistic or Manichean conceptions. The good Creator is baffled, thwarted, and impeded by a brutish or malignant tendency in matter, which on the one hand mars the perfection of creation, and on the other hand inserts in the physical order of things elements of hostility and malevolence to man. It is a thought that at once degrades the Creator, and denudes Nature, as man's abode, of its beauty, comfort, and kindliness. How different is it in the Bible picture of creation! This God has outside Himself no rival, experiences no resistance nor contradiction, knows no failure nor imperfection in His handiwork; but what He wishes He wills, and what He commands is done, and the result answers absolutely to the intention of His wisdom, love, and power. In its relation to its Maker the work is free from any flaw. In its relation to man it contains nothing malevolent or maleficent. It is good. And once again, mark with what skill in the delineation the light is thrown, not on the work, but on the Worker, and the goodness of creation becomes but a mirror to drink in and flash forth the infinite wisdom, might, and goodness of its Divine Maker. Here also the interest is not metaphysical, but practical and religious. A third commanding aim of the narrative appears in the significant and striking use of the formula "and it was so." With absolute uniformity the Divine fiat is immediately followed by the physical fulfilment. There is no painting of the process, no delineation of slow and gradual operations of material forces. Not once is there any mention of secondary causes, nor the faintest suggestion of intermediate agencies. The Creator wills; the thing is. In this exclusion from the scene of all subordinate studies there is artistic design—profound design. The picture becomes one, not of scenery, but of action. It is not a landscape, but a portrait. The canvas contains but two solitary objects, the Creator and His work. The effect is to throw out of sight methods, materials, processes, and to throw into intense relief the act and the Actor. And the supreme and ultimate result on the beholder's mind is to produce a quite overpowering and majestic impression of the glorious personality of the Creator.

Here we have reached the sovereign theme of the narrative, and have detected the false note that is struck at the outset of every attempt to interpret it as in any degree or fashion a physical record of creation. In very deed and truth the concern of the chapter is not creation, but the character, being, and glory of the Almighty Maker. If we excerpt God's speeches and the rubrical formulas, the chapter consists of one continuous chain of verbs, instinct with life and motion, linked on in swift succession, and with hardly an exception, the subject of every one of them is God. It is one long adoring delineation of God loving, yearning, willing, working in creation. Its interest is not in the work, but the Worker. Its subject is not creation, but the Creator. What it gives is not a world, but a God. It is not geology; it is theology.

Why do we so assert, accentuate, and reiterate this to be the central theme of the chapter? Because through the scientific trend and bias of modern inquiry the essential design of the chapter has got warped, cramped, and twisted till its majestic features have been pushed almost clean out of view, and all attention is concentrated on one trivial, mean, and unreal point in its physiognomy. Its claim to be accounted an integral part of a real revelation is made to hinge on its magical anticipation of, and detailed correspondence with, the changeful theories of modern geology. The idea is, in our humble but decided opinion, dangerous, baseless, and indefensible. The chapter may not forestall one single scientific discovery. It may not tally with one axiom or dogma of geology. Nevertheless, it remains a unique, undeniable, and glorious monument of revelation, second only in worth and splendour to the record of God's incarnation of His whole heart and being in the person of Jesus

Christ, our Lord and Redeemer. Consider what this chapter has actually accomplished in the world, and set that against all theories of what it ought to be doing. For our knowledge of the true God and the realisation of mankind's higher life it has done a work beside which any question of correspondence or non-correspondence with science sinks into unmentionable insignificance. Place side by side with it the chiefest and best of the Pagan cosmogonies, and appreciate its sweetness, purity, and elevation over against their grotesqueness, their shallowness, and their degradation alike of the human and the Divine. Realise the world whose darkness they reecho, the world into which emerged this radiant picture of God's glory and man's dignity, and think what it has done for that poor world. It found heaven filled with a horde of gods, monstrous, impure, and horrible, gigantic embodiments of brute force and lust, or at best cold abstractions of cosmical principles, whom men could fear, but not love, honour, or revere. It found man in a world dark and unhomelike, bowing down in abject worship to beasts and birds, and stocks and stones, trembling with craven cowardice before the elements and forces of Nature, enslaved in a degrading bondage of physical superstition, fetishism, and polytheism. With one sweep of inspired might the truth enshrined in this chapter has changed all that, wherever it has come. It has cleansed the heaven of those foul gods and monstrous worships, and leaves men on bended knees in the presence of the one true God, their Father in heaven, who made the world for their use, and them for Himself, and whose tender mercies are over all His works. From moral and mental slavery it has emancipated man, for it has taken the physical objects of his fear and worship, and dashing them down from their usurped pre-eminence, has put them all under his feet, to be his ministers and servants in working out on earth his eternal destiny. These conceptions of God, Man, and Nature have been the regeneration of humanity; the springs of progress in science, invention, and civilisation; the charter of the dignity of human life, and the foundation of liberty, virtue, and religion. The man who, in view of such a record, can ask with anxious concern whether a revelation carrying in its bosom such a wealth of heavenly truth does not also have concealed in its shoe a bird's-eye view of geology must surely be a man blind to all literary likelihood, destitute of any sense of congruity and the general fitness of things, and cannot but seem to us as one that mocks. The chapter's title to be reckoned a revelation rests on no such magical and recondite quality, but is stamped four-square on the face of its essential character and contents. Whence could this absolutely unique conception of God, in His relation to the world and man, have been derived, except from God Himself? Whence into a world so dark, and void, and formless did it emerge fair and radiant? There is no answer but one. God said, "Let there be light; and there was light."

The specific revelation of the 1st chapter of Genesis must be sought in its moral and spiritual contents. But may there not be, in addition, worked into its material framework, some anticipation of scientific truths that have since come to light? What were the good of it, when the Divine message could be wholly and better expressed by the sole use of popular language, intelligible in every age and by all classes? Is it dignified to depict the Spirit of Inspiration standing on tiptoe, and straining to speak, across the long millenniums and over the head of the world's childhood, to the wise and learned scientists of the nineteenth century? It is never the manner of Scripture to anticipate natural research or to forestall human industry. God means men to discover physical truth from the great book of Nature. What truth of science, what mechanical invention, what beneficent discovery in medicine, agriculture, navigation, or any other art or industry, has ever been gleaned from study of the Bible? Not one. These things lie outside the scope of revelation, and God is the God of order. Moreover, in Scripture itself the framework of the chapter is not counted dogmatic nor uniformly adhered to. In the 2nd chapter of Genesis, in Job, in the Psalms, and in Proverbs there are manifold deviations and variations. The material setting is handled with the freedom applicable to the pictorial dress of a parable, wherein things transcendental are depicted in earthly symbols. In truth, this is essentially the character of the composition. We have seen that the delineation, classification, and arrangement are not scientific and not philosophical, but popular, practical, and religious. It is everywhere manifest that the interest is not in the process of creation, but in the fact of its origination in God. While science lingers on the physical operation, Genesis designedly overleaps it, for the same reason that the Gospels do not deign to suggest the material substratum of Christ's miracles. Creation is a composite process. It begins in the spiritual world, and terminates in the material. It is in its first stage supernatural, in its second natural. It originates in God desiring, decreeing, issuing formative force; it proceeds in matter moving, cohering, moulding, and shaping. Revelation and science regard it from opposite ends. The one looks at it from its beginning, the other from its termination. The Bible shows us God creating; geology shows us the world being created. Scripture deals solely with the first stage, science solely with the second. Where Scripture stops, there science first begins. Contradiction, conflict, collision are impossible. In the words of the Duke of Argyll, "The 1st chapter of Genesis stands alone among the traditions of mankind in the wonderful simplicity and grandeur of its words. Specially remarkable—miraculous, it really seems to me—is that character of reserve which leaves open to reason all that reason may be able to attain. The meaning of these words seems always to be a meaning ahead of science, not because it anticipates the results of science, but because it is independent of them, and runs, as it were, round the outer margin of all possible discovery."

May we not safely extend this finding to the entire Bible, and on these lines define its relation to modern thought? Its supernatural revelation is purely and absolutely ethical and spiritual. In questions physical and metaphysical it has no concern and utters no voice. With the achievements of science it never competes, nor can it be contradicted by them. It encourages its researches, ennobles its aspirations, crowns and completes its discoveries. Into the dead body of physical truth it puts the living soul of faith in the Divine Author. Like the blue heaven surrounding and spanning over the green earth, revelation over-arches and encircles science. Within that infinite embrace, beneath that spacious dome, drawing from its azure depths light, and life, and fructifying warmth, science, unhampered and unhindered, works out its majestic mission of blessing to men and glory to God. Collision there can be none till the earth strike the sky. The message of the Bible is a message from God's heart to ours. It cannot be proved by reason, nor can it be disproved. It appeals, not to sight, but to faith, and belongs to the realm of spirit, and not to that of sense. Science may have much to alter in our notions of its earthly embodiment, but its essential contents it cannot touch.

That is not theory, but reality. It is not philosophy, but life; not flesh, but spirit. It is the living, breathing, feeling love of God become articulate. It needs no evidence of sense. In the immutable instincts of the human heart it has its attestation, and in a life of responsive love it finds an unfailing verification. It rests on a basis no sane criticism can undermine nor solid science shake.

Happy the man whose faith has found this fixed foundation, and whose heart possesses this adamantine certainty: he shall be likened "unto a wise man, which built his house upon a rock: and the rain descended, and the floods came, and the winds blew, and beat upon that house; and it fell not: for it was founded upon a rock."

www.ingramcontent.com/pod-product-compliance
Lightning Source LLC
Chambersburg PA
CBHW020420010526
44118CB00010B/340